About Island Press

Since 1984, the nonprofit organization Island Press has been stimulating, shaping, and communicating ideas that are essential for solving environmental problems worldwide. With more than 1,000 titles in print and some 30 new releases each year, we are the nation's leading publisher on environmental issues. We identify innovative thinkers and emerging trends in the environmental field. We work with world-renowned experts and authors to develop cross-disciplinary solutions to environmental challenges.

Island Press designs and executes educational campaigns, in conjunction with our authors, to communicate their critical messages in print, in person, and online using the latest technologies, innovative programs, and the media. Our goal is to reach targeted audiences—scientists, policy makers, environmental advocates, urban planners, the media, and concerned citizens—with information that can be used to create the framework for long-term ecological health and human well-being.

Island Press gratefully acknowledges major support from The Bobolink Foundation, Caldera Foundation, The Curtis and Edith Munson Foundation, The Forrest C. and Frances H. Lattner Foundation, The JPB Foundation, The Kresge Foundation, The Summit Charitable Foundation, Inc., and many other generous organizations and individuals.

The opinions expressed in this book are those of the author(s) and do not necessarily reflect the views of our supporters.

CLIMATE RESILIENCE FOR AN AGING NATION

CLIMATE RESILIENCE FOR AN AGING NATION

DANIELLE ARIGONI

ISLANDPRESS | Washington | Covelo

Library of Congress Control Number: 2023934454

All Island Press books are printed on environmentally responsible materials.

Manufactured in the United States of America
10 9 8 7 6 5 4 3 2 1

Keywords: AARP, affordable housing, age-friendly communities, aging population, climate change, cognitive decline, community-based organization, COVID-19 demographics, disaster preparation, disaster response, elders, emergency management, hazard mitigation planning, healthcare, housing, livable communities, mobility, natural disaster, older adult, resilience, senior citizen, social infrastructure, social network, sustainable energy, transportation alternatives, vulnerable populations

This book is dedicated to my mom, who showed me how.
And to my kids, who are my why.

CONTENTS

—

PREFACE

—

Like 80 percent of Americans, I am worried about climate change and what it means for our well-being and quality of life. In my personal life, I think about where and how I live in terms of how it affects carbon emissions, and I try to make choices that lessen the crisis in some small way. I worry about the world that my four children have inherited and what it holds for their future.

But I worry about climate change, too, as a professional endeavor. Like many other land use planners and policy experts, I chose this profession to identify and implement solutions in land use, housing, transportation, and more that can be used at the community scale to improve life for all, particularly those who have less or who face greater barriers to opportunity. Climate change was not a common area of focus in the 1990s, when I completed my urban planning degrees, but over time it has become the largest and most looming threat to creating the kinds of vibrant, equitable, and sustainable communities that we planners seek to foster.

My first professional job of any significance was in the US Environmental Protection Agency's innovative smart growth office in its early, formative years, when we worked to forge a new path in environmental protection by showing the importance of better land use decisions and how intersectional solutions could be applied to solve for better air and water quality. In that role, I largely focused on what actions communities could take to create more affordable housing while also advancing smarter and more environmentally beneficial land use practices that created opportunity for all, without displacement.

After working in the proverbial shadows for so many years, we saw our longtime efforts to promote smart growth concepts finally take center stage during the Obama administration with the Partnership for Sustainable Communities, formed by the US Department of Housing and Urban Development, the US Department of Transportation, and EPA. I served as part of the leadership team for the duration, representing EPA and later HUD. We worked across agencies to build bridges that broke through conventional transportation, housing, and environmental silos and modeled for states, regions, and localities what cross-sectoral investments and planning could deliver.

The climate crisis we face today calls for the same level of creativity, intersectoral effort, and collaboration to be embraced as standard operating procedure throughout the United States. In fact, I would argue that cross-sectoral collaboration is no longer an option—it is an absolute necessity if we are to build greater resilience in our people and our country to withstand and, we hope, thrive in the face of climate change. I joined HUD in 2014 specifically to work on the front lines of creative cross-sectoral efforts that would help communities recover from climate-fueled disasters with resilience in mind. The National Disaster Resilience Competition was being designed to competitively award $1 billion in disaster recovery funds and demonstrate how communities could undertake disaster recovery efforts that were centered on making low- and moderate-income households safer and better able to withstand future climate-related risks. I was invited to help lead the effort, imparting the lessons we learned through the smart growth movement—the importance of cross-sectoral solutions, the fundamental role of partnerships, and the urgency to deliver multiple benefits through singular investments—to the sixteen-month competitive process, which ultimately resulted in thirteen awards averaging $76 million each. These were potentially game-changing levels of investment and just the first of many efforts by HUD to foster in communities a practice of centering disaster recovery and disaster mitigation funds on the needs of low- and moderate-income people. I recall age being discussed by applicants intermittently throughout the competitive process when they described who lived in their most disaster-affected communities, but age was never the lens through which resilience investments were made.

It was not until I joined AARP in 2017 that I truly began to recognize and embrace the importance of age and the needs of older adults as a differentiating factor in community-scale work. When I assumed the role of director of livable communities in 2017, I had little awareness that AARP even cared about community design, much less why it mattered for older adults. But it quickly became clear why the issue had become a strategic priority for the thirty-eight-million-member organization: because one's ability to live a safe, independent, healthy, secure life at every age is directly affected by where one lives and the kind of communities we construct. I witnessed the power of using the inclusive and relatable "age-friendly" frame to invite disparate voices to the common challenge of ensuring that older adults can work, volunteer, gain access to medical care and groceries, visit family and friends, and stay healthy as a result of better housing, transportation, and infrastructure decision-making. The Livable Communities work took different forms in the fifty-three AARP state offices across the country, and our job at the national office was to develop materials and programs to support their local efforts—and the work of AARP volunteers (the organization's true "special sauce")—and build their capacity to work on new issue areas in which AARP could make a difference, which we did with materials on housing, parks, place making, walkability, and more. My final contribution to the AARP oeuvre was the "Disaster Resilience Tool Kit"—released in July 2022 and co-branded with the Federal Emergency Management Agency—which we developed to help forge better connections between older adults and emergency managers, in response to the troublesome trends that I and others had begun to see in how older adults fared during disasters.

That work was perhaps the most meaningful of my career to date—until this book—because I firmly believe that our climate change trends are on a collision course with our nation's demographic trends. Already, climate change disproportionately affects older adults, threatening their (our!) ability to live healthy and secure lives—and the impacts will only become more widespread as our country becomes proportionally older. I see the results of this demographic and climate clash every time I read a news article that follows the latest disaster, when the data reveal that (once again) older adults made up the majority of people who died, because they were isolated or unable to get to safety. I hear it in stories of people who have the privilege of relocating, moving away from the land they love because of storm or wildfire risk, and I feel it even more deeply in the stories of people who cannot relocate for economic or cultural reasons and are instead fated to live in riskier locations that threaten their ability to age in place.

I firmly believe that more needs to be done now to reduce the risks for our friends, our family members, and our future selves. The time to debate whether climate change is real has passed, and so too has the time to equivocate on whether climate change should inform individual or collective decision-making, for every day spent debating is another opportunity missed to make decisions that make places safer for all. This book argues that older adults should be the lens through which we approach the task of creating more resilient communities. Why? Because older adults are bearing the brunt of climate change impacts now—and older adults who are poor or people of color even more so. Because we all can call to mind an older person whom we care for who would certainly be in need of assistance in the face of a disaster or extreme weather but may be unwilling or unable to ask for help. Older adults should also be the lens because that is our future as individuals, should we enjoy the privilege of aging. If we create communities that work for older adults now, we foster systems that will create safer places for all in the future, too. Climate change is a far bigger challenge than any one person can reasonably be expected to plan for. It is only when we begin to solve for resilience as whole communities that we can ensure that older adults and people of all ages will be able to navigate this uncertain future in ways that preserve dignity and build safety for us all.

ACKNOWLEDGMENTS

—

I would like to thank all of the people who played a key role in making this book possible, particularly Jordan Yin, who is among my biggest champions and gave timely, helpful, and wise counsel as a fellow author (*Urban Planning for Dummies*), professor, and friend; Jason Tudor, who has quietly led AARP's disaster management work for years and invited me to join his efforts when I joined AARP; Ilana Preuss, who helped me navigate the path to becoming an author (check out her book *Recast Your City*) and forged her own unique stamp on how to improve communities; and Heather Boyer, who supported the idea for this book and helped to expertly shepherd my words into their final form.

I am grateful for the assistance of the following individuals who provided valuable information, insights, vision, and encouragement before or during the process: David Azevedo, Jennifer Baker, Donna Beal, Sue Anne Bell, Paul Beyer, Juliana Bilowich, Camille Manning Broome, Caryn Bullis, David Cansler, Heather Chairez, Jerry Cohen, Bradley Dean, Alan DeLaTorre, Peter Edmondson, Stephanie Firestone, Todd Folse, Peter Girard, Erin Grahek, Esther Greenhouse, Beth Harrington, Pat Harris, Alison Hernandez, Pam Jenkins, Kara Kane, Elana Kieffer, Diane Kolack, Wilma Lawrence, Cristina Martin Firvida, Bill McKibben, Nancy McPherson, Steve Mencher, Lisa Monroe, Marla Nelson, Bill Novelli, Asia Ognibene, Greg Olsen, Jonna Papaefthimiou, Kelly Pflicke, Howard Rodgers, Mario Rubano, Laurie Schoeman, Claire Schoen, and Regina Shih. And thanks to Jen Hawse and the Island Press marketing team, who picked up the mantle after the writing process was complete to ensure that this book reached you.

Thank you to my colleagues at National Housing Trust, who were encouraging and supportive of this passion project, and all of whom are incredible leaders and technical experts working every day to deliver more sustainable, just, and affordable housing that improves people's lives.

To my former colleagues and friends at AARP, who work tirelessly on behalf of older adults, and to former colleagues and friends at the US Environmental Protection Agency and the US Department of Housing and Urban Development, who seek to deliver better environmental, resilience, and equity outcomes from our built environment, I thank you for your commitment and collaboration over these many years and for allowing me to learn from and alongside you.

To every volunteer who works to make their community better—whether through a local age-friendly effort, or as a member of a village or a VOAD, or as someone who just stops to check in on older neighbors—thank you: you are the true secret ingredient to creating places that we all want to live in.

A career-vocation is forged by a series of serendipitous events and people met along the way. I credit Geoff Anderson (who hired me not once but twice at EPA), Harriet Tregoning and Marion McFadden (who brought me to HUD and lifted me up while there, respectively), and Priya Jayachandran (who compelled me to join NHT with her leadership and vision) for helping me to land in precisely the right position at the right time for each leg of my journey. I could also fill an entire page with names of AARP staff and volunteer colleagues who inspired me to work toward a more age-friendly future and ultimately formulate the vision for this book.

Finally, to the older adults who have made a difference in my life—especially my grandparents Armand and Lenore, and Tony and Irma, plus beloved friend Flip—thank you for showing me the beauty of love across generations. For Gail, who sparked my teenage interest in affordable housing issues and has spent a lifetime fighting for the unsheltered among us. For my Uncle John, who encouraged me to think beyond the boundaries of my home in San Jose and modeled how to be a disruptor for change. For my teachers at Presentation High School, who instilled in me the mantra of "not words but deeds," and lifelong teacher Porus Olpadwala, Cornell University professor emeritus, who has always led by example with grace and kindness. For Jim and Jeni, I'm so glad you joined our family, and I love you both. For Rose and Miriam, I can't wait to read the books you will write someday. For Matt, thank you for our partnership and our shared life's work of raising our amazing kids. And finally, thank you for the gift of unwavering love and support given to me by people whom I love at their very core and therefore will always think of as ageless: my mom, Denise; my sisters, Nicole and Renee; and my incredible kids, Aiden, Zoe, Finn, and Wyatt.

INTRODUCTION

—

Why It's Essential to Approach Resilience through a Lens of Aging

The changes in our environment are increasingly threatening our ability to live a safe, independent, healthy, secure life at every age. Whether these changes are slow moving (year-over-year alterations in peak heat or cold, shifting seasons, land subsidence or sea level rise, more frequent flooding) or more acute (extreme heat, intense and more frequent storms and flooding, wildfires), climate change is already affecting the way we live every day, especially when it manifests in the form of climate-enhanced disasters. And as our nation grows older, it is ever more important to understand what those changes mean for older adults and the communities in which they live.

When viewed from the perspective of older adults—generally speaking, people sixty-five and older—climate change is having an immediate and sometimes life-threatening impact. Consider the grandparent who can no longer stand and wait at the bus stop to go shopping because of the heat, or the retiree who lives in a home with black mold caused by chronic flooding, which she can't afford to remediate or leave because of her limited fixed income. Consider the countless news stories following any given disaster that reveal that the majority of people who died were older adults who couldn't evacuate, couldn't get the help they needed, or couldn't withstand the power outages, extreme temperatures, or medical disruptions that followed the event. Imagine the fear and despair that these individuals must have experienced. For these people and millions of others, understanding the intersection of climate change and its impact on our ability to age safely and gracefully is critically important.

Older adults can and should serve as the prism through which we plan to build more resilient communities. Of course, they are not the only group that is vulnerable to climate change. Children are affected by disasters, as are people with disabilities, and certainly there is ample evidence that climate change is disproportionately affecting low-income communities and communities of color.[1] But this book argues that older adults can and should be the prism for analysis because of the intersectional nature of older adults—increasingly diverse, increasingly poor, and certainly with a higher prevalence of disabilities—and also because of their incredible projected growth as a share of our population. Already, there are more than fifty million Americans aged sixty-five or older, representing 17 percent of the US population in 2020. In just ten years, this cohort has grown by 38 percent—dramatically faster than the growth rate for people under sixty-five, which grew by just 2 percent[2]—and the share of older adults will continue to grow.

Action is needed now because it is clear that we are not accustomed to designing communities that work for older adults, much less communities that are resilient in the face of climate change.

- People outlive their ability to drive by seven to ten years[3] and often have few viable alternatives. Lack of transportation led nearly six million seniors to delay medical care in 2017. Yet we continue to build communities designed primarily for cars and their drivers.
- More than half of all US households are one- or two-person households, but more than 80 percent of our housing stock is two, three, four, or more bedrooms in size.[4] And among older adults living in the community and not in congregate housing, more than one-quarter live alone.[5]
- Affordable, secure housing is increasingly out of reach for older adults. In 2019, a record number of older households (10.2 million) were cost burdened, paying more than one-third of their income on housing.[6] The percentage of older renters experiencing "worst-case housing needs" (spending more than one-half of their income on housing or living in severely inadequate housing) has steadily increased over the past decade, and it is projected to continue to rise.[7]

If a significant share of older adults can't access secure, affordable housing and transportation that meets their needs on a day-to-day basis, how can they be expected to prepare adequately for a rapidly changing climate and the more intense and frequent disasters it is already bringing? Climate change is certain to continue to alter the way we live over the long haul, necessitating better ways to cool and heat homes, provide reliable power and transportation systems, and manage flooding, drought, and wildfire risks. But the effects of climate change are already evident—and increasingly deadly—in the form of more intense weather events, more extreme and sustained temperatures, and the havoc these wreak on power systems, transportation networks, local economies, community health, housing supply, and more.

Our collective failure to adequately consider older adults is at the heart of the troubling and sadly predictable statistics that we now see emerging after every climate-enhanced disaster all across the United States. Time and time again, the data show that hurricanes, severe storms, extreme cold, extreme heat, wildfires, and flooding are more deadly for older adults than for any other age group. The Center for Disaster Philanthropy notes that older adults represented 70 percent of deaths related to Hurricane Katrina, despite the fact that older adults constituted only 15 percent of the population of New Orleans.[8] In the California Camp Fire of 2018, 85 percent of the fatalities were among people over sixty, in part because of the large number of retirees who had chosen to locate in this wildland-urban interface community.[9] In February 2021, almost two-thirds of the 246 Texans who died as a result of an intense winter storm that brought subzero temperatures and extended power outages were people over sixty.[10]

These tragic outcomes cannot be ascribed just to inadequate individual preparedness because they reflect failures that are systemic. In order to create a new future—one that better acknowledges the realities of older adults today and the larger share of older adults tomorrow—we must invest the time, effort, and focus needed to create more community-wide resilience. The benefits will accrue to all of us, not only because we are all individually aging but also because placing the needs of older adults at the center of community-wide approaches makes places safer for people of all ages.

The Value of an Age-Friendly Lens

During my five years with AARP directing its Livable Communities efforts, I worked with staff and volunteer colleagues to advance the belief that communities can become better places for people of all ages and all abilities by focusing on the needs of older adults. After all, ensuring that parks are designed with adequate seating doesn't serve only older adults, but it does make it easier for them to enjoy. Creating more walkable communities so that older adults can attend to daily needs when they no longer drive, or building a more diverse housing stock so that people can downsize and remain in the neighborhoods they love, leads to a better community for all. Focusing on the needs of older adults in planning efforts invites a diverse array of stakeholders and the general public—who invariably will confront the challenges of aging parents or aging selves—to play a role in crafting a better future for themselves, their neighborhood, and their community.

Applying an age-friendly lens and using older adults as the prism for assessing community investments corrects for the unfortunate reality that the needs of older adults are often overlooked, misunderstood, or simply discounted. Without a formal commitment to become a more age-friendly community, it is unlikely that any state or locality will consider older adults as much more than a cohort that needs to be cared for. When asked how they serve the needs of older adults, local leaders are frequently quick to point to plans for more senior housing or expanded home-based services, like Meals on Wheels, or to recognize that paratransit is needed to fill in the gaps for the most mobility impaired among us. Except for privately developed, self-described "retirement communities" such as The Villages, rare is the locality that centers its planning in the needs of its oldest residents. Far more common are communities that seek to attract millennials as their ticket to economic growth—overlooking the inherent political, volunteer, experiential, and economic power of older adults. That is beginning to change—particularly through the growth of the AARP Network of Age-Friendly States and Communities (an independent affiliate of the World Health Organization Global Network for Age-Friendly Cities and Communities)—but it isn't changing fast enough.

The tragic loss of life, property, and health borne by older adults (and others) during disasters is a by-product of the decisions that communities have made and continue to make about their growth: where housing is located and how it is designed, what transportation options are most readily available and usable throughout a community, how critical infrastructure (including power and high-speed internet service) is deployed and managed, and how emergency plans are devised and implemented.

It is also the by-product of the fact that older adults do not experience extreme weather and climate-fueled disasters in the same way that other age groups do. Many have difficulty with physical mobility or cognitive function or other constraints that impede their ability to evacuate when needed. Others, living alone and isolated for prolonged periods, lack access to communication channels or social networks that would enable them to get timely information and help. Still others may respond in exactly the same way as a twenty- or thirty-year-old does—following the precise orders of their emergency management professionals to take necessary steps to remain safe and secure—and still fare worse because of older bodies' inability to regulate heat or because of a prevailing medical condition.

The reality is that the number of deaths among older adults is in part the result of the built environment and decisions made by local planners, emergency management practitioners, and those who care for older adults—each of which affects the conditions and circumstances within which older adults live but which operate with their own set of terminology, training, and structures in ways that can impede collaboration. (See figure 0-1.) Moreover, there is an uneven understanding among each of these three disciplines about how climate change is affecting their work and how to respond—and often a failure among practitioners to connect the issues in their work. For example, an otherwise thoughtful 2021 article in the journal *Planning*, published by the American Planning Association, describes the intersection between two circles—aging and the built environment—but wholly overlooks any discussion of climate change and the impact it is having (and will increasingly have) on people's ability to age in place.[11]

This book seeks to forge understanding between these three spheres in ways that lead to more collaboration, better decisions, and

Figure 0-1: Resilience for all ages requires connection and collaboration among multiple disciplines, each with its own terminology, training, and structures.

ultimately better outcomes—not only for older adults but for people of all ages.

When we plan for the most vulnerable, and for those with the greatest obstacles to opportunity and well-being, we improve conditions for all. That is the ethos behind the idiom that "a rising tide lifts all boats," wherein community-wide investments, policies, and practices have the potential to improve well-being for all. The imagery of a rising tide has a more complicated meaning these days as we face a climate future in which the tide can both lift communities and threaten them. In my mind's eye, I insert into that imagery representational lifeboats specifically to account for those who are at risk. It causes me to wonder how we are designing the metaphorical (and actual) lifeboats that aim to protect members in a community—and who is included or excluded, by either omission or design. This book argues that we all have a responsibility and an opportunity to design a better lifeboat so that everyone—regardless of age and ability, race, class, or income—can safely ride the rising waters.

Climate Terminology 101

The climate is rapidly transforming in ways that scientists continue to assess and study so that we can prepare for a very different future. Climate scientists have informed us that we should expect more extreme weather events, shifts in seasonal temperatures and durations, and significant shifts in our natural environment and the ecological systems it supports—and all the related health consequences that come with those changes. Our current trajectory is expected to bring even more catastrophic weather events, extinctions of entire species of flora and fauna unable to adapt, and massive ice melts and the commensurate rise of sea levels that will inundate communities around the world.

This book aspires to advance resilience for communities so that places and the people who live in them are equipped to handle these disruptions—whether they come in the form of shocks (acute events) or stresses (slower-moving or more chronic conditions)—that climate change is delivering. Resilience endeavors to ensure that people and places are capable of not just surviving but also rebounding with minimal damage and loss of life.[12]

We can advance resilience by adapting to climate change and by identifying and mitigating the risks posed by climate change in order to change its trajectory and blunt its effects. The book largely focuses on climate *adaptation* measures rather than climate *mitigation* strategies, which seek to reduce the emissions that are causing climate change. When the book does speak of mitigation, it is largely in terms of mitigating risk and making places safer for older adults and, by extension, for all.

However, this book discusses opportunities that both mitigate and adapt to climate change. Investing in energy-efficient homes and promoting more widespread use of solar power reduces emissions from polluting energy sources (mitigation) and lowers the risk of blackouts during storms (adaptation). Creating smaller homes in more densely designed communities fosters social connectedness and walkability (adaptation) but also reduces household energy and water consumption (mitigation). Investments that make walking, biking, and public transit more viable as transportation options pay dividends in improved air and water quality, generating fewer emissions (mitigation), while also creating redundancies in networks that can better accommodate disruptions (adaptation).

It is helpful to clarify what is meant by the various terms used throughout this book. The term "community" is used in a broad and general sense, to include all types of small units of government (e.g., hamlets, villages, towns, cities); to represent groups of people (e.g., members of tribal nations or racial or ethnic groups, older adults, and people with disabilities); and to refer to transboundary regions that define an area (e.g., coastal, rural). Generally, the term "community" is not used to refer to a planned development, such as an age-restricted residential community.

In addition, several climate-related terms are worth defining.

- "Climate change" refers to changes in global or regional climate patterns attributed largely to human-caused increases in atmospheric greenhouse gases.
- "Climate change adaptation" or "climate adaptation" means actions taken to prepare for and adjust to the current and projected impacts of climate change.
- "Climate change mitigation" refers to actions taken to limit the magnitude and rate of future climate change by reducing greenhouse gas emissions, advancing nature-based solutions, or both.
- "Climate resilience" can be generally defined as a system's capacity to maintain functionality in the face of stresses imposed by climate change and to adapt in order to be better prepared for future climate impacts.[13]

Behind all these terms are people. It is sometimes easy to lose sight of that fact when facing the enormity of the climate change crisis, particularly when definitions themselves don't identify *people* as being affected. But understanding who we are as a people, and how we are changing as a people, is an essential first step in achieving resilience.

This book aims to paint a picture of the demographic wave that is coming to our communities—across every state in the United

States—and who older adults are in all their complexity. Far from a monolith, this group, which is hard to neatly categorize, includes people with a wide range of abilities, incomes, mobilities, and needs that must first be understood in order to be addressed. This book explores the unique ways in which older adults are more vulnerable to the climate crisis that affects us all, and what can be done to mitigate the risks for those who are disproportionately affected. It explains the value of applying new planning approaches—including an age-friendly process and a planning framework dedicated to inclusive disability recovery—to create communities that better serve the needs of older adults, not only during disasters but for all the days in between them. It examines how each sector—from housing to energy to health—can incorporate principles that are more responsive to older adults' needs in order to deliver better outcomes. It also examines the experiences of several communities that are piloting new solutions in response to past crises, which can be instructive to other places, and which hold the promise of greater community-wide resilience that ultimately saves lives. Finally, the book concludes with a series of action steps that community members, local and state leaders, and policymakers can take to better prepare for a changing climate in a rapidly aging nation.

01 WHO ARE OLDER ADULTS?

—

Our country faces the challenge of responding to the concurrent trends of a changing climate and an aging nation, both of which have enormous potential to alter the way we live. Each suggests the need to revisit how we design communities, house and support people, and facilitate people's mobility and safety. To solve for both trends, older adults must be the focus for efforts to achieve more climate-resilient communities.

While there are widespread efforts underway to grasp what our future climate reality will look and feel like, our demographic future is less often discussed. Unlike climate change, the aging of our population does not feature prominently in national reporting, scientific study, or corporate commitments. Rather, aging is dealt with as an individual experience, confronted by individuals and families behind closed doors. It is rarely, if ever, discussed in schools or workplaces. And it certainly isn't on display in our youth-obsessed mainstream media. In many ways, this is unique to the United States, where the prevailing cultural norm is to relegate care for the elderly to institutional settings rather than supporting home- and community-based options of the type that are more commonplace in other countries. But to understand climate change, we must understand our demographic future, which reveals what we need to plan for—and why we need to do it fast.

Consider the case of Nadine Demalleville of Carpinteria, California. When forest fires approached her home in 2017, the eighty-year-old former nurse had just five minutes to evacuate from the mobile home where she lived alone with her beloved cats—and yet lacked the ability to leave. Relying upon a wheelchair, Ms. Demalleville had no way to get herself to the emergency shelter twenty miles away, and she would likely have remained in harm's way but for a neighbor who stepped in to help. She arrived safely at the shelter with a lunchbox full of medications but little else.[1]

Ms. Demalleville is hardly an isolated case of an older adult who lives alone with mobility issues and has little means to prepare for disaster. The US population is growing older and will soon approach a demographic tipping point at which we will have more people over sixty-five than under eighteen. To truly respond to the risks brought on by climate change—and if we are ever to achieve climate resilience—we must first make an effort to understand who older adults are and how they respond to those changes. Moreover, focusing on the needs of older adults often delivers universal benefits for people of all ages and abilities, making places more accessible and improving health services for all members of the community.

Understanding the Demographic Trends

When most people think about aging, warm thoughts of grandparents or older relatives may come to mind. For others, thoughts turn quickly to fears of loss of physical mobility or strength, concerns about becoming more forgetful, or worries about access to medical care—or the economic implications of living longer and whether retirement savings (if applicable) will be sufficient. Aging is a deeply personal experience—and yet it is generally poorly understood by state and local leaders, emergency management practitioners, policymakers, and others who are charged with ensuring safe and resilient communities for an increasingly large share of older adults.

In order to plan for our future as an aging nation, we must first seek to understand who older adults are and what it means to age. There are widely varied experiences of aging within the cohort of "older adults" that merit examination as we seek to create more climate-resilient communities that truly serve the needs of all.

Older Adults as a Cohort Can Be Difficult to Identify

Unlike "youth," which enjoys a uniform definition as ending at age eighteen, there is no one way to define or name the oldest members of our society. In some communities, "elders" is the chosen term, denoting respect and honor. At other times, "senior citizens" is used, although it explicitly connotes citizenship along with age, which may not apply to all adults—and brings to mind grocery store discounts or cheaper hotel rates. At times, the words "aged" or "elderly" are used, which clearly signify advanced age, although without a clear sense of when that exactly begins. A more universally acceptable term—and the term primarily used in this book— is "older adults," which is factual without denoting judgment. It is also more inclusive in that it represents age in reference to all adults, and it is elegant in that it has a near counterpart in "young adults"—which together serve as fine bookends for membership in adulthood.

Some people view turning fifty and the magical arrival of the first literature from AARP as the moment when their status as an "older adult" begins. Others may pinpoint the turning point as the year when they qualify for movie discounts or homes in age-restricted "retirement" communities available only to people fifty-five and older. The US government uses several markers to indicate age breaks that unlock benefits aimed at older adults. Individuals are protected by law from age discrimination beginning at age forty, and fifty-nine and one-half is the age at which the Internal Revenue Service permits individuals to access their retirement accounts without penalty. Sixty-two is the age at which people can begin to draw Social Security benefits at a reduced rate (full Social Security age is considered sixty-six or sixty-seven), and sixty-five is the age at which adults qualify for Medicare, the national health insurance program.

Others prefer to describe age in terms of the generations with which we are affiliated. (See figure 1-1.) Older adults generally are members of those groups described as Baby Boomers and the Silent Generation (born in 1946–1964 and 1928–1945, respectively),[2]

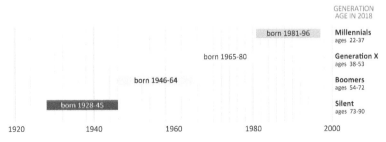

Figure 1-1: Older adults are sometimes defined by generation. (Source: Michael Dimock, "Defining Generations: Where Millennials End and Generation Z Begins," Pew Research Center, Washington, DC, January 17, 2019)

with the most senior among them enjoying membership in the Greatest Generation (Americans born in the 1900s through 1920s). But members of the proverbial forgotten generation, Generation X (born in 1965–1980), will soon begin to turn sixty and join the cohort of older adults.

The lack of clarity in how to define and name older adults as a group hinders our ability to effectively plan for and with them. For simplicity, this book generally cites data related to people sixty-five and older, with some exceptions. There are times when drilling down on the "oldest of the old"—elderly people, eighty or older—is pertinent, particularly regarding challenges in mobility, health status, and ability to live independently. But the real underlying challenge remains the fact that older adults are at times hard to define, which creates barriers to understanding what it means to age.

Americans Are Growing Older but Not Evenly by Gender, Race, or Even Age

Regardless of how one decides to cluster, aggregate, or label this group, the data do not lie: we are growing proportionately older as a country. The US Census Bureau projects that 2034 will be the year when we surpass the aforementioned tipping point, becoming a country of more people over sixty-five than under eighteen—for the first time in US history.[3] Since 1900, the number of people over sixty-five has grown more than seventeen times as large, from 3.1 million to nearly 56 million in 2020—and the number of people eighty-five or older is more than fifty-four times larger.[4] As a result, the Census Bureau asserts that our demographic future has shifted from being best illustrated as a pyramid, with more youth tapering to a smaller cohort of older adults, to a pillar, with a nearly equal share of older adults, far greater than ever seen before.[5] (See figure 1-2.)

If 2034 is the most immediate demographic tipping point, a second and no less urgent one will follow just a few years later, in 2040. At that point, older adults are expected to make up 22 percent of the population—up from just 17 percent in 2020.[6] To put this in context, whereas in 2020 every sixth person was over sixty-five, by 2040 roughly every fifth person will be over sixty-five. By 2040, the United

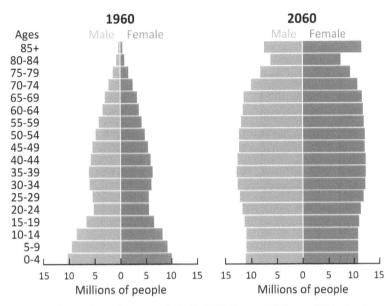

Figure 1-2: Projected population growth, 1960–2060. (Source: US Census, "Older People Projected to Outnumber Children for First Time in U.S. History," March 13, 2018)

States will be home to more than eighty million older adults—more than double the number from just forty years prior.[7]

Is this on the minds of leaders? Yes and no. Pope Francis has been heralded for his conscious effort, as he confronts his own age and ability, to acknowledge this global trend, using his platform to bring awareness to this "veritable new people," as he has termed it, and encouraging communities and individuals to better plan for the needs of older adults.[8] But the fact that his effort is newsworthy suggests that it is not on the minds of nearly enough leaders—both those who lead communities and those who lead efforts to strengthen resilience and preparedness—who more often focus on families and young people as populations for which they plan.

The growth in the share of older adults is in part because we are living longer, but we are not doing so uniformly across gender, race, or ethnicity. Projected life expectancy continues to increase over time—having grown by 10 years between 1960 and 2015, from 69.7 to 79.4 years[9]—although with some significant recent changes related to the COVID-19 pandemic and other factors. In December 2022, the Centers for Disease Control and Prevention reported that the life expectancy for a person born in the United States was 76.4 years—the shortest it had been in nearly two decades—having declined by 2.4 years from 78.8 years in 2019.[10] Prior to the pandemic, the rate of increase in life expectancy was expected to slow in comparison with the past several decades but still increase by more than six years, to a projected average life span of 85.6, by 2060. But average changes in life expectancy vary by gender, race, country of birth, and other factors. Women generally are projected to live longer than men, although the gap has been closing as a result of slower growth in life expectancy for women relative to men. Other group rates have been even more dramatic: the life expectancy of non-Hispanic Black females has remained relatively stable, for example, not increasing over time, illustrating critical breakdowns in access to health and social supports that have benefited some groups over others.[11] From a global perspective, the United States is not faring particularly well, dropping from having the twentieth highest projected life expectancy in 1960 to the forty-third highest by 2060.[12]

The composition of this group is changing in other ways as well, with more "older" older adults. With a population creeping toward a life expectancy of nearly eighty-six years, it is not surprising that the number of people over eighty-five will grow even faster, proportionally, than the rest of the older adult population. The number of people over eighty-five is expected to more than double in the next two decades, from 6.7 million in 2020 to 14.4 million in 2040.[13]

Projected changes in the next two decades also reveal a more racially and ethnically diverse older population. Whereas the relative share of older adults from racial and ethnic minority groups constituted 24 percent of all older adults (13.4 million) in 2020, that will increase to 34 percent of older adults (27.7 million) in 2040. Rates of growth among non-White groups are generally higher than among White older adults. Between 2020 and 2040, the growth rate of older adults among Whites is expected to be just 26 percent, compared with significantly higher rates of growth among American Indians and Alaska Natives (58 percent), African Americans (73 percent), Asians (93 percent), and Hispanics (148 percent).[14] Not only are these trends indicative of a more diverse population, but they are also precursors of more intersectional challenges in aging wherein systemic differences in access to healthcare, financial stability, and opportunities manifest in greater vulnerability to the effects of climate change.

In sum, the next two decades not only will be a time of radical growth in the number of older adults in our communities but also will reveal a more diverse group with different cultural and language traditions, health considerations, and mobility needs—all of which must be understood in order to effectively build more climate-resilient communities.

Facets of Aging and What It Means to Age

While it is important to find a way to neatly define and understand age groups, it is also inherently challenging, given that such classifications can blur the distinctions among older adults. Understanding this complexity of aging is essential if leaders are to be effective in planning for an aging nation. While it may be convenient to presume that "older" means frail or incapable of living independently—or, conversely, that growing older means enjoying a hearty nest egg of retirement savings—the reality is far more complex. Any of these assumptions may be true for some, and none may be true for others—or all may apply, depending on where one is on the aging spectrum. To understand the needs of older adults in all their diversity and to plan for those needs require a more careful analysis of the many facets of aging.

Older adults can include people who are still in the workforce, possibly earning toward retirement and perhaps in peak physical condition. Others, of course, work by choice, many because they have little other choice but to work in order to provide for themselves or family members. Some older adults enjoy empty nests after raising children (or never having them), while others find themselves unexpectedly raising grandchildren. Older adults can be people who are happily retired, dedicating their so-called golden years to pursuing hobbies, traveling, volunteering, starting a new business, or spending time with family and friends. But the older adult cohort also includes people in their eighties and nineties who may be medically frail and reliant upon Medicaid support for care when their savings are exhausted.

Certainly, there are many examples of people thriving as they age. With improvements in health, we are living longer and living more healthfully. There are reams of examples of exceptional older adults achieving feats previously unthought of, disrupting our idea of what it means to age. Madonna and Bruce Springsteen are selling out stadiums on world tours in 2023 at the ages of sixty-five and seventy-three, respectively. Joseph Biden is the oldest sitting president in US history, and Martha Stewart graced the cover of *Sports Illustrated* at age eighty-one. In 2022, an eighty-eight-year-old venture capitalist became the oldest person ever to complete the New York City Marathon.[15]

Still, with age, real differences begin to emerge that affect one's ability to live safely and independently: economic differences, differences in housing tenure and household status, mobility and locational differences, health differences, and differences in access to information and communication.

Economic Differences

Not unlike the situation for the general population, the economic plight of older adults runs the gamut. But unlike the rest of the population, older adults' ability to change their economic outlook by earning an income and building savings is inherently limited by life span and is further challenged by age discrimination prevalent in the workplace.

Nearly 20 percent of older adults are still in the workforce, either by choice or out of necessity. While labor projections foretell declining or stable employment for nearly all age groups over the next decade, the Bureau of Labor Statistics predicts a near doubling in the number of people in the labor market who are seventy-five and older—the only cohort with a significant increase in labor force participation between now and 2030.[16] The road to continued employment is not always easy, however. While federal protections do exist to prevent age discrimination, nearly one in four employees report having experienced age-related discrimination at work.[17]

The tragic reality is that one out of ten people over sixty-five lives below the poverty line, and another 5 percent were classified as "near poor" in 2020.[18] Nearly half of adults aged fifty-five through sixty-six have no retirement savings, with the figure slightly higher for women than for men.[19] Older adults living alone are more likely to be poor than those living with family.[20]

Even among older adults lucky enough to have retirement savings, few express an ability to withstand an economic emergency. A survey conducted in June 2022 revealed that less than 40 percent of Baby Boomers (aged fifty-eight through seventy-two) said they had savings sufficient to cover expenses for three months.[21] Perhaps not surprising, therefore, is the fact that even an unexpected $1,000 expense would be problematic for many. Just 44 percent of Americans are able to handle such a surprise expense—and older adults are consistent with that figure (ranging from 44 percent to 49 percent, depending on age).[22] Whether the cause is a onetime setback (such as amassing food and supplies to shelter in place) or a longer-lasting disruption (such as missing multiple months of work), a significant share of older adults report that they lack the ability to withstand such a financial hit.

Housing Tenure and Household Status

There is a widespread presumption that most older adults live in care facilities—assisted living facilities, nursing homes, or other types of managed care congregate settings. Once again, the reality is quite different: the vast majority of older people live in their own homes, scattered throughout communities—and often alone. In 2019, only 1.2 million of 54 million adults sixty-five and older—about 2 percent—lived in nursing homes.[23] While the majority of older adults live with a spouse, in 2020 roughly 30 percent of adults sixty-five and older living in communities lived alone. Men are more likely to live with a spouse than are women, with just half of women over sixty-five living with a spouse. (See figure 1-3.) Keep this statistic in mind: one in five older men live alone, and one in three older women do.[24] That number is likely to continue to grow as the prevalence of childless older adults surges: nearly 20 percent of the next wave of older adults (currently fifty-five through sixty-four) are childless, compared with 16 percent of sixty-five-through seventy-four-year-olds and just 11 percent of people over seventy-five.[25]

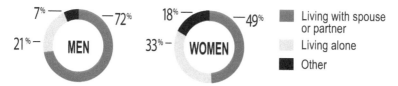

Figure 1-3: Living arrangements of people sixty-five and older, 2021. (Source: US Department of Health and Human Services, Administration for Community Living, "2021 Profile of Older Americans," November 2022)

The majority of older adults own their homes: 77 percent of people over seventy-five owned their homes in 2019.[26] And while that affords some financial stability, it nevertheless requires more than one-third of owners to spend greater than one-third of their income on housing. Homeownership itself brings its own set of challenges, with many homes in need of modifications to make them appropriate placs to age. A 2021 AARP survey revealed that more than one-third of respondents said they needed to make physical changes to their homes, such as modifying a bathroom or installing ramps, to make them suitable for aging in place.[27] Still other homeowners are confronted with buildings in need of significant repairs, which may become unmanageable with increased age. In 2019, more than three hundred thousand homes (3 percent of homes owned by people over seventy-five) had moderate to severe problems with plumbing, heating, electric wiring, upkeep, or all of these.[28]

The plight of the nearly one-quarter of older adults who rent is more dire. With greater vulnerability to rising prices, a record number of older households (10.2 million) were rent burdened, spending more than 30 percent of their income on housing, in 2019. Of those, half were *severely* rent burdened, paying more than half of their income on housing.[29] And the growth in renters sixty-five and older is projected to steadily increase from 7.2 million households in 2019, growing by more than 4 million over the next two decades.[30]

Older renters aren't just at greater risk of being cost burdened; they are also more likely to be evicted and are increasingly counted among the unhoused population. According to an analysis of US Census data by Statista for AARP, more than 180,000 people fifty-five and older were evicted in 2020, and by 2027 that number is projected to rise to more than 300,000.[31] Without viable housing alternatives, evictions can lead to homelessness. In 2020, roughly 216,000 people fifty-five and older experienced homelessness, and that number is projected to grow to more than 280,000 by 2027.[32] This is not a new trend. The share of unhoused individuals aged fifty and over jumped from 23 percent to 34 percent between 2007 and 2017, according to the US Department of Housing and Urban Development's 2017 "Annual Homeless Assessment Report." The same report notes that during this period, the number of people aged sixty-two and older living in emergency shelters or transitional housing rose by about 69 percent, with this age group representing roughly 8 percent of people experiencing sheltered homelessness.[33] Further, people fifty-five and older who use homeless services increased from 16 percent of all service recipients in 2016 to 22 percent in 2020, according to data provided by HUD to AARP.[34]

Whether owned or rented, manufactured housing is an important source of housing for older adults. Of the nearly 6.7 million households living in manufactured housing, nearly half (3.2 million) are headed by people aged sixty and older.[35] While mobile homes are generally perceived as more a more affordable housing option, data reveal that adults living in them are just as housing cost burdened as their peers living in other forms of housing.[36] To the degree that the limited supply of affordable manufactured housing is increasingly threatened in communities—often as a result of investor acquisition or redevelopment—the trend bodes poorly for many older adults, who will be unable to find similarly priced housing.

Mobility Differences (Inside and Outside the Home)

Mobility is a critical quality-of-life feature that, frankly, many people take for granted until they suffer an injury or other physical setback—or are inconvenienced by a transportation interruption, such as inability to drive their car because of mechanical failure or elimination of a relied-upon transit line. But mobility is inherently and fundamentally tied to one's ability to live independently.

The reality is that mobility is an increasingly dire concern for many older adults, particularly as they age. When considering mobility within the home and people's ability to safely navigate their space, consider that 39 percent of adults sixty-five and older reported in 2020 that they had ambulatory difficulty, defined as difficulty in walking or climbing stairs.[37] (See figure 1-4.) One-third of households headed by people sixty-five and older include someone with a mobility disability.[38]

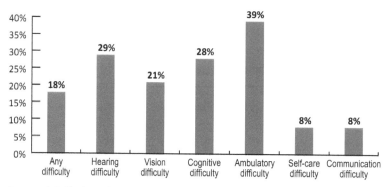

Figure 1-4: Difficulty in functioning among people sixty-five and older, 2020. (Source: US Department of Health and Human Services, Administration for Community Living, "2021 Profile of Older Americans," November 2022)

While interventions are possible to adapt people's homes to physical limitations, it is worth noting that much of our public space still, even with conformity to the Americans with Disabilities Act of 1990 (ADA), presents challenges for older adults with mobility impairments. Aisles in stores and restaurants that are difficult to navigate, a lack of benches and seating to rest while walking, older subway stations that have stairs, and sidewalks with loose bricks or exposed roots are among the types of built environment conditions not well covered by the ADA that affect mobility.

Mobility outside the home also must account for people's ability to get to their desired destinations easily, safely, and affordably. For the majority of older adults, driving remains the transportation mode of choice—but the reality is that fully 18 percent of adults sixty-five and older do not drive, and 35 percent of women over seventy-five don't drive.[39] When driving is no longer an option, walking or biking to destinations can be a solution—but the trends there are not encouraging either, suggesting that we are not building places that ensure safe alternatives exist. In 2020, despite an overall reduction in driving, older adults and people walking in low-income neighborhoods continued to be struck and killed at disproportion-ately higher rates than other populations.[40] Biking reveals similar trends, with data showing that adults aged fifty-five through sixty-nine have the highest bicycle death rates among age groups.[41]

Locational Differences

Older adults are not uniformly distributed throughout the United States, either—particularly with accelerating growth (and loss) trends in some parts of the country.

Rural places are more heavily populated by older adults, with nearly one in five people in rural (nonmetropolitan) areas in the United States aged sixty-five or older, compared with 15 percent in urban (metropolitan) areas. In counties across the United States with a disproportionately older population, nearly 85 percent are located in rural places.[42] While this can be a product of retirees having relo-cated to areas of natural beauty and rich recreational opportunities (termed "recreation/retirement destinations" by the US Department of Agriculture), that describes conditions in only about one-third of these "older age counties." Another one-third is communities of persistent population loss, where younger generations migrate out and do not return.[43] The unique conditions of rural places beget very different levels of mobility and access to healthcare, social connec-tion, and employment.

In 2020, more than half of the country's older adults could be found in just nine states, with the largest shares in California (6 mil-lion), Florida (4.6 million), Texas (3.9 million), New York (3.4 mil-lion), Pennsylvania (2.4 million), Ohio (2.1 million), Illinois (2.1 million), Michigan (1.8 million), and North Carolina (1.8 million).[44] Four states already have the highest percentage of their populations aged sixty-five and older: Maine (22 percent), Florida (21 percent), West Virginia (21 percent), and Vermont (21 percent)—and nine states experienced greater than 50 percent growth in the share of older adults in just ten years (in descending order, ranging from 73 percent growth to 51 percent growth: Alaska, Nevada, Colorado, Idaho, Arizona, South Carolina, Utah, Delaware, and Georgia).[45]

Despite the popular image of snowbirds who move from colder climes to warmer ones for their retirement years, older adults are less likely to move than younger groups, with just 3 percent of older persons moving in 2020 and 2021, as opposed to 10 percent of the population below sixty-five. More than half of those who move remain in the same county—meaning that the locational conditions outlined earlier are unlikely to change significantly in the years to come.[46]

Health Differences

For many, the concept of aging brings to mind concerns about health. While a great many older adults are healthy well into their later years, for most people the prevalence and perception of health concerns rise with age. In 2020, 27 percent of people over seventy-five reported their health as "fair or poor," compared with just 20 percent of those ten years younger.[47] Arthritis (47 percent), cancer (26 percent), diabetes (21 percent), heart disease (14 percent), and COPD, or chronic obstructive pulmonary disease, a suite of respiratory diseases including emphysema and chronic bronchitis (11 percent) were among the more frequently cited chronic health concerns noted by older adults.[48] Nearly 60 percent of people sixty-five and older reported being diagnosed with hypertension during the previous twelve months.[49] Hypertension can compromise the body's ability to circulate blood efficiently and can contribute to deterioration in eyesight, cognition, and mobility.[50] Roughly one in nine people aged sixty-five and older live with Alzheimer's disease, which can cause short-term memory loss, difficulty with motor function, and disorientation.[51]

Aging and disability also affect one's ability to carry out the needed activities of daily living. Nearly 20 percent of older adults reported in 2020 that they could not function at all or had significant difficulty completing activities in one or more of the functioning domains, defined as seeing, hearing, mobility, communication, cognition, and self-care.[52]

Data measuring mental health during the COVID-19 pandemic suggest that older adults generally benefit from lower incidence of anxiety or depression than younger cohorts.[53] A 2022 study found that while two-thirds of older adults reported their emotional and mental health as "excellent" or "very good," roughly one-third nevertheless cited challenges with anxiety, depression, and hopelessness.

Adults over sixty reported significantly less increase in stress related to COVID-19 than did adults aged fifty to fifty-nine.[54] Whether as a by-product of longevity or perspective, adults sixty and older are more likely than adults aged fifty to fifty-nine to be resilient, citing that they "bounce back quickly after hard times and usually come through difficult times with little trouble."[55]

Differences in Access to Information and Communication

In our modern world, access to information and technology is essential—yet it is not as uniformly prevalent among older adults as within other age groups. The degree to which older adults remain without access to high-speed internet or cell phone service—and rely upon landlines or other forms of technology—is a critical determinant of health and well-being. While nearly all other age groups reported internet use at rates of 96 percent or higher, in 2021 only 75 percent of older adults (sixty-five and older) reported that they used the internet, and fewer than two-thirds of people aged sixty-five and older had a broadband connection in the home.[56] Approximately 12 percent of older adults reported that they owned a smartphone but lacked a broadband connection at home. Nearly 30 percent of older adults reported that they used a cell phone but not a smartphone in 2021.[57] Internet access can facilitate greater use of telehealth services, better and stronger communications with friends and family, deeper civic engagement and more volunteerism, and more opportunities for commerce and employment—and it can be a critical lifeline to information in times of disaster.

The task of creating more climate-resilient communities has heretofore not adequately accounted for the needs of older adults, in part because the United States lacks a standard way to define who older adults are. Moreover, there exists a poor understanding of what it means to age and how our needs change as we grow older. Older adults are a wildly diverse and complex cohort in terms of housing tenure, economic stability, health and mobility, and more—and effective planning must be grounded in a clearer understanding of these and other preconditions in order to bolster community-wide resilience.

The diversity of the older adult population as described in this chapter makes it clear that a one-size-fits-all solution to climate resilience is not only failing to serve the needs of older adults—but also placing so many of them at increased risk. When assumptions are made by policymakers, local leaders, care providers, emergency management practitioners, and others about the capacity of older adults to prepare for climate change, extreme weather, and disasters, it interferes with communities' ability to identify, prioritize, and implement solutions that truly reduce their risk.

It is both an act of profound respect for the aforementioned Ms. Demalleville and our country's oldest residents, as well as a moral obligation to strive for a better understanding of who older adults are and what strategies can be deployed to better protect them and the communities in which they reside. But first, it is essential to begin by exploring precisely why climate change presents such a unique and disproportionate threat to older adults' well-being, health, and security, as chapter 2 endeavors to do.

02 CLIMATE-ENHANCED DISASTERS LOOK (AND FEEL) DIFFERENT BASED ON AGE AND OTHER VULNERABILITIES

—

The relationship between the worsening effects of climate change and an aging nation is coincident and colliding—and increasingly hard to ignore. If there were any doubts about the urgency of addressing climate change for an aging nation, the tragedies that unfolded as a result of Hurricane Ian making landfall in the southeastern United States in the fall of 2022 should put those to rest.

The hurricane was one of the deadliest to have hit Florida in nearly a century—and it hit older Americans the hardest. Of the 119 people who died as a direct result of the storm, two-thirds were people over sixty, and more than one-quarter were over eighty.[1] Stories told after the event reveal the challenges of people who felt they could withstand another hurricane, of people who had preexisting medical conditions that impeded their ability to evacuate or shelter in place, and of people who were caregivers for others but overwhelmed by the realities of doing so without the help of readily available emergency responders—in short, people who thought they were adequately prepared until it was too late.[2]

Since Ian, two other catastrophic events devastated US communities in late 2022: repeat atmospheric rivers and rain inundation that caused widespread damage in California, leading to at least sixteen deaths, one-third of them among people over sixty,[3] and winter storms in Buffalo, New York, causing forty-one deaths, 63 percent among people over sixty.[4] (See chapter 5 for an expanded discussion of the State of New York.) These events illustrate the very nature of what this book refers to as climate-enhanced disasters, in which historical trends in rain, snowfall, heat, and hurricanes are upended,

revealing more intense, frequent, and deadly events that disproportionately harm older adults.

The reason older adults consistently and tragically account for
the largest share of deaths resulting from climate-enhanced disasters
is that dimensions of vulnerability intersect and compound. While
some dispute the notion of age itself as a vulnerability, the reality
is that increased age amplifies other vulnerabilities in physical and
mental health, cognition, financial well-being, isolation, mobility, and access that intersect with climate change in very real ways.
This is not to say that all older adults are vulnerable; rather, it is to
acknowledge that aging often results in greater vulnerability in ways
that increase climate risk. Understanding those intersections—and
using them as a starting point for action to build more community
resilience—is at the heart of this book.

Some may challenge the idea that climate exposure disproportionately affects older adults, arguing that there are inherent advan-
tages that offset any increased risk, such as a longer perspective based
on years of experience contributing to a greater sense of resilience
and perhaps even self-reliance. Others may point to potentially
deeper roots in their communities enjoyed by older adults as a result
of a lifetime of service, parenting, or civic leadership. Still others
may point to cultural traditions that place older adults at the center
of families in which elders are looked to and cared for as community anchors. While these may be true, they are likely to be woe-
fully insufficient to offset the increased risk to older adults relative
to other age groups that a changing climate—and increasingly fatal
climate-enhanced disasters—will bring.

The story of eighty-nine-year-old Helen Gatanis is a stark example of how climate vulnerability is affected by age in ways that can
increase risk. Facing what we now know to be the devastating Superstorm (or Hurricane) Sandy in 2012, Ms. Gatanis made national
news for her unwillingness to leave her New Jersey home.[5] Despite
having midstage Alzheimer's disease, Ms. Gatanis lived alone in her
family home with her cat, following the death of her husband several
years prior. She benefited from the support of local eldercare providers, who evacuated her to a nursing home as the storm approached.
But upon realizing where she was, Ms. Gatanis refused to stay in the
facility, insisting that she wanted to be in her home and with her

pet. She was ultimately returned to her home with food and a flashlight by caregivers—but not before she asked why she would need a flashlight, an indication that perhaps she still didn't understand the severity of the risks she would face. Fortunately, local police were able to check in on her despite downed trees and power lines, and Ms. Gatanis emerged unscathed from the storm. Many others in comparable situations have not been so lucky.

Resilience interventions that fail to include age—for example, those that target low-income populations or communities of color alone without an overlay of age—are inadequate. But, in order to be effective, resilience interventions must also go beyond years of age to account for the array of abilities and conditions associated with aging that help to explain this unique cohort. Effectively doing so will bring about a deeper understanding of how age can exacerbate risk in ways that call for different approaches that can ultimately strengthen whole communities.

Understanding the Climate Trends: More Intense, Frequent, and Deadly

For more than two decades, there has been nearly uniform consensus in the scientific community that the climate is changing, and in ways that seem increasingly worrisome with each new report.

The report that is perhaps most widely regarded as the definitive narrative on the risks presented through our changing climate is the National Climate Assessment. First issued by the US Global Change Research Program in 2000 as *Climate Change Impacts on the United States: The Potential Consequences of Climate Variability and Change*, the report is now updated every few years. The 2018 report, the most recent as of this writing, methodically analyzes the probability of change and estimates the impact on the human population, stating:

> The impacts of climate change are already being felt in communities across the country. More frequent and intense extreme weather and climate-related events, as well as changes in average climate conditions, are expected to continue to damage infrastructure, ecosystems, and social systems that provide essential benefits to communities. Future climate change is

expected to further disrupt many areas of life, exacerbating existing challenges to prosperity posed by aging and deteriorating infrastructure, stressed ecosystems, and economic inequality. Impacts within and across regions will not be distributed equally. People who are already vulnerable, including lower-income and other marginalized communities, have lower capacity to prepare for and cope with extreme weather and climate-related events and are expected to experience greater impacts. Prioritizing adaptation actions for the most vulnerable populations would contribute to a more equitable future within and across communities.[6]

The report also provides a preview of the health impacts of climate that well illustrates the wide-reaching implications of our changing environmental conditions.

More frequent and/or more intense extreme events, including drought, wildfires, heavy rainfall, floods, storms, and storm surge, are expected to adversely affect population health. These events can exacerbate underlying medical conditions, increase stress, and lead to adverse mental health effects. Further, extreme weather and climate events can disrupt critical public health, healthcare, and related systems in ways that can adversely affect health long after the event.[7]

However, despite a comprehensive analysis—and acknowledgment throughout the report of the need to prioritize adaptation actions for vulnerable populations—the section dedicated to the built environment and urban systems devotes surprisingly little attention to the impacts on older adults. Age isn't even included as a factor among its key messages for planners and local leaders to consider with regard to built environment solutions that can affect climate vulnerability: "Vulnerabilities are distributed unevenly within cities and reflect social inequalities related to differences in race, class, ethnicity, gender, health, and disability. These populations of concern are at a greater risk of exposure to climate change and its impacts."[8] Older adults—at least those who live alone—are mentioned only in passing in describing the impact of heat on older adults ("Children playing outside, seniors living alone, construction workers, and athletes are also vulnerable to extreme heat").[9]

The complementary and equally well-regarded report by the global Intergovernmental Panel on Climate Change (IPCC) explains the factors that contribute to these projections and calls on governments, industry, and private actors to take greater action now to reduce the severity of the projected events. The IPCC states that greenhouse gas emissions must be reduced by nearly one-half and methane emissions by one-third by 2030 if we are to stave off the worst of the projected effects.[10]

The best available data reveal that carbon emissions do have an impact on climate change, which is being revealed not only by record-setting droughts, devastating floods, and increasingly intense weather events but also in the havoc that a changing climate wreaks upon communities and people around the world.

In the United States, the annual average number of billion-dollar disasters—defined by the National Oceanic and Atmospheric Administration (NOAA) as "weather/climate disaster events with losses exceeding $1 billion each"—in the past five years has been more than twice the annual average for the past thirty-year period.[11] Eighteen events were logged during 2022 (roughly the same number as the most recent five-year trend average): one drought event, one flood event, eleven severe storm events, three tropical cyclone events, one wildfire event, and one winter storm event. In total, the events resulted (in the near term) in the deaths of 474 people and delivered significant economic hardship for the people and places where they occurred.[12]

Climate Effects Aren't Evenly Distributed

While the broad strokes of a changing climate are very clear, the ways in which it affects people and communities are often less clear. A range of factors—such as development patterns, environmental resources and conditions, and proximity to hazards—cause climate effects to be unevenly distributed in ways that imperil some places more than others.

Differences emerge between rural and urban areas, for example. In general, rural places across the United States dependent on

agricultural economies are already seeing evidence of shorter growing seasons, drought conditions, loss of crops and livestock due to
extreme heat, and devastation resulting from flooding or wildfire
events. This disruption threatens to upend the very nature of the
economy upon which rural communities are built, and in some cases
is further contributing to population decline and migration. In rural
places that are dependent on recreational activities, such as skiing
or hunting, warmer temperatures are significantly altering snowfall
and snowpack patterns and affecting wildlife migration patterns in
ways that further disrupt local economies and the quality of life for
residents. Soil and water degradation is likely to increase, creating
additional hazards for agricultural production and the communities
that rely upon it.[13]

In urban places, extreme heat is further exacerbated by the built
environment, with buildings collecting and storing heat throughout
the day and requiring more energy to cool internal spaces. Roads,
highways, and sidewalks all absorb, store, and radiate the heat col-
lected, contributing to the "urban heat island effect" in cities. For
neighborhoods with inadequate tree cover—such as downtown areas
and lower-income communities that have suffered from underinvest-
ment and disinvestment as a result of redlining—temperatures can
be among the highest experienced in urban areas, layering heat on
top of heat. Urban areas can also be hot spots for asthma resulting
from concentrated pollution, which is exacerbated by extreme heat.
Urban areas that are located on waterways or shorelines (as are many
historically important commercial centers) are subject to flooding,
storm surge, and sea level rise where the risks are amplified by imper-
vious surfaces incapable of slowing runoff or absorbing excess water.
Such events contribute to damage and deterioration of infrastructure
and to traffic delays that impede economic activity.

Climate change also does not affect all populations equally. It is
increasingly clear that race, ethnicity, income, and tribal affiliation
deliver a very different experience when it comes to our changing
climate. In 2021, the US Environmental Protection Agency (EPA)
released a comprehensive analysis of how climate change differently
affects a number of "socially vulnerable" populations (see figure 2-1).
Evaluating impacts across a range of risks—extreme heat, air pollution, coastal flooding, and inland flooding—the report concludes

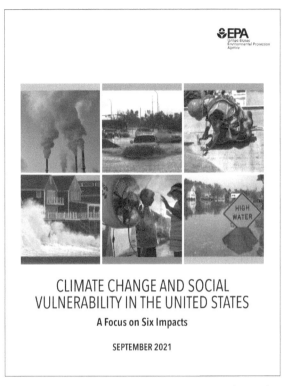

Figure 2-1: Cover of US Environmental Protection Agency report "Climate Change and Social Vulnerability in the United States." (Source: US EPA, 2021)

that several groups that are already socially vulnerable are more likely to suffer in the face of climate change.

- African Americans are more likely to live in areas that will see the highest projected increases in mortality rates caused by climate-driven changes in extreme temperatures, and they are more than one-third more likely to live in areas with the highest projected increases in childhood asthma resulting from climate-driven changes.[14]
- Hispanic and Latino[15] populations are 43 percent more likely to live in areas with the highest projected loss of labor in weather-exposed industries (such as agriculture, construction, transportation, and utilities) as a result of climate-driven increases in high-temperature days. These individuals are also 50 percent more likely to live in coastal areas with the highest projected

increases in traffic delays from climate-driven changes in high-tide flooding areas.
- American Indian and Alaska Native people are 48 percent more likely to live in areas that will be inundated by sea level rise. American Indian and Alaska Native individuals are also 37 percent more likely to live in areas with the highest projected labor hour losses in weather-exposed industries as a result of climate-driven changes.[16]

In general, low-income populations and those with low educational attainment are more likely to be negatively affected by climate change, with as much as a 25 percent greater chance of living in areas with high labor loss caused by climate change, higher rates of asthma, and higher probability of inundation from sea level rise.[17]

Predictably, geographic areas across the United States will also be affected differently. Individuals not only will be exposed to hotter days, more flooding, and more severe storms. They also will experience the effects of these changes on the built and natural environment in the form of worsened health, diminished access to jobs and education, and loss of property—challenges that many already vulnerable communities can hardly afford to bear.

- In the Northwest, climate change is most likely to manifest in extreme heat, coastal flooding, and changes to air quality. The resultant job losses; health effects, particularly increased childhood asthma cases (EPA's report did not estimate asthma rates for people sixty-five and older); and traffic interference will disproportionately affect low-income communities and communities of color.
- In the Southwest, many of the same dynamics are at play, with greater projected losses (due to coastal flooding) of property, again disproportionately affecting low-income communities, communities of color, and those with low educational attainment.
- In the Northern Great Plains, the greatest risk will be posed by extreme heat and the resultant impacts on jobs, disproportionately affecting communities of color.

- In the Southern Great Plains, significant increases in health problems (largely asthma incidence) are projected as a result of extreme heat and deteriorating air quality, with a predominant impact on communities of color.
- Low-income communities in the Northeast are projected to be disproportionately affected by coastal flooding and the resultant traffic interference, impeding access to jobs, education, and economic opportunity.
- And in the Southeast, communities of color are projected to be most significantly affected by high-tide flooding and the related disruption to mobility, access, and opportunity.[18]

Acknowledging these differences, the Biden administration is implementing an initiative known as Justice40 to ensure that 40 percent of the investments in climate resilience benefit communities of color, stating, "For far too long, environmental policy decisions have failed to adequately account for environmental injustice, including the disproportionate, disparate and cumulative impacts pollution and climate change have on low-income communities and communities of color."[19] Justice40 provisions are informing the allocation of hundreds of billions of dollars in climate investment authorized in the Inflation Reduction Act of 2022, as well as an array of programs operated throughout the federal government. While older adults certainly are counted among those groups targeted by Justice40, the lack of an explicit focus on age as part of equity efforts—and the additive complications related to aging for some, on top of economic or other disadvantages—means that the US government potentially fails to miss the mark in truly ensuring a more resilient future for older Americans.

Perception, Preparation, and Risk

Anticipating climate change and climate-enhanced disasters may be thought of as a pragmatic, intellectual effort. Barring any cognitive, financial, socio-emotional, or other barriers, preparedness is an exercise in gauging one's risk exposure and taking steps to mitigate it in advance of an event by carrying out a thoughtful, informed series of tasks.

Experiencing climate change and climate-enhanced disasters, however, is of a different nature altogether. It is a physical, emotional, tactile, intellectual, financial, and sometimes existential experience that is profoundly intertwined with who we are as individuals. And simply stated, older adults experience climate change differently—not just during deadly, extreme events but also in the months or years that follow, given the longer-term impact on health and well-being.

Effective climate resilience requires a clear-eyed understanding of the risks posed by climate change, an understanding of how people perceive and prepare for those risks, and the deployment of interventions to address any remaining gaps. The complexity of the older adult population in the United States makes it difficult to achieve all of these prerequisites for resilience with precision. Not only is there a variation in how older adults perceive risk, and in how risk is influenced by vulnerabilities, but also there is no uniform intervention that works for all. Even evacuation—arguably the most logical response to dangerous conditions—can in some cases lead to greater risk among medically frail older adults[20] and a more rapid decline of those who struggle but were faring adequately in their home of origin.

Increasingly, older adults recognize that natural disasters—including those that are climate enhanced—are likely to affect them. The National Preparedness Poll conducted annually by Healthcare Ready (a nonprofit group focused on disasters and health) reported in 2022 a stark increase in adults' perception of their likelihood to experience a natural disaster. Among all ages, 35 percent of people surveyed were concerned that a natural disaster would affect their community—an increase of ten percentage points in just two years. Natural disaster was reported as the greatest source of concern overall; other options included fear of environmental disaster, exotic disease outbreak, and terrorist attack. For older adults, the perception is even higher, with 44 percent of people fifty-five and older reporting that their greatest concern was that a natural disaster would affect their community.[21] But that increased awareness has not always translated into a clear idea of what to do as a result.

Whether evacuation or sheltering in place is the community response to climate-enhanced disasters, it becomes imperative to understand how perception, preparation, and risk can influence one's willingness and ability to flee—or to take any other action. For longtime residents of areas beset by hurricanes, there may be an unwillingness to evacuate because they have "been through this before" and have confidence in their ability to rely upon themselves, with little appreciation for how physical needs change over time. In Florida, an AARP survey revealed that 78 percent of older adults (defined as forty-five or older) had personally experienced a natural disaster in their lifetime—and that more than half intended to stay in their home during the next emergency, compared with just 13 percent who would move to a public shelter. The same survey revealed that just two in five older adults felt very prepared to deal with the next emergency, and only one-quarter were very confident that they could rebound financially.[22]

For those suffering from cognitive decline (as was the case with Ms. Gatanis) or who lack access to news sources and communication channels for updates and warnings, an incomplete understanding of their risk exposure may hamper their ability to take action. For those who lack transportation or who are unwilling to leave medical equipment or companion pets, evacuation may be wholly infeasible. For those who are caregivers for others—a spouse, an adult child with disabilities, or an aging parent—the question of relocating even temporarily brings with it layers of questions about care, resources, and capacity. For some, the barrier is a financial one. A 2020 study conducted by researchers at the University of Michigan revealed that roughly 25 percent of older adults who responded to their survey would have difficulty affording a temporary relocation lasting for one week or more if asked to evacuate.[23]

For still others, the potential harm and damage associated with climate-enhanced disasters may take a back seat to a deeper, more existential concern about leaving their home. Indigenous communities in Alaska—where the thawing permafrost upon which their homes and roads were built is now leading to land subsidence, contaminated water, and dangerous living conditions—are on the front lines of such existential questions. Some communities are in the process of moving, while others, such as Shishmaref, are resistant, citing long-standing traditional ties to the land, their community, and a way of life that cannot be easily replicated elsewhere.[24] In May 2022, an estimated 60 percent of residents in drought-plagued rural

Mora County, New Mexico—where 30 percent of the population is sixty-five and older[25]—refused to evacuate in the face of devastating fires as a result of their generational ties to the land, traditions of ranching, and deep sense of place. The state's governor, Michelle Lujan Grisham, acknowledged the plight of residents in her state who, for a range of reasons, were unable or unwilling to leave: "I have no doubt that we have people without power who are on oxygen. I have no doubt we have individuals who are running out of food and water."[26] Understanding how older adults perceive risk—climate related and more generally—and are likely to respond is an essential first step in securing the safety of the whole community.

Climate Risk Is Higher in States Where More Older Adults Live

It is likely that confounding questions regarding evacuation and relocation like the ones described in New Jersey, Alaska, and New Mexico will grow, given that the states with the highest number of our nation's older adults are also among those facing the greatest future climate risk. Several of the most populous states in terms of where older adults reside (see chapter 1)—California, Florida, Texas, New York—have already seen increases in the frequency and intensity of deadly events in recent years, ranging from wildfires to hurricanes to extreme cold. These trends are unlikely to abate and, per the National Climate Assessment, are on track to worsen.

Climate Central, a national nonprofit organization focused on communicating climate risks, released a special report on older adults and climate in 2021 in which it explored sea level rise specifically. Noting the near doubling of coastal residents aged sixty-five and older between 1970 and 2010 (see figure 2-2), the report examined how rising sea levels in five states (including Florida and Texas) would affect older residents. In particular, it examined the exposure risk of nursing homes to sea level rise in light of the extreme vulnerability of these residents to death and health setbacks resulting from hurricanes, flooding, and storm surges and how that vulnerability can be exacerbated by evacuation and relocation for the most frail and unwell. The report found that Florida would be the hardest hit by climate change, with a two-thirds increase in the number of units potentially exposed to storms or flooding, equating to nearly six thousand beds

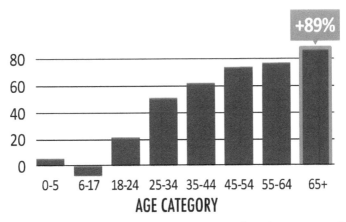

Figure 2-2: Coastal population growth in terms of percentage change between 1970 and 2010. (Source: Climate Central, "Coming Storms: Climate Change and the Rising Threat to America's Coastal Seniors; Part 1: Senior Facilities at Risk," March 3, 2021)

across ninety-one facilities. Nearly one-quarter of these facilities are in locations subject to chronic or frequent flooding.[27]

Whether potential threats involve flooding, wildfires, or other hazards, understanding such risks can help to inform decisions that minimize the need to evacuate. The Climate Central report states that mortality rates cited for older adults following disasters may underreport deaths by as much as one-half as a result of the indirect impacts of evacuation as compared with sheltering in place.[28]

Other researchers have documented the significant risks of morbidity and mortality that can come with evacuation of nursing home residents, illustrating higher rates of death and hospitalization in the weeks following hurricanes compared with similar periods in which there was no hurricane.[29] The disruption in medical care and the physical, emotional, and mental stress of evacuation all complicate the question of how to best mitigate the risks of our most vulnerable residents when they face harm.

Long-Term Care Providers Are Becoming More Attuned to the Risks but with Limited Impact

It may be convenient to conclude that the best solution is to develop stricter requirements for nursing homes and long-term care facilities in ways that would keep older, more vulnerable residents safer.

That could include relocating facilities away from areas of chronic flooding and developing more secure alternatives for transporting residents while ensuring adequate medical care. Many of these and other practices are, in fact, underway. The challenge, however, is that they apply to only a very small share of our country's older adults. Only 2.3 percent of older adults live in nursing homes, and another 1.5 percent live in assisted living facilities.[30]

In the wake of Hurricane Katrina in 2007—and the heart-wrenching images and stories of older adults in harm's way—many long-term care providers throughout the United States responded by developing facility-specific preparedness plans, increasing coordination among providers and emergency management practitioners with new tools that better track facility status and bed availability, and building awareness of the medical needs of older adults. Policy changes also occurred, including the recharacterization of nursing facilities as healthcare providers, entitling them to priority status for power restoration when utilities go down. Greater guidance now exists to help determine when sheltering in place is recommended over evacuation and how facilities can access needed transportation when evacuation is required.[31]

Perhaps most significant, in 2016 the US Department of Health and Human Services' Centers for Medicare and Medicaid Services (CMS) published new requirements for emergency planning and preparation that apply to all facilities that receive Medicare or Medicaid funding (see the chapter 4 section on integrating preparedness into healthcare for more discussion). The Emergency Preparedness Rule aimed to "provide consistent emergency preparedness requirements, enhance patient safety during emergencies for persons served by Medicare- and Medicaid-participating facilities, and establish a more coordinated and defined response to natural and man-made disasters."[32] But in 2019, citing a burden to providers, CMS announced changes to the rule that in some ways weakened it, extending the period for which emergency plans and processes had to be updated from annually to every two years and providing more latitude to providers in how training exercises would be conducted. The so-called Burden Rule stated that providers no longer needed to document the "process for cooperation and collaboration with local, tribal (as applicable), regional, State, and Federal emergency preparedness officials' efforts to maintain an integrated response during a disaster or emergency situation"—they merely had to be able to describe it.[33]

Perhaps it is no surprise, then, that recent events reveal a still fractured system among providers that often fails to adequately protect older adults. Following Hurricane Ida in 2021, it was reported that fifteen elderly people in Louisiana died after being evacuated from a nursing home to a warehouse that was later deemed unsafe and unsanitary.[34] Nursing home owner Bob Dean maintained that he was in compliance with the thinly worded legislation, which relies upon self-reporting by the provider that emergency plans are adequate and requires that plans be reviewed by—but not approved by—the state department of health.

Federal guidelines have been augmented by some state-level actions that seek to strengthen protections for older adults. In Florida, a law was passed in 2017 that requires nursing homes to have on-site power generation sufficient to keep facilities cool for ninety-six hours. Despite initial opposition to the law by the nursing home industry, there is now reported to be widespread compliance with the requirement, along with calls for nursing homes to ensure that all facility areas remain cool—not just common areas.[35] Meanwhile, in Texas, advocates have sought changes to the state law that would prioritize facilities serving older adults for power restoration, noting that the law currently requires nursing homes to have only four hours' worth of fuel on hand for generators and even fewer (or no) requirements for smaller assisted living facilities.[36]

Ultimately, the mix of federal and state guidelines has resulted in a patchwork of regulations and loopholes that does little to build confidence that a robust and consistent approach is in place.

The Default Focus on Individual Preparedness Often Fails to Account for Age

For the vast majority of older adults who live in their homes—often alone—the strategy to reduce risk is often quite different from that governing congregate facilities. The most prevailing default approach focuses on the ability of the individual to prepare for and withstand a disaster, often with very little differentiation based on age or ability.

Emergency managers routinely implore all community residents, regardless of age, to take steps to prepare for emergencies by developing and testing an evacuation plan, having a first aid kit on hand, stockpiling food and water, and securing alternative sources of emergency power and lighting such as batteries, flashlights, and in some cases generators. For able-bodied, financially secure older adults, these recommendations may be perfectly appropriate. But for those with diminished physical capacity, little or no financial reserves, and perhaps cognitive decline (see chapter 1), a strategy that rests principally on individual preparedness is unlikely to suffice.

There is no shortage of resources and articles on the topic of how best to prepare for disasters—particularly in advance of hurricane or wildfire seasons or during National Preparedness Month in September each year. The Federal Emergency Management Agency (FEMA) hosts the robust Ready.gov website, which serves as a treasure trove of checklists, guides, and tips to help build individual preparedness for a wide array of disasters and risks, including some specifically targeted to the needs of older adults, such as reminders to sign up to receive Social Security benefits electronically and create a support network well in advance of a disaster.[37] Even more detailed information is provided for people with disabilities, including specific guidance on power to ensure that in-home medical equipment can continue to operate in an emergency. The American Red Cross similarly offers a rich source of online material targeting older adults, including a checklist urging people to prepare to stay at home for at least two weeks or evacuate, as well as free trainings on preparedness through the Be Red Cross Ready program.[38]

As awareness grows about the unique needs of older adults and people with disabilities in times of disaster, more customized resources are becoming available that augment generalized preparedness information. A 2021 article advises older adults about the trade-offs between standby (whole-house) and portable generators—and how to operate them safely—for those who seek backup power to remain cool or operate medical equipment.[39] Emphasis is beginning to be placed on communicating to caregivers about how to best protect older adults in their care by, for example, maintaining a set of copies of important documents (including power of attorney, a list of prescription medications, and a description of health conditions) in a waterproof bag within easy reach in case of evacuation.[40] And tailored information for caregivers of those with Alzheimer's disease helps account for the impairments in memory and reasoning that can severely limit a loved one's ability to act appropriately in a crisis. One such article cautions caregivers to include incontinence materials in their disaster kit and to prepare for wandering, which can result from the heightened anxiety that comes with relocation.[41]

One's ability to be prepared must, of course, be coupled with access to timely and trusted information to enable better decision-making in times of disaster. The COVID-19 pandemic provided a unique and timely lens into the shortcomings of our focus on individual preparedness (see chapter 3), particularly as it relates to access to information. The 2022 survey conducted by Healthcare Ready noted that the principal source that people fifty-five and older turned to for information about the pandemic was news outlets (39 percent), in contrast to people aged eighteen to thirty-four, whose principal source was social media (22 percent).[42] Researchers at the University of Chicago found a strong correlation between lack of broadband access and an increased rate of death from COVID-19, even after controlling for age, income, and education. They found that an additional 2.4 to 6 deaths per 100,000 people could have been avoided for every additional 1 percent of residents in a county with internet access. The sheer lack of access to broadband—a situation common among older adults (recall data featured in chapter 1)—increased one's chance of dying from COVID-19 as a result of diminished access to information, vaccine sign-ups, food support, and medical care.[43] Both studies point to the need for a comprehensive, coherent, and multichannel approach to disseminating disaster-related information.

Without solving for how to ensure older adults can access timely, relevant, and trusted information, even the best emergency preparedness efforts are likely to be rendered ineffective.

Climate-Enhanced Disasters Differently Affect Older Adults

Any effort to reduce risks for older adults—including but not limited to the well-intentioned efforts described here—must first begin with a deeper understanding of how a range of climate-enhanced disasters[44] affects older adults.

Extreme Heat

Extreme heat is now the leading cause of weather-related deaths in the United States. "It kills more than all other weather-related causes combined, including tornadoes, hurricane, lightning, blizzards, and so on," said Laurence S. Kalkstein, noted climatologist and chief heat science advisor for the Adrienne Arsht-Rockefeller Foundation Resilience Center.[45] A 2020 Climate Central report focusing on heat and older adults noted that twelve thousand heat-related deaths occur in the United States each year—roughly the same number of deaths as caused by gun violence—and of those, 80 percent are among people over sixty.[46]

Extreme heat is uniquely dangerous for older adults because many lack the ability to readily adjust to extreme heat as a result of weakened cardiovascular circulation or preexisting health conditions such as heart disease and diabetes and the medications they may require. The two main ways for the human body to rid itself of excess heat—sweat and dilated blood vessels that efficiently move heat away from internal organs to the skin—become impaired as the body ages. Furthermore, medications taken for preexisting conditions can interfere with feelings of thirst, the body's cue for hydration. And the fatigue and weakness brought on by heat or dehydration can increase the danger that signs of more dire conditions, such as heat stroke, will be missed because the signs can mimic manifestations of chronic conditions, thereby going undiagnosed.[47]

Risk associated with rising temperatures is likely to be widespread, affecting many of the same states where the majority of older adults live, as previously mentioned, as well as other locales that have not yet adapted to warmer conditions. The aforementioned report by EPA focusing on vulnerable populations noted, "Some of the highest projected increases in mortality rates occur in cities in Ohio and Pennsylvania, likely because these cities are not as heat-adapted as many warmer-climate locales."[48] The danger to older adults posed by heat was evident in the Pacific Northwest heat waves in 2021 and 2022, which occurred in a region more characterized by cool and wet conditions, where few homes are constructed with air-conditioning. The 2021 heat wave ultimately caused roughly one thousand deaths across Oregon, Washington, and British Columbia—primarily among older adults.[49] Data released by the Oregon State Medical Examiner revealed the ages of people who died in the heat wave by county: in eight out of ten counties with fatalities reported, the average age of people who died was sixty-two or older (see figure 2-3a). In Multnomah County, Oregon, where the largest number of heat wave–related deaths in the Portland area were reported, accounting for 62 percent of all deaths, the average age was sixty-seven[50] (see figure 2-3b). Next door in Washington State, three-quarters of all people who died were over sixty-five.[51] (See chapter 5 for an expanded discussion of Portland and Multnomah County.)

In 2022, both the United States and Europe experienced their hottest summer on record.[52] In early September, the *Washington Post*'s Capital Weather Gang noted, "In just the past week, nearly

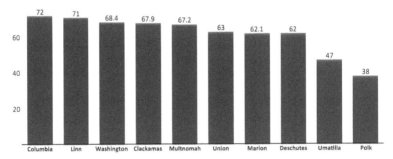

Figure 2-3a: Heat-related deaths in Oregon in 2021, average age by county.

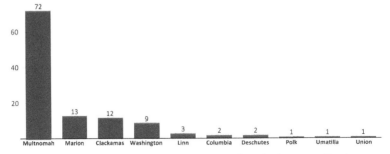

Figure 2-3b: Heat-related deaths in Oregon in 2021, total number by county. (Graphics courtesy of *The Oregonian*)

1,000 heat records have been broken, including more than 270 monthly records. Some places, like Salt Lake City, Sacramento and Reno, Nev., have broken their September records multiple times and by large margins."[53]

For the many older adults who live alone, heat can be more dangerous because no one is present to observe the changes. For older adults who lack cooling systems in the home (as was the case for many in the Pacific Northwest), lack the physical ability or transportation to get themselves to cooling centers, or are financially vulnerable in ways that cause them to limit their use of air-conditioning to conserve costs, heat waves can be and are deadly. Without systems in place to ensure safety—whether by caregivers, family members, eldercare programs, or a social network—older adults who live by themselves are forced to confront these challenges alone. The lack of a robust social infrastructure in the form of nearby neighbors and friends to monitor and provide help literally means the difference between life and death for older adults in times of emergency. Eric Klinenberg famously documented this effect when studying the devastating 1995 heat wave that pummeled Chicago, in which more than seven hundred people died—overwhelmingly older adults—finding that areas with robust civic infrastructure, strong community organizations, and public spaces that encourage social interaction were far less deadly for residents than those without.[54]

Other factors certainly compound the risk. For those who live in urban neighborhoods that lack tree canopy, where temperatures are significantly higher because of the urban heat island effect, otherwise tolerable temperatures can veer into untenable and fatal levels. One paper predicts that "urban heat island warming will probably be equivalent to about half the warming caused by climate change by the year 2050," meaning that significantly higher temperatures beyond those caused by climate change will affect some areas.[55]

Extreme Cold

Older adults lose body heat faster than they did when they were younger, bringing about a greater risk of hypothermia—a condition in which one's body temperature drops below 95 degrees Fahrenheit—which can lead to heart attacks, kidney problems, or liver failure. For older adults already managing chronic diseases, the impacts of hypothermia compound and exacerbate ongoing health risks. New research shows that extremely cold weather appears to increase the risk of dying from heart failure by 37 percent.[56] Among cardiovascular-related deaths, very cold days accounted for nine additional deaths per one thousand deaths, compared with two additional deaths attributable to very hot days. But for those with heart failure, extreme cold was responsible for thirteen additional deaths.[57]

Similar to the situation with extreme heat, older adults who are financially strained may be inclined to conserve costs of heating by setting the indoor thermostat to lower levels, or they may be unable to sufficiently weatherize their homes to conserve costly heat. For those who resort to extreme measures to heat their space—such as turning on and opening ovens, using charcoal grills indoors, or using garage-parked cars to generate heat and power—still other risks emerge in the form of carbon monoxide poisoning. Once again, living alone can compound the risks to older adults when early signs of hypothermia, such as difficulty speaking, shivering, or physical weakness, go unnoticed or unrecognized as being related to the cold. And the lack of a social infrastructure to ensure that older adults have adequate food, water, and heat at a minimum in times of disaster can otherwise leave them very much on their own to deal with life-threatening conditions.

Flooding

FEMA notes that flooding is the most frequent severe weather threat and the costliest natural disaster facing the nation, given that 90 percent of all natural disasters in the United States involve flooding.[58] In homes subject to recurring flooding, moisture can contribute to the slow growth and spread of indoor mold, which can exacerbate existing respiratory problems and contribute to fatigue and dizziness.[59] In areas where acute inundations of water lead to extensive damage, rapid growth of black mold can present even greater risks for those with compromised immune systems (resulting from cancer treatment or infections, for example), in whom exposure can lead to invasive mold infections in the body.[60] Flooding of streets—both "sunny day" flooding and acute or catastrophic flooding—can impede older adults' ability to access needed medical care, required treatments such as dialysis or chemotherapy, prescriptions, healthy food, family, and friends. In an analysis of the impact of climate change on vulnerable populations, EPA determined that older adults were at greater risk of interrupted mobility resulting from coastal flooding due to projected climate change in the Northeast, at risk of property damage resulting from inland flooding in the Southwest and Northern Great Plains, and overall more likely to live in areas with the worst property damage from inland flooding.[61]

Drought, Wildfire, and Smoke

Just as too much water can lead to dire conditions for older adults, so can too little, particularly when it sets the stage for prolonged drought and conditions more prone to wildfire and the attendant impacts of its smoke on air quality. Beyond the obvious impacts on safety for people and structures directly in the path of fire, wildfires produce smoke and air pollution that reach many more people indirectly. For older adults, the effects are critical. Dust from drought and particulate matter found in wildfire smoke can wreak havoc on older adults with compromised immune systems and can lead to greater risk of death from asthma and chronic obstructive pulmonary disease. It can increase the risk of heart attack, especially for those who are overweight or diabetic.[62] Prolonged drought contributed to newly airborne carcinogens exposed in lake beds and riverbeds compromising the air quality around Salt Lake City, Utah, in 2021, for example—adding to already polluted air brought eastward by California wildfires.[63]

The resultant effects of wildfires are long-lasting for both individuals and land. Studies have shown increased rates of post-traumatic stress disorder, depression, and generalized anxiety among adults (and children) following wildfires[64]—all of which exacerbate and complicate efforts to rebuild and reestablish normalcy in areas affected by fire. And when previously forested lands are rendered barren by wildfire, not only are delicate ecosystems disrupted for the flora and fauna that live there, but also water quality deteriorates as erosion and runoff increase. For both people and ecosystems, it can take years or decades to regenerate.

Impacts on Health, Well-Being, and Equity

While each of the climate-related events described brings its own constellation of risks that can affect older adults' health and well-being, it is a worthwhile exercise to also aggregate the impacts of climate change on older adults' health and well-being. As noted previously, the compounding effects are often poorly understood, particularly when examined with an eye to the long-term consequences borne by older adults after disasters. Only by doing so can efforts to strengthen community resilience truly support individuals' desire to thrive as they age—and our collective interest to address and remedy inequities based on race, age, and ability.

Impacts on Health

A 2016 report by the US Global Change Research Program[65] explains that the health impacts associated with climate change are not merely a direct result of "climate drivers" such as those described earlier but also are influenced by exposure pathways—such as poor air quality or diminished quality of food and water—that magnify the effects (see figure 2-4). Further, institutional practices, such as land use or agricultural production techniques, can accelerate or mitigate these pathways along with individual characteristics such as age, gender, race and ethnicity, preexisting health conditions, and other factors.

It is notable that the report dedicates a chapter to "populations of concern," which explains that "the vulnerability of any given group is a function of its sensitivity to climate change related health risks, its exposure to those risks, and its capacity for responding to or coping with climate variability and change."[66] These groups include some communities of color, immigrant groups (especially those with low English proficiency), pregnant women, people with disabilities—and older adults. For individuals in one or more of these populations—as with older people of color, older adults with disabilities, or non-English-speaking older adults—the health risks brought about by climate change are "disproportionate, multiple, and complex."[67] And with complex problems such as these, generalized one-size-fits-all responses to mitigating risk that do not account for age and other factors are unlikely to suffice.

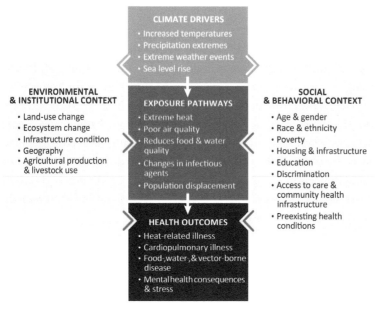

Figure 2-4: Climate change–related drivers of health outcomes. (Source: Allison Crimmins et al., "Executive Summary," in *The Impacts of Climate Change on Human Health in the United States: A Scientific Assessment* [Washington, DC: US Global Change Research Program, 2016])

Regardless of the type of climate event, the interruption of medical care that often follows—including access to needed prescriptions, medical treatments (such as dialysis for kidney failure or chemotherapy for cancer), and health monitoring—can represent significant setbacks to staying healthy. One study evaluated the long-term impacts on mortality among those fighting cancer who had been exposed to a disaster, finding that people who resided in areas most affected by the disaster had a 15 percent increase in mortality compared with those in unaffected areas, highlighting the long-term effects of interrupted treatment.[68] For those on a prescribed diet, interrupted access to healthy foods and safe places to exercise can further compound health risks. Many older adults require in-home care provided by home health workers, family members, or friends to complete basic activities of daily living, such as routine hygiene, self-medication, and self-monitoring. Yet service interruptions are likely in times of disaster, compounding the more dramatic impacts described earlier. One study found that more than three-quarters of home health agencies reported a disruption (many of one week or more) during Hurricane Harvey in Texas, despite having emergency management plans in place.[69]

Impacts associated with disasters tend to have a long tail, manifesting months or years after the event in the form of effects on both physical and mental health. Older adults living in areas where tornadoes touched down across the Southeast in 2011 were shown to have more emergency room admissions and more days of hospitalization in the year following the event than did those who were unaffected by the disasters.[70] Research released in September 2022 delved into the medium- and long-term effects on mental health among older adults following a disaster. Studying those affected by Superstorm Sandy in 2012, researchers found increased frequency of emergency room visits with mental health concerns at three months, twelve months, twenty-four months, and thirty-six months following the disaster as compared with similarly aged people living in unaffected areas, illustrating the lasting effects of exposure to disaster.[71] In surveying older adults one year after the 2020 Oregon wildfires, AARP found that nearly half of respondents indicated that the wildfire took a toll on their mental health, with even higher levels (nearing 60 percent) for those who were directly affected by the wildfires.[72] The research practice regarding how climate change affects mental health is still largely evolving, with a greater focus so far by groups such as the American Psychiatric Association (APA) on how climate affects youth rather than older adults. The APA's Committee on Climate Change and Mental Health has posted several short videos online to help practitioners better consider climate change in their client care; of these, two focus on youth and none mention older adults explicitly.[73]

Disasters Affect Well-Being

Beyond health impacts—and across nearly all types of disasters—there are some commonalities in how the well-being of older adults is affected by climate change.

Financially, older adults whose primary savings are tied up in their home equity and who subsist on a fixed income and little disposable savings (or income) are uniquely at risk of the effects of property damage. They may be unable to afford (or access) flood insurance or enhanced homeowner's insurance and may be unwilling or unable to sell their homes in areas of increased risk. A 2022 survey by AARP reports that older adults in Florida are now more concerned about the rising cost of homeowner's insurance than about the cost of health-care.[74] They may lack sufficient income or the ability to demonstrate future earnings to get a loan approved to complete repairs or make anticipatory risk-reduction investments. They may lack the techno-logical capacity, documentation, or cognitive ability to apply for and secure federal relief. For the increasingly large share of older rent-ers, many of the same risk factors exist (not including the potential loss of home equity). For those who are inadequately insured and lack savings, relocating temporarily or reestablishing residency after a disaster can be a challenge. Following the Almeda Fire in Oregon, one survey revealed that just one-half of renters had rental insurance, which can cover the cost of rent and relocation when the residence is rendered unlivable.[75] Even more stark results were reported in Flor-ida, where just 38 percent of older renters reported having rental insurance, compared with 87 percent of owners who had homeown-er's insurance. The same study revealed a prevalent concern among older adults about their ability to economically withstand a disas-ter, with less than 30 percent feeling very confident that they could rebound financially.[76]

Many older adults are not adequately covered by flood insurance, sometimes because they mistakenly believe it is covered by home-owner's insurance or because they have long since paid off their home and therefore are not required to carry flood insurance by their lender or FEMA. Damage from flooding erodes the value of a home and any accumulated financial equity, as well as creating demands for repair, flood-proofing, or elevation that can exceed older adults' financial capabilities. Unprecedented flooding in and around Yellow-stone National Park in Montana in 2022 revealed that just 3 percent of homeowners had the recommended flood insurance in place to help them recover from the damage.[77]

Others may wish to be insured but cannot afford the additional expense on a limited fixed income—particularly when their homes are in high-risk areas that are increasingly expensive to insure as maps better account for future climate change. Older adults without income, savings, or flood insurance who are faced with rebuilding or repairing their home may be unable to secure the necessary loans to do so by virtue of their limited earning potential. Increasingly for many older adults, the rising cost of flood insurance and the financial risks associated with being uninsured are becoming a principal factor in their ability to "age in place" in coastal areas.[78]

Disasters open the door to other financial setbacks as well. Closures of businesses and interruptions to transportation systems lead to very real job loss for the many older adults who rely upon wage income. In Oregon, 13 percent of older adults living in Jackson County—where a 2020 wildfire razed two towns—reported either temporary or permanent job loss as a result of the disaster. Among those reporting a temporary workplace closure, 68 percent cited a one- to three-month disruption in work, and another 13 percent reported a longer or permanent cessation of work.[79] Wildfires, hurricanes, and other natural disasters are ripe conditions for fraud targeting older adults. The heightened sense of vulnerability, confusion, and need increases the prevalence of phone scams, fraudulent contractors, and fake charity collections—so much so that AARP[80] and the Federal Trade Commission[81] now issue guidance to warn against such risks. All told, disasters can have a dramatic financial effect on older adults and their often tenuous but viable financial plans to age in place, causing significant additional stress and hardship and ultimately expediting their socio-emotional, physical, and financial decline.

Following Hurricane Ian in 2022, the *New York Times* shone a light on the mounting recognition among older adults that climate change is already affecting their well-being and will continue to do so. The article acknowledged the "small yet noticeable shift . . . causing retirees to start reconsidering moves to disaster-prone dream locales."[82] The article is premised, of course, on the notion of choice and the ability of some older adults to select where and how and they age—a luxury not equally available to all.

Inequities Compound the Effects

Not surprisingly, just as age compounds and complicates the impacts of climate change, disasters, and how communities respond, so do factors associated with race and ethnicity, income, and one's housing tenure. Any additional risk exposure that results from membership in a group that is already predisposed to poorer health outcomes or access to safe and healthy housing just adds to the risks that are unique to age.

Decades of racist land use (in the form of redlining) and other government policies have left their mark on communities in ways that lead to low-income people and communities of color being disproportionately located in areas with less access to transportation options, safe and affordable housing, and healthcare. Far too many stories exist across the United States of whole communities being destroyed or uprooted to accommodate new public and private investment in transportation, civic buildings, stadiums, universities, or other "high-value" uses (for some, not all) that promised a pathway to economic growth.[83] As a result, displaced communities were forced to relocate to often less desirable and higher-risk locations— including those prone to greater flooding or located near noxious or toxic uses—increasing their underlying risk of climate impacts and damage associated with disasters. In the years since Hurricane Katrina, these dynamics have been well documented as significant contributing factors to the hurricane's devastating and disproportionate effect on Black and low-income residents of all ages of New Orleans.[84]

The effects of those decisions and countless other policies aimed to enrich often higher-income and White Americans at the expense of lower-income and often non-White Americans are now clearly evident in differing life expectancies based on where people live. Across the United States, a tool funded by the Centers for Disease Control and Prevention reports projected life expectancy based on zip code, revealing a greater than forty-year difference between the communities where the average life expectancy is lowest, at fifty-six years (Stilwell, Oklahoma), and highest, at ninety-seven (Chatham, North Carolina). Stilwell is a largely poor and agricultural area with the largest concentration of Cherokee individuals in the United States (42 percent of residents are Cherokee), whereas Chatham is a higher-income university suburb. Areas with the lowest life expectancy have several things in common, including low levels of education; low-income, predominantly Black populations; and locations in the South.[85]

Housing tenure matters as well, with renters on average at greater risk from climate disasters. The Joint Center for Housing Studies of Harvard University found that 40 percent of the country's occupied rental stock—nearly eighteen million units—is located in areas that are vulnerable to climate-enhanced disasters. Of those, single-family rentals and manufactured rentals are the most likely to be exposed.[86] Residents of publicly supported affordable housing (projects constructed with funds from the US Department of Housing and Urban Development or the US Department of Agriculture or with tax credits issued by the US Department of the Treasury) are also more gravely at risk than are residents of owner-occupied housing or other rental housing. Nearly one-third of HUD-subsidized housing (1.5 million units) is in areas with very high or relatively high risk of negative impacts from natural hazards, compared with one-quarter of all renter-occupied units and 14 percent of owner-occupied units. Of all types of assisted housing, HUD's Public Housing program has the largest share of units (40 percent) in areas of very high or relatively high risk of natural hazards.[87] And sadly, many of the racially disparate outcomes evident in life expectancy appear among residents in publicly supported housing as well: 43 percent of HUD-assisted households of color are in areas with very high or relatively high risk of natural hazards, compared with 28 percent of HUD-assisted White households.[88]

For those who own their homes, land tenure and ownership practices in some parts of the United States can further compound the inequities, disproportionately affecting Black and Latino households. Older adults of color who live in inherited family homes passed informally down through generations—known as "heirs' property"—face greater challenges in trying to rebuild after disasters. It is estimated that as much as one-third of all Black-owned land in the Southeast—and as much as 60 percent by some accounts— is heirs' property, thereby lacking clear and standardized title to prove ownership, which is required by many lenders to access funds to rebuild post-disaster.[89] Without access to capital, these owners' homes remain in disrepair, further depressing housing values, creating unsafe and uninhabitable homes, or opening the door to investor acquisition and ultimately resident displacement. After Hurricane Maria, as many as 40 percent of Puerto Ricans' applications for

FEMA assistance were denied, in part because of homeowners' inability to produce deeds, titles, or other forms of documents proving that they owned the damaged property.[90] FEMA has since instituted policy amendments to account for heirs' property because of emerging patterns of denials for assistance, and it now allows more flexibility in ownership documentation in insular areas, on islands, such as Puerto Rico, and on tribal lands.

Still greater awareness and analysis is needed, however, to fully appreciate and plan for the intersectional ways in which climate change affects older adults. The aforementioned 2021 report from EPA that examined the impacts of climate change on vulnerable groups—people of color, low-income individuals, individuals with low levels of education, and older adults—found that in nearly all climate-related scenarios, low-income and minority individuals fared worse than the general population.[91] While the report represents a significant contribution to our understanding of how underlying factors can exacerbate climate-related risk, it acknowledged its own limitations, stating:

> Additional dimensions of social vulnerability (e.g., linguistic isolation, gender, single parent household, religion, disability, and others) are not included and warrant additional analysis. There are also many ways in which the measures of social vulnerability analyzed could contribute to adverse health outcomes, both independently and jointly, and not all of these pathways and interactions are explored in this report.[92]

It is precisely this challenge—understanding how the many dimensions of vulnerability intersect with and compound climate impacts on older adults—that is at the heart of this book. It is unlikely that community resilience can truly be achieved without a full reckoning of the "pathways and intersections" that lead to greater climate impacts on our most vulnerable community members.

There are frameworks (see chapter 3) that can be utilized in service of trying to better understand the intersection of age, vulnerability, and climate, which are already in use by some communities. Greater use of these age-friendly and disability-inclusive approaches is all the more important because of the shortcomings in federal, state, and local efforts to consider age in climate resilience efforts. But applying an age-friendly or disability-inclusive lens is not enough. Action must be taken across a range of sectors (see chapter 4) in order to reduce risk to older adults and make communities as a whole more climate resilient.

03 MOVING TOWARD CLIMATE RESILIENCE FOR ALL AGES

—

Occam's razor tells us that often the best solution or explanation is the simplest and most obvious one. For communities and a world facing mounting climate challenges that will continue to disproportionately affect a growing population of older adults, the solution seems clear: center climate responses and interventions on the needs of an aging population by using an age-friendly approach.

Global frameworks to advance age-friendly resilience already exist and are being used in a handful of states and localities in the United States and beyond, particularly in response to the global pandemic that has been deadly for so many older adults. Yet much work remains to be done to integrate aging- and disability-centered mechanisms into planning across all levels of government and across all sectors in ways that could materially change the outcome for older adults facing ever more extreme climate-related challenges. For the most part, efforts to create more resilient communities fail the age-friendly test, but with deeper understanding and commitment at the federal level, and greater embrace of inclusive frameworks at the state, local, and community levels, we can begin to move the needle toward greater climate resilience for all ages.

Understanding Age-Friendly Approaches

The World Health Organization (WHO) first identified the need to develop and implement age-friendly approaches in 2007 on the basis of input received around the world about what conditions should be present in the built and social environments to help people to live their best lives at every age.[1] Since then, WHO has led a global network of cities, states, and countries that are dedicated to the task of creating age-friendly communities, resulting in nearly 1,500 communities (roughly half of which are in the United States) participating across fifty one countries.[2] WHO explains the approach as follows (emphasis added):

> Age-friendly environments foster *healthy and active ageing*. They enable older people to: *age safely* in a place that is right for them; be *free from poverty*; continue to *develop personally*; and to contribute to their communities while retaining *autonomy, health and dignity*. Because older people know best what they need, they are at the centre of any effort to create a more age-friendly world. . . . The physical and social environments in our cities and communities are powerful influences on the experience of ageing and the opportunities that ageing affords. Cities and communities around the world are already taking steps towards becoming more age-friendly. An age-friendly world is possible and will be built by all of us—community by community, city by city, and region by region.[3]

The value of a response such as this—in which problems are addressed through an aging lens—is not limited only to facing the challenge of a changing climate. That same foundational approach of centering solutions in the needs of older adults lies at the heart of the age-friendly approach that seeks to better inform community decisions about housing, transportation, and civic engagement around the world.

While the original goals of WHO's Global Network for Age-Friendly Cities and Communities were not explicit in addressing the challenges associated with climate change, every element of the age-friendly vision is now dependent upon communities' and countries' willingness and capacity to effectively manage these growing new challenges.

- *Healthy and active aging* is not possible in areas where extreme heat and poor air quality resulting from wildfire smoke prohibit outdoor activity.
- *Aging safely* is not possible in locations where climate-related risks threaten people's ability to live securely or create conditions that compromise health and well-being.

- For older adults living in or on the cusp of *poverty*, climate change presents a very real and present threat to their financial well-being, particularly as a result of damage to their homes and property and inability to access jobs or support services.
- The ability to *develop personally* is inherently tied to older adults' ability to live with *autonomy*, *health*, and *dignity*—all of which are directly affected by climate-related disasters of greater frequency and intensity and the compounding effect of climate change on top of the physical and intellectual changes that occur as we age.

Age-friendly approaches are being implemented differently across the world as diverse actors across the fifty-plus participating countries adapt the WHO framework to their unique political conditions and cultural traditions. In the United States, the WHO age-friendly framework is implemented as the AARP Network of Age-Friendly States and Communities, with AARP serving as an organizational affiliate for WHO. Both the US-based and the global models hew closely to the same core principles, which serve well as a foundation for identifying solutions to the climate challenge with the needs of older adults in mind. The age-friendly framework is premised on eight domains of livability (see table 3-1), which represent both built and social environmental elements that merit intentional planning and coordination in order to create places that best serve the needs of older residents.

In both the WHO and AARP models, the process of implementation is similar. Action to advance each of these domains requires the commitment of elected leaders, along with a variety of stakeholder organizations, working together over a multiyear period. Often key to the process is the local Area Agency on Aging (AAA), which represents the city- or county-based entity charged with administering support provided by the Older Americans Act, such as in-home services and supports (e.g., meal delivery), caregiver information, legal support, and sometimes utility assistance programs. But stakeholders also frequently include representatives from planning, transportation, healthcare, universities, and an array of community-based interests.

The process begins with one year of community engagement to assess the needs of older adults through surveys and listening

Table 3-1: AARP's Age-Friendly Domains Defined

Domain	Definition
Outdoor Spaces and Buildings	People need public places to gather indoors and out. Green spaces, seating, and accessible buildings (elevators, zero-step entrances, staircases with railings) can be used and enjoyed by people of all ages.
Transportation	Driving shouldn't be the only way to get around. Pedestrians need sidewalks and safe, crossable streets. Dedicated bicycle lanes benefit nondrivers and drivers alike. Public transit options can range from the large scale (trains, buses, light-rail) to the small (taxis, shuttles, rideshare services).
Housing	The vast majority of older adults want to reside in their current home or community for as long as possible. Doing so is possible if a home is designed or modified for aging in place or if a community has housing options that are suitable for differing incomes, ages, and life stages.
Social Participation	Regardless of a person's age, loneliness is often as debilitating a health condition as a chronic illness or disease. Sadness and isolation can be combated by opportunities to socialize and availability of accessible, affordable, and fun social activities.
Respect and Social Inclusion	Everyone wants to feel valued. Intergenerational gatherings and activities are a great way for younger and older people to learn from one another, honor what each has to offer, and at the same time feel good about themselves.
Work and Civic Engagement	An age-friendly community encourages older people to be actively engaged in community life and has opportunities for residents to work for pay or volunteer their skills.
Communication and Information	Age-friendly communities recognize that information needs to be shared through a variety of methods, since not everyone is tech savvy and not everyone has a smartphone or home-based access to the internet.
Community and Health Services	At some point, every person of every age gets hurt, becomes ill, or simply needs some help. While it's important that assistance and care be available nearby, it's essential that residents are able to access and afford the services required.

Source: Adapted from AARP Livable Communities, "AARP Network of Age-Friendly States and Communities," 2020, 6–7, https://www.aarp.org/content/dam/aarp/livable-communities/age-friendly-network/2020/AARP-NAFSC-Booklet-20200326.pdf.

sessions, followed by one year to collaboratively develop an action plan, and finally two to three years of implementation. The five-year process makes for a defined, manageable period of time that helps to drive action. Upon completion, many age-friendly communities refine their vision, renew their pledge, and continue their work in recognition of the fact that becoming a truly age-friendly community requires commitment to an *ongoing process* rather than arrival at a single point in time.

A key element of age-friendly efforts—one worth replicating regardless of membership in any program or adoption of any framework—is the notion of giving older adults greater voice in the process of designing their communities. In both the AARP and WHO frameworks, the value of older adults as contributing members of their societies is celebrated, honored, and encouraged. In the United States, a great many of the leaders of local age-friendly efforts are older adults themselves, who work in tandem with elected and administrative leaders to implement solutions that have been identified through the process. Done well, age-friendly efforts embody the mantra of "No about us without us."

As a result, communities participating in the age-friendly network in the United States point to changes in public policy, new private-sector investments or services, and other successes—such as greater education, engagement, and collaboration—as evidence of their impact.[4] Age-friendly member communities ranging from Portland, Oregon—the first US city to enroll (read more in chapter 5)—to Pittsburgh, Pennsylvania, count among their successes changes in housing and transportation policy, new investments in services and programs, and greater coordination among community-based and public organizations in ways that better serve older adults.[5]

AARP's model expands upon WHO's model by making way for state governments—in addition to local and regional ones—to commit to an age-friendly future. The first US state to make an age-friendly commitment was New York, in 2017 (see chapter 5), followed by more than ten others in subsequent years, thereby unlocking new policy, funding, and alignment opportunities that augment and strengthen the local context for change. At present, more than seven hundred states, cities, and counties participate in the program, supported by the efforts of AARP staff and a diverse array of AARP volunteers committed to creating places that better serve all ages and help older adults to thrive.

The widespread adoption of the age-friendly framework—with its emphasis on broad stakeholder engagement, local- and state-level action, and centering of older adults' needs—represents a powerful potential framework to bring still greater focus on climate resilience and aging. While there is early evidence of some age-friendly members incorporating climate-related considerations into their efforts, more can and must be done.

Age-Friendly Communities Show What Is Possible

Countless age-friendly communities around the world illustrate how thoughtful, locally led approaches that explicitly account for age in decision-making can better serve older adults, particularly in the face of new challenges. Among the hundreds of communities and states enrolled in the AARP Network of Age-Friendly States and Communities, many celebrate how they were able to quickly pivot their preexisting plans, programs, and relationships to respond to the COVID-19 pandemic in ways that better served their oldest residents. Age-friendly members converted volunteer driver programs into food delivery efforts; mobilized volunteers to ensure that older adults, particularly difficult-to-reach seniors living alone, were informed about how to access care, companionship, and information; and advocated with decision makers to ensure that the needs of older adults were considered.[6] That same ethos can be applied—and to some degree already is—to better address climate-related disasters.

Many members of the age-friendly network have begun to explicitly integrate disaster preparedness, emergency management, or climate resilience efforts into their efforts. In some cases, that work is woven into the implementation of the Community and Health Services, Communication and Information, or Respect and Social Inclusion domains. Others have instead added a ninth domain dedicated to Emergency Preparedness (or a similarly named category) to better structure the work, raise the visibility and importance of the issue, or create more accountability for change. (See figure 3-1.)

At present, roughly fifty of the more than seven hundred age-friendly communities featured on the AARP Livable Communities

Figure 3-1: Eight domains of age-friendly livability. (Source: AARP Livable Communities, "8 Livability Domains" graphic)

Map include a focus on disaster as part of their age-friendly action plans in order to drive greater focus and attention to how to best protect older adults.[7] In 2018, Los Angeles was one of the first age-friendly cities to add Emergency Preparedness and Resilience as an explicit ninth domain to its plan, Purposeful Aging Los Angeles.[8] Several other age-friendly communities now include a growing and intentional focus on emergency and disaster preparation as result of the COVID-19 pandemic and climate-enhanced disasters, such as those featured below.

SAN FRANCISCO, CALIFORNIA

The City and County of San Francisco's Action Plan for an Age and Disability Friendly San Francisco explicitly identifies "resiliency and emergency preparedness" as one of its areas of focus, in which it commits to strengthen individual-level preparedness, community-level resilience, and greater understanding among emergency responders of the needs of older adults and people with disabilities. In the plan, San Francisco commits to the following specific actions:

- Develop [an] outreach campaign to encourage registration with AlertSF. Provide outreach through Community-based organization (CBO) partners to encourage registration with AlertSF.

- Ensure that there is a strategy in place for evacuating people with mobility challenges in multi-story buildings.
- Assess how to best reach vulnerable residents who are not connected to [existing] social service networks.[9]

Austin, Texas

A member of the age-friendly network since 2012, Austin acknowledged in its 2021 age-friendly progress report that the COVID-19 pandemic and Winter Storm Uri (February 2021) exposed gaps in its age-friendly approach, stating, "We learned from these tragic events and are currently working to improve our plan and our strategies." In the report, Austin's mayor, Steve Adler, stated, "The needs and gaps of our aging community [have] been exacerbated by COVID-19. I'm so proud to be mayor of a city that can not only identify challenges but can work collaboratively to meet the needs of older adults, especially in the midst of a crisis."

In its plan, Austin identified two specific actions related to emergency preparedness:

- The Commission on Seniors has initiated a new working group to explore the need for specific City of Austin emergency preparedness plans for older adults.
- The Aging Services Council is addressing emergency preparedness in the community by collecting input from aging-related nonprofits, creating and distributing emergency toolkits and increasing coordination among service agencies to make it easier for older adults to get help and others to give help (to older adults).[10]

Longwood, Florida

A member of the age-friendly network since 2017, Longwood commits to several specific activities with an eye to reducing risk for older adults during disasters, including educating residents on disaster management and emergency preparedness. It also commits to more coordinated efforts to relocate elderly residents to shelters and to utilize a service called Reverse 911 to inform people—particularly those without internet service or home computers—about risks of danger during storms and to advise them about local shelters.[11]

WASHINGTON, DC

Now in its third phase of age-friendly work since joining the WHO network in 2012, Washington, DC, noted significant progress in its five-year progress report to WHO, in which Emergency Preparedness and Resilience was identified as a ninth domain. Spurred by expected growth in the number of residents aged sixty and older by fifteen thousand in ten years, the district points to the following initiatives undertaken as a result of its age-friendly commitment:

- An opt-in AlertDC system now reaches registered residents through email, phone, and text, with updates on traffic and public safety. In fiscal year 2016, the system gained 10,709 new subscribers, and in 2017 it increased by an additional 3 percent to reach a total of 170,000 residents.
- In June 2017, the Text to 911 program was implemented, allowing residents to text 911 to receive emergency services if they are unable to call.
- The district is helping to train older residents through the Community Emergency Response Team volunteer program, which requires five three-hour classes for certification on how to respond in emergency situations. The program also empowers older adults and persons living with a disability to become active residents in an emergency.[12]

Alternatives and Complements to the Age-Friendly Framework

Certainly, the approach that these communities have utilized does not represent the entirety of what can be done in terms of intentional planning for older adults' resilience. Nor is the age-friendly framework the only pathway to better planning for the needs of older adults. USAging—the national membership group representing AAAs—administers the Dementia Friendly America program, which aims to equip communities to better support people living with dementia and their caregivers. Per USAging, member communities commit to convening cross-sectoral teams (including government, clinical, and community-based organizations and people in communities living with dementia and their care partners); to including people with dementia and their caregivers in communities; to adopting dementia-friendly practices; and to ensuring that both organizational capacity and an accountability structure is in place.[13] Several age-friendly communities, including Tempe, Arizona,[14] work under the auspices of both age-friendly commitments and dementia-friendly aspirations.

A 2021 article in *Nature Aging* posits that a more expansive framework is called for in order to create places that truly foster healthy living and longevity. The article explores several US communities that have been most effective in demonstrating how to create "longevity-ready cities," which not only embrace the age-friendly framework but go further by both acknowledging and addressing "the cumulative effects of exposures to the ambient urban environment" that can negatively affect healthy aging, including air and drinking water pollutants, heat stress, and limited access to green spaces.[15] The proponents depart from the conventional approach focused on older persons used by many age-friendly communities and instead identify opportunities to enhance aging at multiple points across the life span, thereby better integrating healthy aging goals within broader community health efforts. One example cited is that of California's Master Plan for Aging (MPA), adopted in 2021, which the article's authors note "is not simply for the current older population, but rather is a blueprint for aging across the entire life course, acknowledging the role of different life stages in reducing disparities in life expectancy." The MPA focuses on efforts to increase affordable and safe housing options, improve community walkability, enhance the safety of public transportation, improve access to parks and other community spaces, and integrate climate and disaster preparedness.

Born of a different but complementary global initiative to the WHO's age-friendly framework, the Disability Inclusive Disaster Risk Reduction (DIDRR) framework presents a way to engage diverse stakeholders in order to better plan for the needs of people living with chronic medical conditions, mobility limitations, or cognitive decline—specifically with disasters in mind.[16] (Read more later in this chapter under "The Global Case for Inclusive Disaster Recovery.")

RAND Corporation—a nonprofit organization dedicated to advancing solutions through research—has also developed and promulgated a tool kit, "Building Resilience in Older Adults," that offers a framework for action.[17] The tool kit invites age-friendly communities, "villages" (which are distinct nonprofit volunteer-led groups serving older adults), and public health departments to complete checklists and self-assessments to determine opportunities to build community resilience.

Regardless of which approach or framework is utilized, much more intentional work is needed to map the needs of older adults across all sectors of community resilience and institutionalize approaches, policies, and partnerships that—at every juncture— mitigate their risk. (See chapter 4.) Nevertheless, these frameworks all represent what can happen when disparate actors come together to identify and implement community-driven solutions that keep the needs of older adults and people with disabilities front and center. Arguably, the age-friendly framework—with its focus on broad stakeholder engagement, formalized process, inclusive framing, and widespread adoption globally—represents an important opportunity to advance resilience with more intentional focus on climate change and its impacts. It is precisely this type of locally driven, aging-focused, intentional action that will ultimately deliver more resilient communities in the face of a changing climate, not only for older adults but for people of all ages.

Learning from COVID-19 to Deliver Better Outcomes

The global COVID-19 pandemic—while not a climate-enhanced disaster—was useful as a test case for how well countries and communities integrated the needs of older adults into their disaster preparedness and response efforts. Sadly, it revealed that the United States generally does not have adequate structures in place to respond to disasters in the face of an aging and increasingly diverse population. Lessons from the pandemic can, however, be applied to our understanding of how disaster management efforts should be implemented and how individual and community resilience to future disasters can be improved.

As of October 2022, people aged sixty-five and older represented 75 percent of the cumulative 1.1 million people in the United States who had died as a result of COVID-19 infections, according to the Kaiser Family Foundation—which also reported that "people 65 and older have consistently accounted for a larger share of COVID-19 deaths than those younger than 65, and represented 88% of all deaths in September 2022."[18] In the United States, the rates of COVID-19 deaths have been shown to be higher among older adults from communities of color, attributable to a range of factors including access to care, access to quality housing, and more.[19] Both outcomes are due to the fact that outreach strategies deployed to promote vaccination, support ongoing medical care needs (particularly in congregate living facilities), and provide a range of other ad hoc interventions to protect health and well-being were not sufficient to blunt the impact of the pandemic on older adults.

A global study put these findings in context, comparing the impact of COVID-19 on older adults in the United States with its impact on peers in other high-income countries. The study found that older adults in the United States fared worse during the pandemic than their global counterparts in terms of maintaining uninterrupted medical care for chronic conditions, accessing help with activities of daily living, and maintaining economic well-being, with an even greater loss of savings reported by Black and Latino older adults in the United States.[20]

As evidenced by the efforts of many age-friendly communities, the pandemic served as a reminder of the value of centering the needs of older adults in decision-making. Increasingly, leaders at national, state, and local levels—including but not limited to the age-friendly leaders featured earlier in this chapter and those discussed in chapter 5—are exploring how to learn from the pandemic to develop more effective approaches for future disasters.

COVID-19 as a Catalyst for Action

The years immediately following a disaster are often a fertile time for change. Faced with COVID-19, many localities seized the moment to establish new goals regarding preparedness, and at the federal level the pandemic spurred new conversations about how to identify and implement solutions that could more effectively protect older adults in times of disaster.

Three congressional hearings during and following the pandemic demonstrate an attempt by our country's lawmakers to solve for the disproportionate impact that the pandemic had on older adults in ways that might lead to more inclusive disaster management planning. In 2021, the US Senate Special Committee on Aging convened a hearing titled *Inclusive Disaster Management: Improving Preparedness, Response, and Recovery*, which was meant to advance several pending legislative bills introduced in the 117th Congress. In 2021 and 2022, the US House Committee on Homeland Security's Subcommittee on Emergency Preparedness, Response, and Recovery convened two relevant hearings: the first was titled *Ensuring Equity in Disaster Preparedness, Response, and Recovery*, and the second was *Supporting Underserved Communities in Emergency Management.*

One of the featured legislative proposals was the REAADI (Real Emergency Access for Aging and Disability Inclusion) for Disasters Act, which aimed to invest in technical assistance and training to assist states and localities in providing better support for people with disabilities and older adults during and after disasters; to implement pilot projects to demonstrate innovative solutions in resilience that benefit older adults and people with disabilities; and to better ensure that emergency shelters meet the needs of all. One of the most important provisions was one that would ensure that people who are forced to relocate to a different state as a result of a disaster would still be able to access their Medicaid-funded support services, which otherwise are governed by state-specific eligibility requirements.[21] The 117th Congress ended without passage of the REAADI for Disasters Act, but leaders in the Senate who are committed to providing better support for aging Americans intend to reintroduce the bill in the 118th Congress, as well as incorporate elements of the act in efforts to reauthorize the Pandemic and All-Hazards Preparedness Act (PAHPA), which expires in September 2023.[22]

Prior efforts show what is possible when legislators focus on how to improve federal responses to better respond to the needs of older adults. Two new national committees now exist, authorized in the (similarly named but distinct from PAHPA) Pandemic and All-Hazards Preparedness and Advancing Innovation Act (PAHPAIA) of 2019, to ensure that lessons learned from the COVID-19 pandemic and other disasters lead to improved federal action for older adults and people with disabilities in the face of climate-related risks. The National Advisory Committee on Individuals with Disabilities and Disasters (NACIDD) and the National Advisory Committee on Seniors and Disasters (NACSD) are charged with advising the Administration for Strategic Preparedness and Response (ASPR), within the US Department of Health and Human Services, on disasters from the perspectives of seniors and people with disabilities, respectively.[23] In its inaugural meeting in April 2022, NACIDD noted that the challenges associated with COVID-19 were more pronounced for people with disabilities. These individuals were often triaged out of medical care and access to equipment, such as ventilators, to serve COVID-19 patients; were poorly served by information dissemination plans (particularly those who lived in congregate facilities for those with physical or mental disabilities); and had difficulty accessing vaccines and sign-ups. Putting a finer point on the challenges, one committee member summarized, "Much of the information released by federal and state governments was not accessible for the blind or visually impaired, or for the deaf and hard of hearing. Testing sites and vaccination sites were inaccessible to many people with disabilities across the nation. Accessible information was also scarce."[24]

Similar to NACIDD, NACSD is charged with evaluating and providing "input with respect to the medical and public health needs of seniors related to preparation for, response to, and recovery from all-hazards emergencies, and [providing] advice and consultation with respect to state emergency preparedness and response activities relating to seniors."[25] At a joint meeting held with NACIDD in August 2022, NACSD identified four shared priorities for deeper examination, which will ultimately lead to recommendations for ASPR and by extension all federal agencies: behavioral health (interstate licensing for healthcare providers during disasters, telehealth, and needed research); infrastructure (workforce training and improved climate resilience in long-term care facilities); partnerships (traditional and force-multiplier collaboration on readiness and response); and communications (disaster literacy, equity in disaster planning, misinformation risks).[26]

Notably, both committees identified two key areas for cross-cutting collaboration: communications and telehealth. The groups jointly acknowledged, "Communications—including getting materials to the end users that need them—have always been among the biggest issues in preparedness, mitigation, and post-event notification."[27] Further, telehealth merited special focus by virtue of the challenge to more effectively integrate telehealth into long-term care facilities to both improve health and relieve pressure on strained emergency care systems, and to ensure that telehealth is fully accessible to people with disabilities.[28] Certainly, improvements in both arenas would help to reduce climate-related risk for older adults and people with disabilities in future events.

Climate Planning and Disaster Resilience Tools Generally Fail the Age-Friendly Test

Local age-friendly commitments of the variety described earlier are increasingly important not only because of the compounding effects of demographic and climate-related changes underway but also because the federal government can be slow to implement change. Despite the congressional focus on disasters and the important work underway within cross-agency committees, aging considerations are still generally absent from many climate and disaster resilience tools. Even with the increased frequency and severity of disasters—and their recurring and consistently disproportionate impact on older adults—there is scant evidence that those responsible for leading disaster planning efforts are adjusting course to better consider age as a critical factor in building community resilience. Recalling that we are midway through a forty-year shift in which the number of older adults in the United States will double to reach more than eighty million people (see chapter 1), there has been remarkably little intentional focus on or exploration of the intersection between climate change and older adults within the practices of gerontology and eldercare, public health and emergency management, disaster recovery and mitigation, and climate science.

Inconsistent Messaging within Public Health and Aging Advocacy Fields

Part of the reason for the lack of a focus on aging within climate planning and disaster resilience efforts may be that there is inconsistency in messaging and focus among those who otherwise champion the needs of older adults and caregivers through advocacy, education, and engagement.

Among the field of organizations whose mission is to support the needs of older adults, the American Society on Aging (ASA) has emerged as one of the more ardent advocates for an intentional focus on climate change. ASA is one of the country's largest groups dedicated to the support of aging policy and practice, and it dedicated the Summer 2022 edition of its *Generations* journal to the topic of climate change as a clear marker of its commitment to the issue. ASA's president and chief executive officer eloquently made the case for engagement, stating, "While the field of aging may be a latecomer to the climate change discourse, we have an opportunity to harness our unique voices to drive change."[29] The journal focused on the intersections between aging and climate, how to build age-friendly and climate-resilient housing, ways to engage older adults in the solutions, and why beliefs influence response to the challenges.[30] ASA has continued its focus on educating individual and organizational members on how climate change affects their work by weaving the issue into articles and thought leadership efforts on health equity, as well as by inviting climate-focused proposals for sessions at its annual conference.[31] Climate issues—including passage of the REAADI for Disasters Act[32]—are among ASA's stated advocacy priorities in which it calls for inclusion of older adults in healthcare and environmental justice; stronger emergency preparedness, response, and recovery; and more age-inclusive volunteerism.[33]

Other groups are still finding their voice. Some groups seek to educate practitioners about specific climate-related needs or intermittently share with members information related to climate change, whereas others say nothing at all about climate change. In February 2022, LeadingAge (which largely serves care and housing providers) and the University of Massachusetts Boston jointly published a report on why climate change differently affects older adults and how service providers can better adjust their practices to reduce risk.[34] The work builds on prior efforts by LeadingAge to help service providers navigate the emergency preparedness requirements of the Centers for Medicare and Medicaid Services (as described in chapters 2 and 4).[35] In April 2022, the National Council on Aging (NCOA) published an article encouraging older adults to plan ahead to protect their health.[36] In June 2021, AARP published a set of articles on climate change and the impacts on older adults in its *Bulletin*[37] seeking to educate its thirty-eight million members about the topic, and in July 2022, it released a guide for local leaders, in partnership with the Federal Emergency Management Agency (FEMA), on how to advance disaster resilience for older adults.[38] AARP state offices have independently sought to educate members about disaster preparedness (and in some cases climate change)[39] and engage in some state-level advocacy to encourage stronger action by nursing homes and utilities to better protect older adults.[40] AARP has also supported a handful of related advocacy efforts at the federal level, including testimony to Congress "to keep older Americans healthy, safe and informed during and after increasingly powerful natural disasters"[41] and participated in the aforementioned 2022 House Committee on Homeland Security hearing on underserved communities. Still, climate change itself remains largely absent from much of AARP's public messaging and strategy. Meanwhile, the Leadership Council of Aging Organizations (LCAO), an invitation-only membership group of prominent aging groups and coalitions, does not mention climate change at all as part of its three priority areas (health, community service, and income security) or as a topic within its recent news and featured action sections on its website.[42]

This inconsistency leads to inaction. When there is not consensus among the leading voices who represent the interests of older adults about the degree to which they should address climate change, it provides room for doubt to emerge among practitioners, funders, policy officials, and decision makers about whether climate change is affecting older adults and how they should respond. And equivocation among those who are poised to make better decisions on behalf of older adults is a luxury that we can no longer afford.

A similar dynamic is evident among public health practitioners, in which there is a disconnect between national groups and local practitioners on how to both address the intersection of climate change and aging and take the necessary steps to reduce risk for older adults. Within the larger medical community, there is little doubt that climate change represents a significant and urgent health crisis. The Medical Society Consortium on Climate and Health, representing six hundred thousand health practitioners, has issued several statements urging more action from public, private, and non-profit actors to address the intersection of climate change and health and has clearly articulated the health benefits of climate interventions. Health Care Without Harm, a nonprofit dedicated to integrating sustainable solutions into healthcare practices, has developed a thoughtful guide on climate resilience strategies featuring case studies that explicitly consider aging in order to spur greater adoption in communities.[43] The American Public Health Association's Center for Climate, Health and Equity works to bring a health equity lens to help shape climate policy, engagement, and action to better address the needs of an aging population.[44] And the American Medical Association adopted a policy in June 2022 declaring climate change a public health crisis that threatens the health and well-being of all people—a move that is expected to accelerate existing efforts and identify new opportunities for action.

Yet despite this policy leadership at the national level, a 2018 article in the *RAND Health Quarterly* surveying local public health agencies and aging-in-place efforts (such as age-friendly communities and senior villages) found that most public health agencies generally do little to tailor preparedness activities to the needs of older adults. The article summarized the findings as follows:

> Public health departments focused on disaster preparedness, as well as preventing and managing chronic disease among the local population, but they did not have programs targeted specifically to older adults. Public health departments did have programs for individuals with functional limitations (which can encompass some older adults, but not all), but public health leaders did not view programming for all older adults as their responsibility.[45]

Age Not Adequately Considered in Federal Disaster Requirements or Tools

Special focus is merited for the federal agencies charged with leading recovery and resilience efforts—namely FEMA and the US Department of Housing and Urban Development (HUD)—among which increasing but still inadequate attention is paid to the unique risks associated with age. While there are several examples of disaster *preparedness* materials that consider the needs of older adults (as discussed in chapter 2), for the most part federally supported efforts to mitigate risks from climate hazards do not sufficiently incorporate an understanding of how an aging population affects community resilience. In 2022, FEMA released a report in partnership with AARP that included interviews with practitioners that revealed little understanding, as yet, of how best to tailor mitigation solutions and interventions to reduce risk for an aging population. That report noted, "To date, most work that considers the impacts that disasters have on older adults has focused on preparedness and response, rather than mitigating risk."[46] FEMA also supports the Resilient Nation Partnership Network, which seeks to foster inclusive and collaborative partnerships to improve resilience, and it engaged older adult and disability advocates in the development of its 2021 "Building Alliances for Equitable Resilience" publication.[47]

Notwithstanding these efforts, FEMA's procedures and processes still generally are not designed explicitly to reduce climate risk exposure for older adults or expedite their recovery from disasters. FEMA's shortcomings in both regards were the subject of a 2019 study by the US Government Accountability Office (GAO) following Hurricanes Harvey, Irma, and Maria in 2017.[48] The final report, titled "Disaster Assistance: FEMA Action Needed to Better Support Individuals Who Are Older or Have Disabilities," included seven recommendations to the agency to drive better outcomes.[49] (See table 3-2.)

It appears that opportunities are also missed in some core work by the agency that could drive a deeper understanding of how the needs of an aging population specifically affect community resilience and therefore more effective hazard mitigation strategies. One of FEMA's most potent tools to reduce risk—its "State Mitigation Planning Policy Guide,"[50] which governs all state hazard mitigation plans that are prerequisites for some federal funding—shows improvement over past guidance documents with a clearer focus on risks associated with "demographics; population; land use; and existing disparities in underserved communities,"[51] but it fails to mention age or the needs of older adults explicitly. Rather, FEMA paints a broad picture of

Table 3-2: GAO Recommendations to FEMA for Executive Action

Recommendation	Status of Action
1. Develop and publicize guidance for partners working to assist individuals who are older or have disabilities in requesting data and working with FEMA staff throughout the data-sharing process to obtain individual assistance data.	Reported as completed/ implemented by FEMA
2. Implement new registration intake questions that improve FEMA's ability to identify and address survivors' disability-related needs.	Reported as completed/ implemented by FEMA
3. Improve communication of registrants' disability-related information across FEMA programs.	Reported as completed/ implemented by FEMA
4. Establish and disseminate a set of objectives for FEMA's new disability integration approach.	Reported as completed/ implemented by FEMA
5. Communicate to regional administrators and regional disability integration specialists a written plan for implementing its new disability integration staffing approach.	Not yet complete as of December 2022
6. Develop a plan for delivering training to FEMA staff that promotes competence in disability awareness.	Not yet complete as of December 2022
7. Develop a timeline for completing the development of new disability-related training the agency can offer to its partners that incorporates the needs of individuals with disabilities in disaster preparedness, response, and recovery operations.	Reported as completed/ implemented by FEMA

Source: Adapted from US Government Accountability Office, "Disaster Assistance: FEMA Action Needed to Better Support Individuals Who Are Older or Have Disabilities," GAO-19-318, May 14, 2019, https://www.gao.gov/products /gao-19-318.

"socially vulnerable" populations without identifying characteristics, such as a growing share of older adults. FEMA guidance also shows improvement over past versions in its new requirement that groups consulted in plan development—such as emergency management, economic development, housing, and health and human services— must include those that support underserved communities.[52] But it nevertheless fails to explicitly call out the unique and intersectoral risks that accompany an increasingly older (both proportionally and on average) aging population. A state mitigation plan could conceivably meet requirements according to the newest (and arguably improved) FEMA guidelines with no analysis or discussion of aging.

The guidance for *enhanced* plans, which avail the qualifying state of more funding, do provide encouragement for the type of integrated, multisectoral approach to resilience that is advocated for in this book—despite failing still to explicitly call for a focus on age. The guidance states, "To be enhanced, states must demonstrate a history of integration with a wide range of agencies and stakeholders with mitigation capabilities and/or shared objectives to reduce risks from future natural hazards and increase resilience in the state, including underserved communities."[53] To that end, FEMA could significantly accelerate climate resilience for an aging nation by emphasizing the critical importance that both standard and enhanced state mitigation planning expressly consider age.

FEMA requirements for local hazard mitigation plans are equally vague in their consideration of older adults. While the guidance does encourage a focus on socially vulnerable populations in the same way the state guidance does, and calls for the involvement of housing, healthcare, or social service agencies that support underserved and vulnerable populations, the local plan guidance also fails to expressly mention age or the needs of older adults. Even in the guidance for plan updates—arguably the most consequential element of local plans, given their focus on changes in underlying conditions and newly assessed risks—there is no explicit focus on the needs of older adults. Rather, the plan invites localities to identify "conditions that may affect the risks and vulnerabilities of the jurisdictions (for example, climate change, declining populations or projected increases in population, or foreclosures) or shifts in the needs of underserved communities or gaps in social equity."[54]

HUD is an important yet often overlooked agency charged with disaster recovery and mitigation, given its role in administering both Community Development Block Grant (CDBG) funds targeted for these specific functions, CDBG-Disaster Recovery (CDBG-DR) and CDBG-Mitigation (CDBG-MIT), respectively. The 2019 notice for the just-launched CDBG-MIT program defines mitigation as "those activities that increase resilience to disasters and reduce or eliminate the long-term risk of loss of life, injury, damage to and loss of property, and suffering and hardship, by lessening the impact of future disasters."[55] And while these are precisely the sort of interventions that are needed in order to prevent the death rates among older adults that have persisted to date, the CDBG-MIT notice offers no guidance to suggest that age be a consideration by grantees in administering CDBG-MIT funds. HUD is bound by its national objective to support low- and moderate-income households, but it is also charged with directing funds to meet "urgent needs" beyond those specifically addressed in authorizing legislation—such as significant demographic changes. In addition, the nearly $7 billion in CDBG-MIT funds must be directed only to the "most impacted and distressed areas" as defined by the *Federal Register* notice (and specific to covered disasters). There is no mention of age at all in the notice. The only mention of disability is in provisions included for people with disabilities as related to relocation and displacement.[56] There is promise of change, however, in HUD's December 2022 request for input on a range of matters related to implementation of the CDBG-DR program, including the questions "What CDBG-DR rules, waivers, or alternative requirements, if any, should be modified or eliminated so that grantees are prioritizing assistance to low- and moderate-income persons and areas, vulnerable populations, and underserved communities?" and "What barriers do protected class groups [including age], vulnerable populations, and other underserved communities face in accessing, applying for, and receiving CDBG-DR assistance in a timely manner?"[57]

HUD released a "Community Resilience Toolkit"[58] in 2022 that serves as a useful resource to help guide and inform communities seeking to invest in community resilience. It focuses on low- and moderate-income communities in keeping with HUD's mission and congressional mandate and speaks only in general terms about other vulnerable populations, with few express mentions of older adults. Those interested in expanding community resilience are asked to "consider low- and moderate-income populations, those living in older or compromised structures, older adults, individuals with mobility issues, households with limited English proficiency, and households that lack personal transportation."[59] To its credit, the tool kit does acknowledge the impact of heat and the importance of aligning with Area Agencies on Aging to identify solutions, working with care providers, and planning for evacuation for those with mobility issues (including people with disabilities and older adults). To the degree that age is more consistently, intentionally, and clearly communicated by HUD for communities responding to or planning for disaster, better community resilience will result for all.

Beyond HUD and FEMA, the growing "U.S. Climate Resilience Toolkit"—which is meant to be a one-stop, whole-of-government online repository for tools and insights related to mitigating climate risk—also contains remarkably few tools that bring attention to the intersections between age and resilience. Of the more than five hundred digital tools featured on the website, of which roughly half are dedicated to assessing risks and vulnerabilities, a scan revealed very few that even include the option to overlay age when assessing a community's risk exposure. The most useful include the following:

- The Centers for Disease Control and Prevention and the Agency for Toxic Substances and Disease Registry's Social Vulnerability Index includes an option to identify people sixty-five and older.[60]
- EPA's EJScreen[61] includes an option to examine populations over the age of sixty-four.
- EPA's EnviroAtlas[62] includes an option to examine populations over sixty-four.
- The USDA's Food Environment Atlas[63] allows for a scan of populations sixty-five and older.
- The US Census Bureau's OntheMap for Emergency Management[64] incorporates real-time data from past and projected events across several agencies to aid in preparation. Importantly, it includes a screen for populations over sixty-five living alone, as well as for households containing one or more people aged sixty-five or older.

Greater leadership from and focus among federal leaders who are responsible for climate planning and disaster resilience to elevate age as a necessary consideration will be essential to enhancing resilience for older adults. Such federal leadership would encourage, guide, support, and inform the expanded state and local work that is also needed in order to effect change in the places where people live. At the same time, as this chapter highlights (and as further discussed in chapters 4 and 5), there are already examples of state and local leadership that can, conversely, inform and guide federal leadership.

Opportunities for Improved Federal Policy

Without a doubt, congressional hearings and national committees represent important steps in the right direction. But their effectiveness will ultimately be judged by the degree to which they result in new policy adoption that changes how the federal government considers and responds to the needs of older adults in disasters. It is conceivable that the work of committees and legislative efforts could accomplish the following:

- Charge FEMA with explicitly requiring that changes in the population share comprised of older adults and an assessment of related needs are addressed in state and local hazard mitigation plans.
- Require HUD to collect data on age and assess the effectiveness of action plans funded by CDBG-MIT and CDBG-DR resources on the basis of how well they respond to the needs of older adults.
- Encourage all agencies that provide competitive resources to states and localities to bolster more resilient infrastructure and community-scale mitigation investments to consider the degree to which older adults are served by the proposed investments as an evaluation factor.
- Task the GAO with broadening its scope not only to explore how older adults fare in terms of accessing FEMA disaster assistance but also to evaluate other agencies' successes or shortcomings in considering age in climate-related planning and programmatic efforts.
- Provide incentives to state and local departments of emergency management, health, housing, transportation, and community development to more explicitly coordinate and plan for the needs of older adults during disasters, including but not limited to providing funding to encourage the development and implementation of age-friendly plans.

As with all challenges that transcend borders, there are lessons to be learned from other countries. Doing so can help build the political will, expertise, and commitment necessary to achieve these actions and the many others required across all levels of government, within the private sector, and among community-based organizations to deliver more resilient places for people of all ages.

The Global Case for Inclusive Disaster Recovery

The nature of a global crisis means that the United States is not alone in recognizing that disaster relief and recovery efforts fail to adequately address the needs of all. But recalling that Americans fared more poorly during the COVID-19 pandemic than our global peers, and that gaps in integrating age persist across our federal landscape, it appears that the United States could benefit a great deal from exploring how other countries are working to achieve more inclusive disaster recovery.

Multisectoral Efforts and Local Leadership Are Critical

In the mid-2010s, the United Nations outlined an approach known as the Sendai Framework for Disaster Risk Reduction 2015–2030—named after the location of a devastating earthquake and tsunami in Japan—in order to achieve more inclusive disaster resilience. The development and promulgation of the Sendai Framework recognizes the many levels of action needed to achieve change, noting that "the State has the primary role to reduce disaster risk but that responsibility should be shared with other stakeholders including local government, the private sector and other stakeholders."[65] Adopted by UN member states in 2015 (including the United States[66]), the framework outlines four key steps that lay the groundwork for an improved disaster resilience approach in the United States and beyond:

1. Understand disaster risk.
2. Strengthen disaster risk governance to manage disaster risk.
3. Invest in disaster risk reduction for resilience.
4. Enhance disaster preparedness for effective response and to "build back better" in recovery, rehabilitation, and reconstruction.[67]

The Sendai Framework lays a great deal of responsibility at the door of localities, which are recognized as the level of government most directly charged with managing risk for their residents and best positioned to understand the localized nature of disaster risk. In so doing, the framework asks localities to better engage those who are traditionally left out of disaster response and resilience planning efforts and to ensure that there is broad and multisectoral representation in the process.

> There has to be a broader and a more people-centered preventive approach to disaster risk. Disaster risk reduction practices need to be multi-hazard and multisectoral, inclusive and accessible in order to be efficient and effective. While recognizing their leading, regulatory and coordination role, Governments should engage with relevant stakeholders, including women, children and youth, persons with disabilities, poor people, migrants, indigenous peoples, volunteers, the community of practitioners and older persons in the design and implementation of policies, plans and standards. There is a need for the public and private sectors and civil society organizations, as well as academia and scientific and research institutions, to work more closely together and to create opportunities for collaboration, and for businesses to integrate disaster risk into their management practices.[68]

Opportunities Exist to Better Include the Needs of People with Disabilities

The UN call for member states to employ multisectoral, locally led strategies to deliver more inclusive disaster recovery has already begun to advance solutions in how to mitigate disaster and climate risk for older adults, especially those with disabilities. Leaders in Queensland, Australia, cited their country's commitment to the Sendai Framework and its charge to explicitly regard people with disabilities as contributing stakeholders in disaster risk recovery as their motivation to develop and promulgate the Disability Inclusive Disaster Risk Reduction (DIDRR) framework.[69] Researchers worked in close partnership with local government leaders to establish the framework and resulting tool kit, which provides clear and useful insights to emergency managers, local leaders, and individuals to better prepare for disasters with the needs of people living with chronic medical conditions, mobility limitations, or cognitive decline in mind. The following are some of the most important and telling findings from the Queensland report:

> People with disability rely on different levels and types of function-based support every day. Access to these supports can be compromised during and after a disaster. This challenges self-reliance and the capacity of people with disability to take effective action during a disaster, increasing their risk and impacting recovery. . . .
>
> People with disability are being left behind in disaster preparedness activities worldwide. The first UN survey on disability and disasters found the majority of respondents with disability (85.57%) from 137 countries had not participated in community-level disaster risk reduction (DRR). Only 20% were able to evacuate effectively, rising to 38% when appropriate information was available. . . .
>
> DRR approaches are delivered to citizens by emergency managers through public awareness and education campaigns that are generalised to an *entire* population. These broad approaches fail to acknowledge and cater for the individualised support needs and capabilities of people with different types of disabilities in an emergency. This oversight has devastating consequences. Research shows that people with disability are more vulnerable to hazard events; they are up to four times more likely to die or be injured during disasters than others.[70]

The DIDRR framework demonstrates the value of a more integrated and inclusive disaster resilience approach—one that requires the involvement of people with disabilities, community and disability support services that support those individuals, and local disaster management groups to develop and implement approaches that better meet their needs. It encourages an explicit consideration of several functional needs as a lens through which disaster management approaches should be evaluated.[71]

The DIDRR framework—in use globally but less prevalent in the United States—could be a mechanism to further strengthen the age-friendly framework to ensure that efforts are more inclusive of the needs of people with disabilities during disasters. Many of the functional needs are closely aligned with the previously described age-friendly domains (see table 3-3). The DIDRR framework does not represent a significant deviation in how to evaluate and plan for inclusive disaster resilience and recovery; instead, it offers an opportunity to refine and expand community-led efforts in many of the age-friendly domains in order to bring a greater focus within them on functions that are deemed essential for truly inclusive and resilient communities. For example, the DIDRR framework's explicit focus on Assistive Technology and Personal Support could be integrated into the Community and Health Services domain. More clear consideration of Living Situation—including who older adults live with (or without)—can and should inform a more inclusive Housing domain. And Assistance Animals is a potentially new and important addition to the age-friendly framework—under Transportation or Housing, for example—as it relates to accommodations that must be considered well before disaster strikes so that people with assistance animals are adequately served.

The Importance of Community-Based Organizations in Inclusive Recovery

In nearly all of the frameworks discussed, community-based organizations (CBOs) play an absolutely essential role. While they largely fall outside of federal, state, and local planning and budgeting, CBOs are critical pieces of the implementation puzzle, given that they function closer to the ultimate beneficiaries. Whether they take the form of Voluntary Organizations Active in Disasters (described later in this section), community-based stakeholders in an age-friendly action plan, or leaders of a dementia-friendly initiative, the importance of these frontline groups cannot be overstated.

The DIDRR framework enhances our understanding of the critical role that CBOs play in inclusive disaster recovery. The DIDRR

Table 3-3: DIDRR Functional Supports and Related Age-Friendly Domains

DIDRR Functional Support	Description of Functional Support	Related Age-Friendly Domains
Social Connectedness	The people you do things with; your relationships with friends, family, and other people; help you give to other people	Social Participation; Respect and Social Inclusion
Transportation	How you travel where you want or need to go (e.g., car, bus, train, taxi, walking)	Transportation
Assistive Technology	The help you get from equipment but not from people	Community and Health Services
Management of Health	Taking care of your health	Community and Health Services
Personal Support	Help you get from other people	Community and Health Services
Communication	Getting, giving, and understanding information	Communication and Information
Assistance Animals	Help from animals; how you care for them	Transportation; Housing
Living Situation	Where you live and who you live with	Housing

Source: Adapted from M. Villeneuve et al., "Disability Inclusive Disaster Risk Reduction (DIDRR) Framework and Toolkit," University of Sydney, New South Wales, Centre for Disability Research and Policy, 2019, 16, https://collaborating4inclusion.org/wp-content/uploads/2019/11/DIDRR_Framework_document_FINAL.pdf.

framework—which has been applied well beyond its place of origin in Australia—is premised on an understanding of the essential role of nongovernmental support agencies in providing care for older adults and people with disabilities. These organizations can range from government-funded nonprofits that assume the role of delivering meals to homebound seniors to private in-home care providers who help with activities of daily living to "villages" that provide membership-based support with transportation and social engagement to volunteer organizations that mobilize in times of disaster. The decentralized nature of these organizations can lead them to be forgotten about or excluded from discussions and plans to prepare for disaster—but they invariably play a critical role.

One analysis of the DIDRR framework as it was applied in Puerto Rico as it recovered from Hurricane Maria (which hit the island in 2017) underscores the need for a more inclusive approach to response and recovery that better supports the roles CBOs play in providing critical frontline care. The study found the following:

- CBOs were working under financial, logistic, and resource limitations, partly because they were working far beyond the scope of their original mission.
- Government officials were unresponsive to their requests for help or information.
- Only 50 percent of CBOs serving the elderly and people with disabilities reported providing classes or training for clients or caregivers on emergency preparedness.
- Homebound older adults faced major physical barriers in obtaining CBO assistance.
- Roughly three-fourths of CBOs incorporated emergency preparedness training following Hurricane Maria.
- Fewer than half of the emergency preparedness training sessions received by CBO staff included specific information on supporting the elderly, the deaf and hard of hearing, the blind or visually impaired, people with disabilities, people with cognitive or developmental disabilities, or people with mental health conditions.
- Clients were facing major mental health issues, but CBOs emphasized that staff also needed mental health support.[72]

FEMA recognizes the important role that CBOs play in disaster response and recovery and provides direct training through its Community Emergency Response Team program, which equips frontline individuals and organizations to build the capacity to support disaster efforts led by FEMA. FEMA staff include voluntary agency liaisons who work year-round in all ten FEMA regional offices, allowing the agency to have a CBO-focused presence throughout the country and to establish liaisons with organizations at a local level even during nondisaster times. FEMA also collaborates with an array of nongovernmental, faith-based, and civic organizations independently and through the Voluntary Organizations Active in Disasters (VOAD) network, which harnesses civic and faith-based groups to serve as information hubs, organizing structures, and service providers in times of disaster, ultimately serving as a critical augmentation of disaster response efforts. VOADs are represented nationally by the National Voluntary Organizations Active in Disaster (National VOAD) organization, which supports ongoing coordination among more than seventy national organizations and provides capacity building to fifty-six state and territorial VOADs, which in turn represent hundreds more local and regional member organizations across the United States.[73]

Groups such as these represent critically important opportunities to ensure that local expertise and insight are applied in pursuit of more inclusive disaster response and recovery for older adults. In some cases, aging interests (such as AARP state offices and councils on aging) are already represented and integrated into state, regional, and local VOADs, but there is a need to do so more systematically and intentionally across all levels of the VOAD infrastructure, as well as through expanded use of FEMA's Multi-Agency Sheltering/ Sheltering Support Plan Template, which can be used to identify additional potential community partners to represent aging interests. Communities can enhance resilience for older adults by ensuring that VOADs and other CBOs that can effectively harness aging interests have a seat at the table in discussions of how to build community-wide resilience for all.

Making Frameworks Work for Older Adults

This chapter has focused on the ways in which an age-friendly lens or disability-inclusive framework can be applied to improve and enhance emergency preparedness, disaster recovery, and resilience efforts. It also has assessed how the prevailing federal disaster and preparedness frameworks fall short in terms of the needs of older adults.

The throughline across it all is that greater intention and focus must be brought to bear in any climate-, disaster-, or emergency-related planning effort to place the needs of older adults in the center and to make older adults the organizing principle for community action.

But good intentions and clear focus are not enough, nor are plans, frameworks, and guidelines. In order to truly influence community resilience in ways that better serve the needs of all, systems of accountability must be constructed to ensure that these intentions lead to action. Just as environmental commitments by organizations can be discounted as greenwashing when they lack the evidence to show how their commitments to reduce water pollution or energy use or carbon emissions are faring, so too are there risks that communities or individuals may apply an age-friendly label to efforts without any accountability infrastructure to ensure they are effective. This "greywashing" of climate resilience efforts could manifest as, for example, new requirements to list age as a factor in decision-making but without any simultaneous requirement to bring older adults' voices to the decision-making table. It might be seen in cities that describe themselves as age-friendly on their website but lack any mechanism to hold themselves (or their elected officials) accountable to demonstrate impact. Arguably, greywashing might also be the correct term for any single-sector solution, implemented unilaterally, that fails to acknowledge the compounding and intersecting facets of climate and age in ways that necessarily require greater collaboration with an array of stakeholders.

Ultimately, the best measure of success of efforts to create more resilient communities will be when older adults are no longer disproportionately affected by disasters. But that is an aspirational goal that will require sustained focus by many, as discussed in the next chapter. In the meantime, leaders and stakeholders can move toward climate resilience for an aging nation by ensuring that the voices of older adults are integrated—that climate resilience planning is done with them rather than for them—and that any efforts that result are accompanied by a built-in accountability system to ensure that they do, in fact, lead us toward safer communities for all.

04 STRATEGIES FOR AGE-FRIENDLY RESILIENCE

—

The health and safety we enjoy as individuals and the opportunities for employment, education, and recreation available to us are shaped to a large degree by the built environment in which we live. For the past seventy years, the vast majority of new housing development has followed the example of Levittown, New York. Levittown now serves as the poster child for a seemingly endless wave of car-dependent greenfield suburban sprawl developments that not only helped to generate the carbon emissions that contribute to the climate crisis we now face but also modeled a form of growth that provided opportunity for wealth creation for some households and not others. Cookie-cutter single-family detached homes were constructed that put the American ideal of homeownership within reach—if you were of the right race, gender, marital status, profession, and household size. The Levittown model of development established a pattern of growth that upended our early twentieth-century traditions of walkability and urbanism; contributed to a growing sense of isolation, disinvestment, and deterioration of community for many; and still reverberates in the racial wealth gap that persists today. If Levittown is the example of how we got here, it's high time that we look for a new model of where we go in the future—one that reflects the sort of systems focus that is required to create true community resilience that better serves our demographic future.

Babcock Ranch may serve as that new type of model community (see figure 4-1). Built on principles of climate resilience, sustainability, and choice, this eighteen thousand–acre master-planned community of two thousand homes near Fort Myers, Florida, was designed to withstand the area's hurricanes—and succeeded, given the negligible impact to its five thousand residents during Hurricane

Figure 4-1: Aerial image of Babcock Ranch, Southwest Florida, January 2022. (Source: Shutterstock)

Ian in late 2022.[1] Babcock Ranch homes were constructed according to FORTIFIED building standards, and thus were able to withstand the category 4 storm and use energy from on-site 150-plus megawatt solar arrays (plus battery storage) sufficient to power up to thirty thousand homes—all of which are connected by buried power lines to ensure reliability during extreme weather events. The site uses stormwater management best practices and filter marshes to reduce flooding, protect watersheds, and reduce on-site water demand. It incorporates a range of housing options—from condos in multifamily apartment buildings to single-family attached villas to single-family detached homes—all built to be energy efficient and meet Florida's Green Building standards. Technology is used to connect people to one another and to resources through high-speed fiber-optic internet service in all homes and free WiFi in common areas. Public amenities include parks and trails throughout the surrounding fifty thousand acres of preserved land, an on-site health center, a neighborhood school, and a community center that doubles as a reinforced storm shelter capable of serving area residents beyond Babcock Ranch. Transportation options within the development include fifty miles of an active trail system to encourage walking and biking and pilot use of autonomous vehicle shuttles for residents[2] and prospective home buyers.[3]

Babcock Ranch is surely not perfect, nor is it wholly replicable, given that it is a greenfield development of all-new construction. Planned developments such as Babcock Ranch tend to be home to a wealthier, more educated, and Whiter population.[4] But it nevertheless serves as a powerful illustration of the value of an intentional, cross-sectoral, community-wide approach to resilience—one that needs to be applied to all places, particularly places where older adults already live and most urgently in areas that already face acute climate risks (see chapter 1). Doing so requires action by the private sector (including utilities, nursing homes, and for-profit healthcare entities); all levels of government (including but not limited to federal agencies, state legislatures and departments, and local governments); quasi-governmental public utility commissions and multi-jurisdictional planning and transportation authorities; and community-based organizations (CBOs) that work and operate closest to the people we collectively aim to protect. It will take all of these entities and more to commit to a shared vision of community resilience if we are to achieve it.

Committing to Community-Scale Resilience

Systemic change is needed because the ability to prepare to survive or even thrive in the face of climate-related disasters goes well beyond the capacity of any one person or any single entity. The long list of disasters in which older adults constitute the majority of deaths shows us that the failures to reduce risk for older adults are systemic. Older adults need reliable and affordable energy, safe and secure housing, responsive and redundant transportation, stronger social infrastructure, better emergency response support, and more adaptive approaches to healthcare—but as previous chapters have illustrated, communities today in their current form often fall short. Of course, there is a role for individual preparation, too. But addressing these failures in the broader system by committing to community-scale resilience is essential to reduce deaths during disasters, as well as to help older adults thrive every day in the face of an ever-changing climate.

Building community resilience requires committing to community-scale actions that reduce risk. Investments in hard infrastructure that seek to enhance the safety and stability of entire districts—such as the levee system in New Orleans to manage flooding, the seawall being constructed around Lower Manhattan to protect the region from future storm surges like the one it experienced during Hurricane Sandy, and other such large-scale projects—are of course critical to increasing resilience and will always remain so. So too are policy solutions like the adoption of stricter building requirements that reduce energy use and ensure new construction can better withstand hurricanes, tornadoes, or wildfires. Equally important are efforts to map and better assess risk using available tools—particularly when coupled with a robust public engagement process—to help states and localities effectively deploy scarce resources. Any and all of these can add to the incremental resilience of a community and its residents, regardless of age.

A commitment to achieve true resilience for all ages requires still more focused effort in which communities center their planning in an understanding of how aging individuals experience risk. Doing so can and must be integrated into planning for disasters, as well as in the making of everyday investments in public infrastructure. States and communities can take meaningful steps to advance resilience in their traditional budgeting processes, in planning for transportation and housing, and in prioritizing investments for needed infrastructure. Entities that are members of the AARP Network of Age-Friendly States and Communities (see chapter 3) may have an advantage in that they have an established process for developing and implementing an action plan centered on older adults' needs that could be deployed to target a goal of reducing climate-related risk for all ages.

But there truly is a role for every sector and every community to advance resilience for older adults. Any and all levels of government would be well served to strengthen their focus on older adults by committing to one or more of the interventions described in this chapter. But the responsibility does not lie only with the public sector. Private and nonprofit entities—ranging from healthcare providers to utilities to housing developers to aging advocates and beyond—must do their part by first acknowledging the impact that climate change is having on the people they serve and then committing to deliver more sustainable and resilient outcomes. Only by embracing greater collaboration with diverse partners can we create a better future for us all.

Improvements in the sectors discussed in the following sections (listed in no particular order of precedence) should be considered by leaders who acknowledge the changing demographics of their communities, understand the additional risks inherent in business-as-usual responses that fail to adequately consider age, and seek to take concrete steps to bolster community-wide resilience for all. These strategies (see table 4-1) are by no means exhaustive—future study and analysis will surely identify more ways that community resilience can be improved—but they are meant to spur action that can and will make a tangible difference in the lives of older adults.

Table 4-1: Strategies for Age-Friendly Resilience

Invest in Redundant, Resilient, Affordable, and Sustainable Energy Systems
Offer consumer-centric service and fee structures that give ratepayers more control over their energy costs.
Invest in redundant energy systems, including an "all of the above" approach to providing energy during peak periods.
Ensure affordable energy for all, including provisions that protect customers from shutoffs due to nonpayment.
Create a resilient grid infrastructure, including an electric grid that can better withstand extreme weather events.
Invest in energy efficiency and in housing and transportation alternatives that reduce the load on the grid.

Provide Adequate, Affordable, Secure Housing
Build more small and attached homes that reduce energy burden and encourage social interaction.
Provide policy and funding support for resilient multifamily housing.
Support efforts to weatherize, harden, or elevate homes, including those regulated by condominium and homeowner associations.
Map the targeted risk exposure of housing across communities and implement programs to mitigate risk in the most vulnerable areas.
Support preparedness training among on-site service coordinators in targeted multifamily housing developments.

Expand Transportation and Mobility Options
Provide diverse, affordable, accessible, and reliable transportation options to key locations.

Table 4-1 continued

Maximize use of shared resources among localities and transportation providers to serve a broad range of purposes.

Integrate transportation solutions during disasters (including evacuation) into human service delivery transportation plans.

Strengthen Social Infrastructure

Strengthen social networks, particularly intergenerational ones.

Develop a clear understanding of where older adults live and how to support them in times of disaster, particularly those with special needs.

Establish a range of media, including low-tech modes, to communicate with residents.

Increase access to broadband service and technology training.

Integrate Climate Education and Preparedness into Healthcare

Support facilities and caregivers (both paid and unpaid) in better handling disasters.

Focus attention on home health aides in their role in preparing for disasters.

Encourage medical providers to discuss the risks associated with a changing climate in the course of regular medical care.

Deploy a range of resources to provide healthcare, including telehealth and mobile health clinics.

Make Emergency Management More Effective

Ensure that hazard mitigation and other plans better account for age in assessing and responding to risk.

Better integrate disaster preparedness with age-friendly and disability-inclusive efforts.

Increase investment in and use of multipurpose resilience centers.

Account for people with dementia and cognitive impairment in disaster planning.

Invest in Redundant, Resilient, Affordable, and Sustainable Energy Systems

Energy is an essential part of modern life, but it takes on new life-sustaining importance for many older adults during times of disaster. Blackouts (either planned or the result of disasters or system failure) and brownouts (reduced voltage in response to crisis or surge conditions) that interfere with the provision of reliable and safe energy can heighten risk for those who rely upon refrigeration for medication, home-based medical equipment such as oxygen machines, elevators to enable them to leave their apartment homes, and heating and cooling. Lack of affordable power can further endanger older adults who may be unable to bear the financial cost of heating and cooling their homes—particularly when after-the-fact surge pricing borne by utilities is passed along to consumers—thereby exposing them to even more difficult environmental conditions. Especially in days of increased price volatility associated with energy, the costs of maintaining power for basic essentials can mean older adults are forced to make difficult trade-offs. Among US households earning less than $40,000 per year and headed by someone sixty-five or older, 17 percent went without basic necessities for at least one month during the prior year to pay an energy bill.[5]

The following approaches can be deployed to reduce energy-related risk for older adults.

Offer Consumer-Centric Service and Fee Structures That Give Ratepayers More Control over Their Energy Costs

Customer-centric utility practices would make it easier for ratepayers to enroll in payment plans that spread out seasonal spikes or peak costs throughout the year—a critical benefit for those on fixed incomes. A customer-centric orientation would also mean that utilities are committed to delivering clear, timely, and effective communication about planned outages well in advance so that those who rely upon medical equipment or indoor heating or cooling can make alternative arrangements.

Utilities can increase resilience by structuring rates to give older adults and other customers more visibility into and control over the cost of using energy. Greater transparency in real-time usage would also support more consumer-centric operations. Fee structures that utilize high base charges are regressive for lower-income households. Lower fixed customer charges and more tiered usage-based rates let customers better regulate their energy use in ways that can support their safety and well-being. Support for the purchase and installation of in-home electricity usage monitors would provide valuable insights for those on fixed incomes who may be mindful of overspending on utilities. Monitors would help ratepayers keep track of their utility use and better determine when cost or other concerns might drive them to seek out alternative locations to stay cool or warm, as needed.

It is worth noting that any effort by utilities to switch energy fuel sources to low-carbon and renewable alternatives is also consumer-centric by reducing emissions that contribute to climate change.

Invest in Redundant Energy Systems, including an "All of the Above" Approach to Providing Energy during Peak Periods

Redundant energy systems would ideally expand investment in micro solutions, such as rooftop and community solar power and geothermal energy, along with adequate battery storage to ensure that locally generated energy can serve the needs of older adults who are unable or unwilling to relocate in times of disaster (see figure 4-2). A redundant energy approach would also require that utilities establish an array of energy sources that are affordably priced through purchase agreements that put safety and reliability, not profitability, at the forefront.

Figure 4-2: Solar array in an affordable housing development, Channel Square Apartments, Washington, DC. (Photo courtesy of Todd Nedwick, National Housing Trust)

Communities and utilities can also commit to redundant energy by encouraging the safe use of in-home generators (either whole-house or portable) to be deployed more extensively along with training on how to operate them, particularly for those with power-dependent medical equipment in the home or those with diminished mobility. AARP identified whole-house backup generators as the new "hot home accessory" in a 2021 article in which it offered guidance on how to appropriately select and place the equipment while also urging caution for those using portable generators instead.[6] Redundant energy would incorporate adequate, affordable, and accessible large-scale battery storage at the home or community scale to allow basic health and safety needs to be met for longer periods of time. Further, a commitment to redundant energy would support the work of CBOs that deploy portable, on-demand solar power sources to those in need during times of crisis (see the case study on New Orleans in chapter 5).

Increasingly, federal funds are available for such investments, particularly in publicly subsidized housing and for uses aimed to serve low- and moderate-income households. For example, supplemental funding related to the COVID-19 pandemic made available by the US Department of Housing and Urban Development (HUD) to support multifamily properties covers the cost of installing generators in housing for the elderly and people with disabilities.[7] The Inflation Reduction Act of 2022 provides more than $350 billion in energy and climate resilience investment resources, including tens of billions of dollars in incentives and grants to reduce energy consumption, bolster investment in rooftop and community solar installations, and install on-site battery storage in affordable multifamily properties. Eligible properties include those specifically designed to serve the needs of older adults and people with disabilities funded by Section 202 and Section 811 programs, respectively.[8]

Ensure Affordable Energy for All, including Provisions That Protect Customers from Shutoffs Due to Nonpayment

Commitment to providing affordable energy for all would require that states and tribes make it easier for low-income households to access federal resources designed to reduce the cost of energy, such as the Low Income Home Energy Assistance Program (LIHEAP), and also expand the use of this block grant–funded program in more seasons. LIHEAP has existed since the 1980s and was designed to help low-income individuals pay for their immediate home energy needs—generally, high heating costs in northern states and high cooling costs in southern states. For example, Pennsylvania historically has provided LIHEAP assistance only for heating.[9]

Yet as the climate changes, northern residents in states such as Pennsylvania are experiencing rising costs of cooling with more hot weather days. The federal government has acknowledged the importance of LIHEAP in addressing extreme heat, stating, "Historically, LIHEAP resources have predominately been used for heating assistance, but the uptick in extreme heat events underscores a need for a more robust cooling strategy."[10] In support, a new heat map and new program guidance on how to use LIHEAP for energy-related home repairs have been released[11] to inform stakeholders' efforts as they seek to help the program make the transition to a new climate future, particularly for the many older adults on fixed incomes or living below the poverty line.

Affordable energy also means that lack of ability to pay doesn't lead to cutoffs in peak use time. New York and Arizona are among the states that have passed a moratorium on utility disconnections due to lack of payment during peak weather conditions. Still other states have used federal and other resources provided in response to the pandemic to eliminate utility debt for those most affected by the economic downturn brought on by COVID-19. Such efforts could be further expanded to account for high utility costs brought on by climate change.

Create a Resilient Grid Infrastructure, including an Electric Grid That Can Better Withstand Extreme Weather Events

Resilient energy systems would replace those that were designed decades ago for a very different and less extreme set of weather conditions with an energy grid that is better able to withstand stronger winds and storms without blackouts or system failures, and less likely to contribute to risk of wildfire in areas already experiencing highly flammable drought-enhanced conditions.

Electric wires could be buried underground, investments in repairs and upgrades could be made to fortify transmission lines and generators, and the long transmission lines could be eliminated in favor of more distributed energy sources (or buyouts for remote customers). Doing so would meaningfully reduce disaster risks and potentially avoid a recurrence of California's devastating Camp Fire wildfire of 2018, in which eighty-four people died—more than 80 percent of whom were older adults—for which Pacific Gas and Electric Company (PG&E) pled guilty to involuntary manslaughter related to sparks created by its transmission lines.[12] History nearly repeated itself in 2022 when PG&E transmission lines ignited the Dixie Fire, which burned one million acres in California but fortunately did not result in any civilian deaths.[13]

Resilient grid infrastructure also encourages redundancy (see the earlier discussion), drawing on an array of sources, and severability, which allows smaller systems to function independently of the broader grid. Microgrid solutions—such as rooftop and community solar arrays—that can be disconnected from the grid can be important parts of that diversification, particularly when paired with adequate backup battery storage.

The cost of such investments, however, should not be passed along entirely to ratepayers in the form of surcharges or higher rates, which few older adults on fixed incomes could easily absorb. Responsibility lies with utilities and the public sector to ensure that such investments are made in the name of future community resilience. In California, PG&E proposed significantly higher utility prices in 2021—equivalent to $1 per day for some households—in order to make needed resilience investments to mitigate future wildfire risk, an approach that was not welcomed by many Californians, given the degree to which it would impact consumers rather than PG&E's shareholders.[14]

Invest in Energy Efficiency and in Housing and Transportation Alternatives That Reduce the Load on the Grid

Energy efficiency accelerates resilience because it reduces the load on the grid and lowers the overall cost of utilities. Greater energy efficiency can be achieved through incentives, education, and investments by the public sector and utilities that encourage use of traditional weatherization approaches to make home heating and cooling more effective, such as more energy-conserving windows and doors. Home audits can identify areas where greater insulation is needed and target leaks in the building envelope that lead to inefficient use of heated or cooled air. Increased energy efficiency of homes is also achieved through the replacement of equipment and appliances with models that are less energy intensive, such as upgraded water heaters, heating, ventilating, and air-conditioning (HVAC) systems, refrigerators, and others that have the Energy Star certification. These efforts are particularly important for older adults, who may have lived in the same home for decades with little cause to upgrade their systems along the way (as might be needed at the time of the sale of a home), or who struggle to prioritize the most effective investments they can make—particularly with limited savings. When coupled with investments in solar energy and storage, decarbonization (which aims to eliminate fossil fuels in homes by utilizing only renewable sources of electricity) and energy efficiency improvements can significantly lower the cost of utilities for residents, reduce demand on the grid, and improve indoor and outdoor air quality.

Investments in energy efficiency can also be incentivized through local zoning that encourages housing that requires less energy per square foot, as is the case with smaller, attached, and multifamily home construction. Zoning can also incentivize increased density and urban design elements such as wider sidewalks, narrower streets, and dynamic public spaces, which make other low-carbon modes of travel—such as public transit, walking, biking, and rolling—more feasible. Similarly, state and regional plans that provide greater funding and incentives for local and regional authorities to invest in public transit, biking, and walking as increasingly viable alternatives to energy-intensive car-dependent network systems are also community-scale investments in resilience. These smart growth approaches well serve the needs of older adults and people with disabilities, particularly when housing and mobility options are crafted that intentionally incorporate accessibility measures and foster a range of options in where to live and how to get around for all residents.

Provide Adequate, Affordable, Secure Housing

Affordable, safe, and secure housing should be a human right. It is a precondition for health and well-being, it is a foundation for growth and contributions to one's community, and it can contribute to both a sense of identity for residents and a sense of belonging when shared with others. It provides protection from the elements, the threat of possessions being lost, and feelings of being unmoored—until it doesn't. Housing can be a safe harbor for self, family, friends, and pets during times of crisis so long as it remains affordable—a condition out of reach for many older adults (see chapter 1). Security in housing also means that improvements to housing design, location, and supportive services are implemented that would allow older adults to more safely age and shelter in place in times of disaster and better adapt to our changing climate.

The following approaches can be deployed to increase resilience for older adults through housing.

Build More Small and Attached Homes That Reduce Energy Burden and Encourage Social Interaction

For decades, roughly 60 percent of all housing units in the United States have been single-family detached homes,[15] with the size of the homes growing larger over time and nearly doubling since 1975.[16] But zoning changes and incentives for greater production of small, attached, and adjacent homes—including "missing middle" solutions[17] of the type described in Daniel Parolek's book *Missing Middle Housing*—can advance climate goals and enhance resilience. A wave of local and state policy change to diversify the housing stock is underway across the country, from Minneapolis, Minnesota, which effectively outlawed single-family housing with passage in 2018 of the Minneapolis 2040 plan, to California, which now permits up to four housing units on parcels previously designated for only one home following passage in 2021 of the California

Housing Opportunity and More Efficiency (HOME) Act. Not only do smaller and attached homes deliver energy benefits, requiring less energy to heat and cool than single-family detached homes, but they also can facilitate more social interaction among residents in ways that reduce risk. Resilient housing strengthens social connections by ensuring privacy while providing opportunities for residents to bump into each other informally in ways that foster community. Whether through shared driveways, foyers, clustered mailboxes, or communal courtyards, smaller and attached housing encourages residents to watch out for one another during times of disaster.

Research shows that there is a protective effect at work in senior villages and communities (such as fifty-five-plus or retirement communities) that fosters interaction, leading residents to more frequently check on neighbors during heat waves and ultimately delivering better health outcomes.[18] Congregate and community-focused housing also delivers efficiencies in disaster relief efforts, making it easier to distribute supplies, establish cooling centers, or transport individuals as needed—rather than doing so in a decentralized, house-by-house manner.

Communities truly committed to ensuring that the needs of older adults and people with disabilities are met will work to advance housing solutions that are accessible and resilient, including through adoption of accessory dwelling units (ADUs). ADUs are particularly well suited to the needs of older adults because they provide opportunities for people to downsize in existing communities, to house family members or caregivers, or to generate rental income. ADUs and smaller homes can still be designed to meet "universal design" standards, with wider doorways, wider hallways, and kitchens designed to serve people in wheelchairs. Indeed, the single-story nature of many smaller units is ideal for those with mobility challenges, particularly when they thoughtfully integrate and account for accessibility and resilience needs.[19] Following Hurricanes Harvey and Ike, students at Prairie View A&M University in Texas designed a prototype ADU, Prairie Dwelling 360/H House, that is capable of withstanding hurricane-level winds and generating renewable power on-site.[20]

Provide Policy and Funding Support for Resilient Multifamily Housing

Many communities would benefit from increased production of multifamily housing in addition to the smaller, denser housing solutions described earlier. Whether market based or subsidized—including through HUD's Section 202 and Section 811 programs, which serve low-income older adults and people with disabilities, respectively—multifamily housing provides benefits for the residents and the community as a whole. These higher-density developments are less energy intensive and land consumptive than single-family detached alternatives and offer even greater promise to serve as leading examples of sustainable, resilient, and decarbonized housing solutions that can pave the way toward a more climate-resilient future for all. At a minimum, multifamily housing requires that local zoning allows for its construction, but it can be accelerated—and made more attainable for lower-income households—through policy and funding incentives that support the integration of green and resilient features in affordable housing.[21]

Increasingly large-scale affordable housing developers—such as National Housing Trust,[22] Mercy Housing, and WinnDevelopment—recognize the essential nature of bringing sustainability solutions to their residents in order to reduce energy cost burden, improve indoor air quality, and reduce climate risk for low-income households least able to rebound from disaster. One of the nation's largest organizations dedicated to affordable housing, Enterprise Community Partners, has developed a comprehensive set of standards to encourage the multifamily affordable housing industry to build more sustainably. The Enterprise Green Communities (EGC) and EGC Plus (EGC+) certifications use criteria to evaluate the sustainability and resilience of multifamily affordable buildings by assessing community engagement, location efficiency of the site, energy and water efficiency of the building, integration of sustainable and healthy materials, and much more. The 2020 criteria are further enhanced by greater encouragement of net zero investments that significantly reduce energy use, as well as consideration and integration of climate-related hazard risks.[23] Together with other third-party building standards—such as the U.S. Green Building Council's LEED (Leadership in Energy and Environmental Design); Passive House; and Energy Star Multifamily New Construction— these programs offer a clear road map to bring sustainability and resilience investments to residents of affordable multifamily homes.

Enterprise also supports a valuable online tool, "Climate Safe Housing: Strategies for Multifamily Building Resilience," to foster greater integration of climate resilience into multifamily housing, as a complement to its EGC certification.[24] The tool is based on lessons learned from Hurricane Sandy (see the New York State case study in chapter 5), as stated in the tool's introduction.

> Superstorm Sandy led to a generational awakening in New York and across the country to the risks of climate change. Rolling blackouts, catastrophic power failures and uncontrolled flooding made a few things immediately clear: climate change impacts every community, and no facility or structure is immune to what's coming. When critical community resources are overwhelmed by water, wind or fire, every household is affected—for hours, days, months or even years.[25]

The online tool that resulted from the Sandy experience seeks to provide information to building owners to identify and address these and other risks in order to guide effective resilience investments. It thoughtfully identifies the level of "criticality" of a range of building functions—from access to potable water to resident elevator access to sump pumps—as measured against an array of climate risks, and offers solutions for each.

The Inflation Reduction Act of 2022 offers unprecedented opportunity and funding for climate investment in affordable housing—if the programs are designed to allow it.[26] The complex requirements of affordable multifamily housing merit a clear understanding at the federal and state levels of how new funding programs for energy efficiency, renewable energy, resilient retrofits, and more can best be integrated into the new development or rehabilitation of affordable multifamily homes. Without an intentional focus to ensure that these resources can be accessed by owners and developers of affordable housing—including Section 202 and Section 811 properties for older adults and people with disabilities—there is a risk that this generational investment in climate resilience will bypass those best positioned to benefit from it.

Support Efforts to Weatherize, Harden, or Elevate Homes, including Those Regulated by Condominium and Homeowner Associations

Stronger building codes can deliver a more resilient housing stock when applied to new construction and substantial rehabs. Existing housing can also be made more resilient through investments in weatherization (see the earlier discussion), hardening, or elevation, which can be undertaken by individuals or organizations and incentivized by public entities. In areas at risk of flooding, interventions can include those that facilitate wet flood-proofing (which allows homes to safely take on water) and dry flood-proofing (to repel the intrusion of water) and prevent flooding through the installation of sump pumps and backwater valves. In areas where extreme heat or extreme cold is becoming more prevalent, housing should be retrofitted to include heat pumps or other mechanisms to better maintain healthy indoor air temperatures. Outside the home, improved drainage to direct water away from the perimeter, tree planting to increase natural cooling, and investments in xeriscaping solutions, better adapted to drought or aridification so as to conserve water, can all serve to make housing more resilient.

Investments in resilient housing may, for example, take the form of hardening, in which building roofs, siding, doors, and windows are constructed using materials and installation techniques that are better able to withstand hurricane-force winds or tornadoes. Other measures may include elevating homes and critical systems such as water heaters and HVAC systems to enable them to better withstand storm surges or flooding. Elevation efforts must take account of accessibility requirements such as ramps or external elevators so as not to preclude or prevent the free movement of people with disabilities, while also considering the maintenance, cost, and power required to ensure their safe operation.[27]

With each passing disaster, more examples emerge of buildings that are better able to withstand disaster conditions when built to higher standards—including those designed to serve low-income households. Babcock Ranch, discussed earlier in this chapter, was designed with this ethos in mind, as was the thirty-five-unit Les Maisons de Bayou Lafourche affordable housing development in Lockport, Louisiana. Both withstood the impacts of Hurricane Ian and survived almost wholly intact while other units in the surrounding area were rendered uninhabitable.[28] (See figures 4-3a and 4-3b.) The Les Maisons project was made feasible through the state's Piggyback Resilience Initiative Mixed-Income (PRIME) program, in which the Louisiana Housing Corporation (LHC) competitively awards funds originally provided by HUD to help the state recover from previous disasters and build back more resiliently. LHC in turn awards funding to developers of affordable housing to incentivize the construction of more resilient mixed-income housing—critically important, given the disproportionate climate vulnerability of low-income households (see chapter 2). More than three-quarters of the units at Les Maisons house low-income families, several are designed for people with mobility impairments, and priority consideration for units is given to older adults and people with disabilities.[29] The one-, two-, and three-bedroom semi-attached homes were constructed to the FORTIFIED Commercial Standard Gold designation and included hurricane category 3–resistant roof, siding, and foundation, among other features.[30] The development had just been completed—and was only partially occupied—when Hurricane Ian hit in the fall of 2022. One resident, a seventy-seven-year old woman, having previously been displaced from her rental home following Hurricane Ida in 2021, expressed relief at how well the development fared.[31]

State and local governments can accelerate construction of more resilient housing by adopting stronger building codes, providing incentives for resilient housing in their award of resources (including but not limited to Low-Income Housing Tax Credits), and leading by example in constructing new public facilities. However, this is not the job of public officials alone. Elected representative bodies that govern nonpublic communal standards for housing—such as condominium associations, homeowner associations, and manufactured home communities—should consider how best to facilitate or even encourage changes that individual homeowners wish to make through amended governing documents or other procedural changes,

Figure 4-3a: Recently constructed affordable units in Lockport, Louisiana, developed to FORTIFIED standards survived Hurricane Ida with nearly no damage.

Figure 4-3b: Nearby apartments built to code (less than one mile away) in Lockport that were not built to FORTIFIED standards suffered severe damage during Hurricane Ida, causing displacement for residents. (Photos courtesy of Todd Folse, Louisiana Housing Corporation)

rather than prioritizing compliance with business-as-usual practices that might impede or even prohibit investments in resilience.

Map the Targeted Risk Exposure of Housing across Communities and Implement Programs to Mitigate Risk in the Most Vulnerable Areas

Efforts to map and manage the most vulnerable locations for residents are an essential and fundamental part of reducing risk and building community-wide resilience. Federal agencies serve as the front line of such mapping efforts, although several private-market tools (such as Risk Factor) have begun to emerge as well. The Federal Emergency Management Agency (FEMA) maps flood vulnerability in its effort to show minimum standards for floodplain management and identify the highest-risk areas so that appropriate flood insurance rates can be established for the National Flood Insurance Program. Increasingly, FEMA has encouraged homeowners and local officials to take action on the basis of flood map data through its comprehensive Risk Mapping, Assessment and Planning effort.[32] Actions can include elevating homes, acquiring and relocating homes in the floodplain, and ensuring that open public or private floodplain parcels will be kept free from development. Steps such as these can reduce the cost of flood insurance available to area residents, which is particularly important for older adults who may lack adequate financial resources to insure their homes (see chapter 2) and who face rising insurance premiums.[33] Indeed, flood insurance rates increased for more than 75 percent of policyholders with FEMA's 2021 release of Risk Rating 2.0, which endeavors to "calculate premiums more equitably across all policyholders based on the value of their home and individual property's flood risk."[34]

But risks extend well beyond flooding. The National Oceanographic and Atmospheric Administration (NOAA) launched a new tool in July 2022 that allows communities to explore their vulnerability to a range of risks, including wildfires, cyclones, winter storms, and more, at the census tract level.[35] NOAA joined forces with the National Drought Mitigation Center and the US Department of

Agriculture to map areas at risk of drought throughout the United States at the Drought.gov website.[36]

State, regional, and local land use planners should enhance resilience by taking steps to reduce or eliminate construction in areas subject to these risks. That may include withholding public infrastructure from such areas to discourage construction or utilizing public resilience funding to buy out landowners and homeowners and institute easements to prevent future development. These areas can also serve as focal points for more stringent building requirements—including fortified homes, elevated buildings, and stronger stormwater management practices—that directly mitigate risk for the ultimate residents of the homes constructed.

Support Preparedness Training among On-Site Service Coordinators in Targeted Multifamily Housing Developments

Resilience for low-income seniors and people with disabilities housed in federally supported housing developments—such as those funded through HUD's Section 202 and Section 811 programs, respectively, or those in housing funded in part by Low-Income Housing Tax Credits—can be significantly bolstered by the integration of on-site service coordinators able to assist in times of disaster. On-site coordinators are essential in steady-state conditions by ensuring that residents can access needed health services, food, transportation, and opportunities for social engagement. But in times of extreme weather, trained on-site coordinators can serve as critical resources to deploy timely information, check on the well-being of residents who may otherwise be isolated, and facilitate the delivery of emergency care or services. On-site resident services, however, are not uniformly included in these types of housing developments, and public funding for such services is often awarded competitively and is almost chronically under-resourced.

Health and long-term care facilities are already subject to federal requirements to provide such on-site support (as discussed in chapter 2 and in the healthcare section later in this chapter), but a scaled and comparable set of practices could be applied to any housing development that serves a disproportionate number of older adults or people with disabilities. A January 2022 publication by LeadingAge titled "Enhancing Service Coordination in HUD-Assisted Senior Housing Communities: Lessons for Implementation" provides a useful starting point to explore how the existing framework for service coordination could be enhanced by integrating a focus on climate resilience and disaster preparedness.[37] It is easy to imagine how existing tasks—such as establishing partnerships with CBOs or making referrals for support services—could also serve to strengthen connections and resources for older adults in ways that reduce their climate risk before, during, and after disasters.

Owners and managers of multifamily housing developments—including but not limited to those that are publicly financed—should consider how to strengthen the capacity of on-site resident service coordinators to help residents better prepare for disasters. Efforts could advance basic emergency preparedness (such as stockpiling of food, water, prescriptions, and batteries) but also could include a focus on helping residents maintain medical care during disasters through telehealth or ensuring that redundant communications systems are in place that reach residents and keep them informed.

Expand Transportation and Mobility Options

The decisions that people make about how to get around are bound by which public infrastructure investments are prioritized as much as they are by individual choice. This becomes acutely clear in times of disaster, when an already complicated set of decisions about whether and when to evacuate becomes even more fraught for those who lack the ability to drive themselves. Recalling that older adults outlive their ability to drive by seven to ten years and that nearly 20 percent of older adults sixty-five and older (and 35 percent of women over seventy-five) do not drive at all,[38] it becomes critical to ensure that a range of options exist to support older adults' daily well-being and also help them better prepare for and respond to disasters. Yet researchers have found that one-third of the fifty largest cities in the United States do not have evacuation plans, and among those that do, fewer than one-half mention carless or vulnerable populations.[39]

A 2013 report by the Transportation Research Board (TRB) found that for the most part, transportation planning has not been effective in accounting for "transportation disadvantaged populations" and those with functional needs during disasters. A survey administered among transportation planners and emergency professionals did not indicate a high prevalence of practices related to planning for such populations, particularly in regard to planning for disaster recovery.[40] The report notes that while 85 percent of regions represented in the study indicated that they had vehicles accessible by wheelchair available, only 25 percent of regional emergency plans included these vehicles. The TRB report noted, "Despite being in regions that had transportation options for transportation disadvantaged populations and people with access and functional needs, survey respondents did not have a strong level of agreement that these segments of the population evacuated safely in the last large-scale emergency."[41]

Clearly, transportation planners can and must do better. The following approaches can be deployed to increase resilience for older adults through improved transportation solutions.

Provide Diverse, Affordable, Accessible, and Reliable Transportation Options to Key Locations

The transportation options available to any one person are inextricably linked to where the person lives. The prevalence of single-family detached housing across the United States has resulted in communities that largely require residents to drive themselves to work, school, or services. Public transit serves as an essential mode for many— particularly for people with disabilities, members of lower-income households who can't afford a car, and others who choose not to or cannot drive—but it is most likely to serve higher-density areas and major transportation corridors. In these and in other communities where housing density does not support transit, additional direct service models may be available, such as volunteer driving programs, paratransit (sometimes limited to areas already served by public transit), taxis, or rideshare programs. The design of the built environment has a direct impact on how viable it is for people to walk, roll, or bike to their destination, depending on the prevalence of protected bike paths and lines, proximity to amenities, and safety of the pedestrian environment—including lighting, comfortably wide sidewalks, and adequate ramps.

A more intentional commitment to expand transportation choices and align public infrastructure investment with housing in both existing and new developments can reduce the risk to older adults of being dependent on family or friends for transportation, hesitating to evacuate in the face of mounting risks, or being stranded while they await help during a disaster. Such a commitment would ensure that a range of options exist to serve daily needs—including those that make it safer to walk, roll, or bike, as well as volunteer-led programs and responsive public transit and paratransit systems—and that older adults are capable and comfortable using these systems well before a disaster strikes. Ensuring that a dynamic transportation system exists can also contribute to greater overall physical fitness, better mental health, increased freedom and independence, and improved well-being in ways that bolster older adults' ability to manage climate-related risks.

Local and regional planners and developers (particularly of housing targeted at older adults and people with disabilities) should work to create more and diverse housing within easy reach of public transportation, building people's "muscle memory" should it be needed in times of crisis. Doing so can facilitate greater access by residents to the means to transport themselves out of harm's way. When transportation is intentionally designed to connect as many people as possible with key locations—hospitals, senior centers, schools, clinics, grocery stores, and even movie theaters—these systems can provide essential solutions in times of crisis to keep people cool, warm, fed, sheltered, and cared for.

Housing situated in areas that are connected by streets as well as multiuse paths means that there are safe and accessible means to remain mobile in a climate-neutral way—or to get help and support or move oneself in times of disaster. FEMA has promoted Disaster Relief Trials as a way for bike-friendly communities to help residents learn how to deploy bicycles in times of emergency.[42] In Southern Oregon, during the days immediately following the Almeda Fire,

Figure 4-4: Bike brigade volunteers provided food and water to residents trapped in evacuation zones in Jackson County, Oregon, after the 2020 Almeda Fire. (Photo taken by April Ehrlich to accompany the article "Ashland Cyclists Bring Water, Food to People Stuck in Evacuation Zones," published September 11, 2020, on ijpr.org. Copyright 2020 Jefferson Public Radio. Used with permission. Any unauthorized use or duplication is strictly prohibited.)

which closed roads and left many without power or services, bicyclists formed a bike brigade to use available bike paths to deliver fresh water and supplies.[43] (See figure 4-4.)

Maximize Use of Shared Resources among Localities and Transportation Providers to Serve a Broad Range of Purposes

Effective planning for transportation needs during an emergency would capitalize on all available resources to deploy supplies, evacuate people to safe locations and medical care, and ensure that critical services such as hospitals, utilities, and water infrastructure remain operational, particularly for those in greatest need of assistance. Such a practice would establish shared-use or joint-use agreements—which codify a commitment between two or more entities to share resources in times of need—with nearby localities as well as private entities (such as churches, hospitals, employers, and universities) that independently provide transportation services for members, students, or clients. Maximizing use of shared resources would also effectively leverage the role of transportation network companies (TNCs), such as Uber or Lyft, for those who do not or cannot drive in advance of, during, and in recovery from disaster.

Planners can and should preemptively coordinate with a wide range of private, public, and nonprofit actors to account for all available transportation modes in their emergency plans, ensuring that accessible modes are available. In 2017, during the wildfires in California, both Uber and Lyft partnered with local nonprofits to offer free rides to those in need to reach evacuation centers, hospitals, and filtered air centers. Research suggests, however, that there were low levels of use of car-sharing offers and that there remains significant hesitation among older adults about using such a resource.[44] Emergency managers therefore should thoughtfully integrate users' most prevalent concerns related to personal safety, accessibility, availability, and reliability in their planning for any and all transportation providers, including TNCs.

Transportation assets are not only useful for moving people. They can also serve important roles in delivering information, supplies, or comfort. Cities ranging from Austin[45] to Philadelphia[46] to Chicago[47] now repurpose their public transit buses as mobile cooling centers during heat waves to provide relief or offer free transportation to cooling centers to address the needs of older adults, people with disabilities, and people experiencing homelessness.

Integrate Transportation Solutions during Disasters (including Evacuation) into Human Service Delivery Transportation Plans

The transportation needs of older adults and people with disabilities are most directly addressed through funding provided under the US Department of Transportation's Enhanced Mobility of Seniors and Individuals with Disabilities (Section 5310) program. That funding is used to purchase, maintain, and operate accessible vans and vehicles to deliver paratransit services, volunteer driving programs, and other supportive elements (such as call-in centers or accessibility improvements to sidewalks) that make public transportation solutions more readily usable to people with disabilities. A requirement of Section 5310 funding is that localities complete Coordinated Public Transit Human Services Transportation Plans, which are intended to be informed by end users and articulate a vision for how their needs can best be served by a range of entities (including but not limited to those receiving Section 5310 funding).

Such plans should address how services will operate in times of disaster, yet the practice of doing so is uneven. The Federal Transit Administration (FTA) does not require that plans address transportation needs in times of emergency or disaster, instead urging collaboration with other state agencies and "other groups" to include emergency management agencies.[48] The National Center for Mobility Management does not address the need to do so, either, as indicated in 2021 guidance on how to write human service transportation plans.[49] As a result, any charge to expressly consider transportation needs during disaster is left up to the state or regional entity that oversees local or regional plans.

State, regional, and local entities can and should more explicitly require consideration of transportation needs during disasters and extreme weather events in human service transportation plans. The Washington State Department of Transportation serves as a model, requiring that entities within the state address disaster transportation planning in order to qualify for state funding, asking that "transportation providers collaborate with state, county, or other emergency management agencies for disaster preparedness, response, recovery and mitigation."[50]

In Florida, which routinely experiences hurricanes, flooding, extreme heat, and other events that may prompt evacuations, there appears to be a less-than-comprehensive consideration of the mobility needs of older adults and people with disabilities during disasters. A July 2021 report, titled "State of the State: Transportation Coordination and Mobility Management Efforts in Florida," by the National Center for Mobility Management leads with the statement, "Florida has long been at the forefront of innovative thinking regarding coordinated transportation, especially for the 'transportation disadvantaged.'" Yet the report—which seeks to provide an overview and explanation of Florida's coordinating structure—fails to mention the role of transportation during disasters almost entirely, with only a passing reference to the benefit of a coordinated system as a "powerful platform to coordinate transportation, especially in times of crisis."[51]

Strengthen Social Infrastructure

In order to build community-wide resilience for older adults, it is essential to invest in efforts to strengthen social infrastructure as a complement to the prevailing focus on individual preparedness. The needs of older adults are far less likely to be overlooked within finer-grained social networks that can recognize and respond to vulnerabilities in times of disaster—if those networks are encouraged and supported before disaster strikes. Particularly for the large share of older adults who live alone, have underlying health or financial conditions, or both (see chapter 2), ensuring that there are effective communication systems, social networks, and mechanisms to proactively monitor the well-being of older adults can mean the difference between life and death.[52]

The following efforts to strengthen social infrastructure can be deployed to increase resilience for older adults.

Strengthen Social Networks, Particularly Intergenerational Ones

Fostering opportunities for older adults—especially those living alone and no longer in the workforce—to connect with others is an essential but often undervalued investment in community resilience. When the COVID-19 pandemic hit, many in the United States gained a deeper understanding of what it means to be confined to one's home and unable to engage easily in social interactions. As past disasters have shown, stronger social networks can mean the difference between life and death to the degree that they are a means to share information and respond to needs that are either expressed by the older adult or visible to the visitor. They are also often a determinant of mental well-being that can carry individuals through difficult times.[53]

Investments to strengthen social networks can come in many forms. A significant share of age-friendly communities and states (see chapter 3) prioritizes efforts to promote social interaction, engagement, and connectedness among older adults and across generations through activities such as the following:

- Creation of new volunteer opportunities for older adults
- Installation of benches, pathways, and signage in parks to foster physical activity and interaction among neighbors
- Intergenerational mentoring programs focused on supporting students' academic success and older adults' use of technology
- Robust programming at and expansion of senior centers
- Virtual programming to foster lifelong learning and healthy living
- Volunteer-led intergenerational walking and bicycling programs
- Social events such as dances and lunch-and-learn programs
- Support for inclusive activities, such as pickleball, that engage people of all ages[54]

An array of public, private, and nonprofit actors contributes to this element of resilience, ranging from private philanthropy to public parks departments to educational institutions and many more. Even when not designed for emergency conditions, these types of investments pay dividends for older adults—particularly when in-home options exist to support individuals unable to leave their homes during periods of more extreme heat or cold. They can also be repurposed to address more emergent and urgent needs in times of disaster. For example, Greenwich, Connecticut, recognized the value of intergenerational connections in its age-friendly plan well before the pandemic, launching a partnership between the Commission on Aging and the Greenwich Country Day School in which students visited the local senior center to provide one-on-one technical support to older adults to help them learn how to retrieve email, activate privacy settings, send photos, and use the internet. During the COVID-19 pandemic, that program was adapted to become a virtual program called CONNECTT (Connecting Our Neighbors, Naturally Enriching Our Community Through Technology) that expanded to offer online classes and discussions aimed at promoting well-being for older adults. A dial-in option was made available for those without in-home internet access, and the program naturally evolved to encompass other strategies that strengthen community resilience, including a volunteer "friendly voice" phone call program to ensure regular touch points with older adults.[55]

Develop a Clear Understanding of Where Older Adults Live and How to Support Them in Times of Disaster, Particularly Those with Special Needs

Given that the vast majority of older adults do not live in congregate settings, it becomes essential that emergency managers develop a clear understanding of where older adults live and what their needs are well before disaster strikes. The most widely available tool to do so at an aggregate level is the Social Vulnerability Index (SVI), operated by the Centers for Disease Control and Prevention (CDC). The SVI maps sixteen factors, including population aged sixty-five and older, income, race and ethnicity, housing type, and transportation access to illustrate areas with higher levels of vulnerability to disasters.[56] The tool does not display parcel- or household-level details but instead illustrates census tracts that are more vulnerable to inform planning efforts. The SVI helps emergency, health, and transportation planners to better understand community needs, including how to appropriately staff response efforts, shelter those in need, and evacuate people with special needs.

At a more granular level, emergency managers can seek to gain a better understanding of where older adults live and what their needs are by better coordinating with providers of home-based care, such as Area Agencies on Aging (AAAs), those who deliver Meals on Wheels, faith-based organizations or senior centers that offer visitation programs, or home healthcare providers. Doing so would create an opportunity to share contact and basic medical information—with the permission of the participant—in ways that allow frontline emergency responders to check in on and support those who may otherwise be left behind. An infrastructure to share information can also help agencies charged with caring for older adults to maintain continuity of operations should disaster strike command centers. One example cited by the CDC in a 2012 publication seeking to promote greater protection for older adults comes from Florida, where the AAA sent confidential electronic client files to neighboring county AAAs—from Miami-Dade to St. Petersburg and ultimately to Tallahassee—as Tropical Storm Fay progressed across the state, all the while ensuring that emergency management professionals could access files on older adults in need of assistance.[57]

The creation of opt-in special needs registries allows for a similar outcome wherein older adults and people with disabilities are encouraged to self-register with city- or county-run programs. In turn, the state or locality commits to providing more customized emergency response services (such as notifications) as well as more effective disaster planning informed by registrants' needs. Depending on the level of support provided by the host agency, the range of services available to registrants can vary widely. In Florida, for example, the state-led Special Needs Registry promises individuals customized alerts and better overall planning for their needs,[58] while the more localized registry offered by Orange County, Florida, goes further by offering transportation assistance upon request and special medical shelters during disasters.[59] Special needs registries can also be used to provide critical medical and health information to disaster response teams when the registrant agrees to share such information.

Establish a Range of Media, including Low-Tech Modes, to Communicate with Residents

Given the low rate of adoption of smartphone technology and the far from universal access to in-home internet service among older adults (see chapter 1), it becomes essential to ensure that low-tech communication means are not only established in advance of a disaster but well utilized as an effective means of sharing information. This can and should include an "all of the above" approach to communication with older adults that can be activated in times of disaster, including but not limited to phone trees or hub dialer programs that generate direct phone calls to older adults; home-delivered print flyers, door hangers, newsletters, and resource guides; leveraging of in-home healthcare aides and volunteer programs that provide direct services in the home to assess needs; and partnerships with local radio, newspaper, and television outlets to disseminate information targeted to older adults.

The use of 211 or 311 lines—which are available to nearly 95 percent of US residents[60] and both of which provide community-serving public information—allows for any individual to gain streamlined access to information about health and human service needs on an ongoing basis. In times of disaster, 211 lines can play a critical role for older adults seeking information about available resources without tying up 911 emergency lines. For those without in-home internet access or smartphones, this may be the only proactive step that they can take within the bounds of their home to get updated information. It therefore becomes essential that the state or local organizations and social service providers responsible for managing 211 lines rapidly adapt to changing conditions during disasters, posting new information through on-demand recordings and expanding availability of immediate operator assistance. The failure of officials in Portland, Oregon, to update their 211 line with information related to heat waves, including how to access cooling stations, was cited as having contributed to a critical delay in disseminating information as temperatures rose to 108 degrees Fahrenheit during the 2021 heat wave.[61] (See chapter 5 for a broader discussion of Portland's resilience efforts.)

Even standard emergency alert systems must be thoughtfully managed in times of disaster. Some residents in Southern Oregon reported that they received no alert about the impending risk of wildfire in 2020, which later was identified as the result of failure to test and activate the Integrated Public Alert and Warning System (IPAWS), FEMA's primary alert system, which allows emergency managers to deliver alerts to all cell phones in a designated range—not just for those who opt in to receive notifications. A secondary software-based system that requires preregistration by residents also was not effective in reaching residents, leaving some older adults reliant upon happenstance meetings with police officials who were in the area to disseminate evacuation notices.[62]

Local governments and community-serving nonprofits can support resilience by cultivating a multichannel approach to communications well before disaster strikes, as well as by better educating residents about emergency alert options. Mendocino County, California, for example, clearly spells out for residents the opt-in alert systems available to them, indicating which ones are purely text-based and which include landline phone notifications. The county's FAQ page also invites people to voluntarily provide information about access, functional, or language needs that may better support emergency response efforts.[63]

Increase Access to Broadband Service and Technology Training

Broadband access and use are often assumed preconditions that drive many disaster-related efforts, starting with alerts (see the previous discussion) and extending to online applications for disaster assistance. As discussed in chapter 1, older adults' level of access to high-speed internet or broadband services lags behind that of other groups, with just 64 percent of people aged sixty-five and older reporting in-home access and only 75 percent reporting that they are internet users.[64] Irrespective of age, broadband access and use also differ by race and location. More than 22 percent of American Indian and Native American households report no home broadband internet subscription or home computer, compared with 16 percent of Black households, 12 percent of Hispanic households, and less than 10 percent of White households.[65] Rural residents also have lower levels of access to broadband than their suburban and urban counterparts.[66]

Efforts to advance digital equity by addressing race, age, location, language, income, and other sociodemographic-based barriers to internet use therefore become essential investments in community resilience. Local and state leaders and service providers should focus on lowering the cost of service, expanding the physical infrastructure required to reach more locations, and providing training in how to use internet-enabled services. Federal programs funded through the 2021 Infrastructure Investment and Jobs Act (IIJA) and prior pandemic relief programs make it increasingly financially feasible for states and localities to bridge this digital divide with new broadband investments to reach those previously unserved or underserved. At present, more than 43 percent of the fifteen million subscribers to receive a federal subsidy to reduce the cost of internet through the Affordable Connectivity Program, funded by IIJA, are people aged fifty or above.[67]

Digital equity plans—required to implement some of the IIJA resources—represent critically important opportunities to ensure that the needs of older adults are addressed through the expansion of broadband infrastructure, subsidies, and training.[68] Digital equity plans should assess and respond to the barriers that impede older adults' access to full digital engagement. Philadelphia's January 2022 digital equity plan provides a model of an approach that intentionally seeks to target investments to address the needs of its senior residents while recognizing the intersectionality of race, language, and cognition to digital access.[69] While results of the plan are yet to materialize, it serves as a model for other localities planning for investments in digital equity by acknowledging how age and cognition affect one's ability to fully access online tools and resources and by advancing strategies to address those needs.

Integrate Climate Education and Preparedness into Healthcare

Efforts to expand community resilience must better integrate an awareness of how climate change affects health into efforts to bolster community health. There is little doubt among the medical community that climate change represents a significant and urgent health crisis. In 2019, a diverse array of more than seventy groups representing nurses, physicians, and public health officials under the banner of Climate Health Action stated that "climate change is the greatest public health challenge of the 21st century," calling on government leaders to recognize climate change as a health emergency and prioritize a set of actions to advance health and equity.[70] But that national commitment and ethos has not always made its way into the frontline care provided by health professionals in the course of tending to the needs of older adults (see chapter 3), nor has it been fully integrated into our disaster planning and preparedness.

In order to strengthen community resilience, it is critical to instill a broad understanding across all actors in the community health field—including private, philanthropic, and nonprofit sectors and different levels of government—of how to integrate climate and disaster considerations into healthcare for older adults.

Support Facilities and Caregivers (Both Paid and Unpaid) in Better Handling Disasters

As discussed in chapter 2, the 2016 Emergency Preparedness Rule issued by the Centers for Medicare and Medicaid Services (CMS) was an important step in integrating disaster preparedness into healthcare. It required all providers—including hospitals, long-term care facilities, hospice facilities, and nursing homes—that are eligible for participation in Medicare or Medicaid to take action to better protect residents in times of disaster. While the rule does not require change unilaterally in every healthcare facility—such as private facilities that opt not to meet Medicare requirements and do not participate in Medicaid—it is nevertheless instructive for all facilities and caregivers. In particular, the rule requires providers to do all of the following:

- Develop an emergency preparedness plan based on facility and community risk assessments and utilizing an all-hazards approach
- Develop emergency preparedness policies and procedures based on risk assessment, communication plan, and the emergency plan
- Develop an emergency preparedness plan that addresses a comprehensive communication plan
- Develop an emergency preparedness training and testing program based on the risk assessment, communication plan, and emergency plan, including annual training for all staff on all emergency preparedness policies and procedures and two annual exercises[71]

The guidance also applies to home health agencies that provide skilled nursing care and home health aide services in the patient's home and participate in the Medicare program. The guidance does not, however, apply to family or other unpaid caregivers, although the same requirements would be prudently applied to anyone providing care for an older adult, as discussed later. While these caregivers can be difficult to reach because they do not always self-identify as such, are under tremendous stress (often edging on burnout), and frequently act in isolation or outside of formal care networks, it is critically important that they too be supported in preparedness.

Communities seeking to build community resilience should assess the ability of healthcare providers covered by the 2016 CMS Emergency Preparedness Rule to respond to disasters as well as that of private facilities and informal caregivers not covered by the rule. Such efforts could involve local and regional philanthropic, private, or public investment in surveys, interviews, and research that evaluate how preparedness is being integrated into healthcare practices. It would promote stronger awareness within the industry and among patients (and their families) to best understand how investments in emergency plans, training, and stronger communication are manifesting in risk mitigation for older adults. It would also provide additional resources to augment public investments in preparedness in recognition of the critical role that facilities play in helping older adults under their care to better withstand the impacts of disasters.

Focus Attention on Home Health Aides in Their Role in Preparing for Disasters

Home health aides and caregivers are direct providers of regular, sometimes daily, care, so it is critically important to bolster their role in supporting older adults in times of disaster. Not only are these caregivers in the best position to monitor well-being, deliver timely information, and assess risks to the individuals, but they also can and do play an essential role in helping older adults to become more resilient through preparation. Home health aides and other paid or volunteer caregivers can help those in their care to document current medical conditions, required prescriptions, and other health considerations so that people in need can be easily transported in the event of evacuation or relocation to a shelter, or create documentation that can be used to rapidly inform those who are providing disaster response support in the home.

The COVID-19 pandemic shone a light on the challenges facing home healthcare workers and illustrated the difficulty of providing consistent care while also tending to their own well-being and health in the face of a pandemic. These dynamics are also likely to be present during climate-enhanced disasters, making it ever more important to ensure that clear guidance and systems are in place well before disaster strikes. The US Department of Homeland Security recognizes the importance of such preparation in its "Disaster Planning Guide for Home Health Care Providers,"[72] and nonprofit groups such as Healthcare Ready lead important work to bolster coordination among government entities, local partners, for-profit companies, and healthcare organizations to prepare for and respond to disasters.[73] Research has documented the value of bolstering the capacity of home-based care providers in an assessment of the Veterans Health Administration's Home Based Primary Care (HBPC) program. The HBPC program serves as a model for the broader home healthcare industry in that it effectively guides practitioners to better support their patients on preparedness through the use of checklists and tools. The program covers core elements of preparedness but also ensures that care providers address matters that are often overlooked, including helping older adults to plan for backup power for medical devices, identify transportation options in case of emergency, and register for emergency shelters.[74]

Leaders in the home health and hospice care industries can and must accelerate the adoption of practices that advance community resilience among practitioners in their field. While information on best practices exists, as described earlier, to date only sparse guidance is available on preparedness and disaster resilience for members of key national organizations such as the National Association for Home Care and Hospice and the Home Care Association of America.

Encourage Medical Providers to Discuss the Risks Associated with a Changing Climate in the Course of Regular Medical Care

Climate change is not among the most common topics for discussion during older adults' routine appointments with their healthcare providers, but it should be. Evidence suggests that 64 percent of Americans rarely or never discuss climate change, according to the Yale Climate Opinion map[75]—a figure that could be improved if climate change were appropriately discussed by doctors and nurses as a contributing or related factor affecting individuals' health. Increasingly, resources are being made available to support nurses, doctors, and home health aides in addressing the impacts of climate change during consultations that aim to ensure well-being or address chronic medical conditions.

Physician-serving groups such as the American College of Physicians, the U.S. Health Care Climate Council, and My Green Doctor now offer patient-oriented guides on climate change for use by member practitioners. Florida Clinicians for Climate Action named "educate and inform" as one of its three primary activities and seeks to support clinicians as agents for change to inform Floridians about the risks of increased and more extreme heat, longer allergy seasons, extreme weather events, and other climate-related drivers affecting patients' health.[76] And the group EcoAmerica works to track and improve climate literacy among all people by proving materials that can be used by healthcare providers and other sectors. But the task is not without risk; doctors acknowledge that climate change remains a polarized and politicized issue with many patients, potentially diminishing their willingness and ability to broach the topic.[77]

Mental health practitioners can and should also better integrate climate change topics into the course of their routine care. As noted in chapter 2, the American Psychiatric Association (APA) has acknowledged that the "impacts of climate change are significant sources of stress for individuals and communities."[78] The APA has developed several video resources (two of which are focused on youth) to guide practitioners in discussing climate change during therapeutic care for older adults.

Deploy a Range of Resources to Provide Healthcare, including Telehealth and Mobile Health Clinics

Ensuring that routine medical care for chronic medical conditions—such as dialysis for those with kidney disease, treatments for those battling cancer or heart disease, and supplementary oxygen for those with chronic obstructive pulmonary disease, emphysema, or serious infections—is available during and immediately after disasters is an essential part of building community resilience. Studies have shown that the interruption of care for chronic conditions contributes to higher fatalities among older adults and that hospitalizations for those suffering from chronic disease increase after disasters. (See chapter 2 for a more detailed discussion of the impacts of disasters on health.) Communities seeking to build climate resilience should invest in an array of interventions to ensure that ongoing treatment is more readily available and accessible by older adults before, during, and after disasters.

Mobile clinics can and should be a part of the solution. At present, roughly two thousand mobile clinics are in operation throughout the country, providing both preventive and primary care as well as dental care, vaccinations, and telehealth access.[79] Given their ability to be rapidly deployed to provide care in hard-to-reach areas where people are sheltered in place or temporarily relocated, mobile health clinics provide tremendous potential for more specialized care. The possibilities for greater use of mobile clinics were expanded in October 2022 when the Maximizing Outcomes through Better Investments in Lifesaving Equipment for (MOBILE) Health Care Act was signed into law. The legislation offers community health centers more flexibility to use federal funds to establish new mobile delivery sites.[80]

Telehealth access can also be a critical means for doctors to help their patients manage chronic disease through more rapid and frequent monitoring. For those with in-home internet access, education and support to ensure older adults' full use of telehealth technology can help fill critical care gaps during times of crisis, provided that reliable power and internet service are available. For those without in-home internet, mobile units can provide a means for patients to connect with doctors, as can temporary shelters that thoughtfully prepare for telehealth use by ensuring power and internet connectivity, planning for privacy for patients, and offering assistance to patients unfamiliar with telehealth technology.

Make Emergency Management More Effective

Effective emergency management requires that actions are taken quickly in the face of complex challenges—drawing on federal, state, local, private, philanthropic, and nonprofit resources—in order to protect human health and well-being. The United States utilizes a whole-of-government doctrine to achieve the National Preparedness Goal of "a secure and resilient Nation with the capabilities required across the whole community to prevent, protect against, mitigate, respond to, and recover from the threats and hazards that pose the greatest risk."[81] The goal is achieved through a National Preparedness System composed of six parts—from risk identification through testing and assessment—that provide the overall process for all elements of the community to take action. The goal and system are integrated in a series of frameworks that align with each of the five preparedness mission areas—prevention, protection, mitigation, response, and recovery—which encompass thirty-two core capabilities ranging from critical transportation to mass care services to health and social services. Ultimately, this complex and interrelated set of policy documents issued by FEMA seeks to clarify responsibilities, roles, and objectives among government and nongovernmental actors and to support coordination. It is a comprehensive doctrine and structure that can be daunting to understand for those outside of the emergency management or public safety professions, from which many FEMA staff and leaders hail.

As such, the comprehensive and complex nature of the national preparedness doctrine may also be its greatest impediment to achieving the kind of community stability that it seeks. In order to build true community resilience, all individuals must see themselves in the approach and understand how their mission—whether it is caregiving, designing bus routes, or building affordable housing—advances our nation's readiness for disasters. The National Response Framework (NRF), one of five such required frameworks aligned with the mission areas previously identified, seems to acknowledge this ongoing challenge. In its charge to govern how the nation responds to disaster, the NRF (now in its fourth iteration) underscores the "paramount importance of sustaining essential community lifelines," defined as services that enable the continuous operation of critical functions that are essential for human health and safety.[82] The NRF notes that recent disasters have illuminated threats to community lifelines that call for new approaches to response planning and operations: "Communities cannot meet these challenges solely by scaling up existing plans and capabilities. Rather, new mechanisms are needed to supplement and integrate those already in place and facilitate cross-sector coordination, while respecting the roles of private sector partners and authorities of agencies at all levels of government."[83]

This call for new approaches seems ideally suited to the type of age-friendly and disability-focused frameworks described in chapter 3. It also opens the door to new solutions in emergency management such as those described in the remainder of this chapter that can deliver better outcomes for older adults.

Ensure That Hazard Mitigation Plans Better Account for Age in Assessing and Responding to Risk

NOAA reports that the United States sustained 348 weather and climate disasters between 1980 and the end of 2022 in which the overall cost of damages reached or exceeded $1 billion—resulting in a staggering $2.5 trillion in losses.[84] For those states and localities that seek to reduce the economic and human cost of disaster by investing in proactive risk mitigation, public funds are available from FEMA once the jurisdiction completes a hazard mitigation plan. However (as discussed in chapter 3), these state or local hazard mitigation plans do not explicitly require that demographic changes and the needs of older adults are considered when assessing risk and devising plans to enhance community resilience.

Jurisdictions can and should explicitly address the needs of older adults when developing plans to mitigate community-wide risk, even though this is not presently required by FEMA. Doing so ensures that FEMA funding resources dedicated to reducing risks from floods, wildfires, hurricanes, and other disasters—specifically, Hazard Mitigation Grant Program, Pre-Disaster Mitigation, Flood Mitigation Assistance, and Building Resilient Infrastructure and Communities funds—are implemented in ways that address the differing needs of residents in the community. Furthermore, state emergency management offices seeking to be successful in competitive programs should focus their application on their state's changing demographics and cultivate partnerships that ensure that FEMA-funded interventions can effectively reduce risk for older adults. Beyond FEMA funds, other federal resources dedicated to support resilient disaster recovery and mitigation, such as HUD's CDBG-Mitigation and CDBG-Disaster Recovery funds, can be more effectively implemented when grantees specifically focus on age in their development of HUD-required action plans.

For example, the 2022 action plan submitted to HUD by the State of North Carolina relating to implementation of its CDBG-Mitigation (CDBG-MIT) grant identifies the importance of home buyout programs in areas largely affected by Hurricane Matthew and Hurricane Florence, stating that approximately "2,200 owner-occupied properties are strong candidates for buyout activity."[85] The state analyzed the population associated with these target buyouts to ensure that they met HUD's required focus on low- and moderate-income households. In addition, it determined that nearly 90 percent of the targeted census blocks had an above statewide average share of households with individuals over sixty years of age. The state attested to its intention to ensure that the needs of these and other vulnerable populations are met by "considering individuals with access and functional needs that will require assistance with accessing and/or receiving CDBG-MIT disaster resources," including seniors and people with disabilities.[86] Further, the state affirmed its commitment to equitable distribution of funds by stating that the North Carolina Office of Recovery and Resiliency "commits to continuing to assess each new or alternative buyout zone proposed by participating communities to ensure that the buyout zone works in favor of those community members which have historically not had the same opportunities to recover or benefit from long-term resilience and mitigation."[87]

Better Integrate Disaster Preparedness with Age-Friendly and Disability-Inclusive Efforts

The National Response Framework's call for new solutions that better support community stability provides an opening for new ways to approach emergency preparedness and climate resilience that better serve the needs of older adults and people with disabilities. Both the AARP age-friendly framework and the Disability Inclusive Disaster Risk Reduction (DIDRR) framework discussed in chapter 3 serve as ideal mechanisms to leverage diverse actors at the local level, give greater voice and agency to community-based and volunteer organizations, and bring authentic engagement to emergency and disaster planning efforts. That fusing of efforts can be initiated by emergency management professionals who seek to lead new age-friendly efforts within their work, or by those who oversee age-friendly efforts and aim to more intentionally integrate climate and disaster preparedness in theirs. Arguably, both are needed.

The age-friendly approach, in particular, provides an ideal mechanism to better protect older adults in light of mounting climate-related crises. With its community-driven, multi-stakeholder, and phased approach, it presents an opportunity to organically integrate disaster and emergency preparedness officials into an ecosystem of committed actors that are already committed to strengthening community stability. The DIDRR framework is also well suited to foster improved emergency management efforts with its intentional, community-led, and multi-stakeholder focus on how to reduce risk for people with disabilities in the face of climate-related and other disasters. In addition, a handful of nonprofit organizations are dedicated to the task of better integrating the needs of people with disabilities into community resilience and disaster planning efforts, including the Partnership for Inclusive Disaster Strategies, which offers training and guidance—led by people with disabilities—for those seeking to be more inclusive in their planning.[88]

While at present there are few resources that speak directly to how to best integrate climate resilience into age-friendly efforts, a number of resources point the way. The "Disaster Resilience Tool Kit" created by AARP and FEMA in 2022 serves as a useful starting point for communities seeking to invite greater participation of emergency professionals in efforts that serve the needs of older adults. Similarly, FEMA's "Guide to Expanding Mitigation: Making the Connection to Older Adults," released in 2022, articulates the urgent need for emergency management professionals to better focus on older adults.[89] Emergency preparedness has already been identified as an emergent ninth domain and is being used as an organizing principle by several age-friendly communities, along with elder abuse, public safety, and dementia-friendly efforts (see figure 3-1).[90]

Greater support for the integration of climate resilience and disaster preparedness within the World Health Organization and AARP age-friendly frameworks can build on the efforts already underway by several age-friendly communities (see chapters 3 and 5) and accelerate climate resilience planning for older adults. A December 2022 keyword search among publicly available resources provided to AARP from the nearly seven hundred members of its age-friendly network revealed that the vast majority of age-friendly communities were not as yet using the framework to address climate resilience, disaster preparedness, or emergency response. Just fifty members were focusing on "disaster," nearly thirty were listed as having program materials posted related to "emergency," and fewer than ten on "preparedness" or "emergency preparedness"—while none as yet appeared to focus explicitly on climate change or resilience.[91]

Among these member communities that are already seeking to integrate resilience, preparedness, or response, efforts primarily focus on increasing communications and alert systems, strengthening emergency response during disasters, and ensuring that evacuation plans consider the needs of older adults and people with disabilities. These are important steps forward but will likely be insufficient, given the range of interventions that are possible to foster community resilience and stability and reduce risk to older adults in the face of climate-enhanced disasters.

Increase Investment in and Use of Multipurpose Resilience Centers

In recent years, there has been a rise in interest in "resilience centers" (also known as resilience hubs or resilience pods), created by local governments, nonprofits, or developers of affordable housing to serve community needs. The Urban Sustainability Directors Network (USDN) hosts perhaps the definitive online resource dedicated to the use of resilience hubs, supporting their adoption as part of a community resilience framework that seeks to provide value every day, during disruption, and during recovery.[92]

Resilience hubs are generally located in spaces such as community centers, senior centers, or common areas in multifamily housing developments, where they can serve as accessible, trusted focal points for residents. Hubs can be places to educate residents about risks and how best to prepare for disasters, deliver services that promote health and well-being, and support disaster response and recovery efforts, ranging from offering food, water, and phone charging stations during a disaster to helping residents complete applications for federal assistance afterward. In their ideal state (per the USDN), resilience hubs model best practices in climate-resilient construction through net zero energy practices, biophilic design that promotes health and well-being for users, and integration of community solar installations to provide power for residents of nearby homes.[93]

Such interventions can be permanent fixtures or temporary and mobile deployments. In Miami, for example, the 2021 launch of its resilience pod featured a forty-foot repurposed shipping container that can be brought to local parks to educate residents about community-specific risks and share resources, guidance, and tools for residents to "be prepared, get connected, and take action."[94] In Tempe, Arizona, the EnVision Tempe center, set to open in 2023, will be the city's first resilience hub and will serve as a heat relief location for residents on extremely hot days or in the event of a power outage. The city expects to eventually outfit the facility with solar power and battery storage, making it the first in a projected citywide network of resilient energy hubs throughout the city.[95] In Tallahassee, Florida, the city targeted a number of existing community facilities—including several that already serve older adults with programming and services—for use as resilience hubs by not only enhancing year-round social services but also intentionally integrating emergency preparedness and disaster recovery resources.[96] And in New Orleans, a series of sixteen Community Lighthouse facilities are being constructed to serve as resilience hubs in areas of greatest need (see chapter 5).

While there is some evidence to suggest that resilience centers are being thoughtfully designed to address the needs of older adults, there are also indications of potential missed opportunities. Researchers from the University of Alberta who assessed resilience hubs across the United States in 2022 noted that the two most common functions featured in hubs were community emergency response training and an information desk, whereas far fewer also offered services and programs directly targeting older adults, such as group meetings and technology classes. The assessment also noted a wide gap in integrating transportation and mobility needs into the planning, design, and implementation of resilience hubs, perhaps serving as a barrier to older adults' full use of such resources. The report noted the following:

A wide range of transportation services (e.g., public transit, shared mobility, paratransit service, point-to-point transportation to/from key destinations) could be included as services or characteristics of a resilience hub. The lack of transportation examples indicates that while there may be the co-location of hubs and transportation, mobility services are not considered critical components of hubs in their current form. This also suggests that transportation—including connections to/from hubs—is not being considered as part of their functionality or usability.[97]

Account for People with Dementia and Cognitive Impairment in Disaster Planning

Dementia—a disease of the brain that causes progressive deterioration of memory, thinking, and communication, of which Alzheimer's disease is one cause—is not unique to older adults, but it is far more prevalent among them, necessitating more careful and thoughtful planning in order to reduce their risk. In 2022, 6.5 million Americans lived with Alzheimer's disease, and nearly three-quarters were people over seventy-five. Recall from chapter 1 that approximately one in nine people aged sixty-five and older have Alzheimer's disease.[98] And data suggest that, when compared with non-Hispanic Whites, Blacks and Hispanics are at increased risk for Alzheimer's disease.[99]

Many of the symptoms of dementia across all phases (early onset as well as later stages) can result in higher risk exposure for the individual:

- Early stages: difficulty remembering recent conversations, names, or events; apathy; depression; difficulty with motor function, especially slow gait and poor balance; visual hallucinations and visuospatial impairment
- Later stages: impaired communication, disorientation, confusion, poor judgment, behavioral change; difficulty speaking, swallowing, and walking.[100]

As a result, people with dementia and their caregivers find transitions—changes in routine or prescribed patterns—to be particularly difficult to manage. Those are made even more acute during times of disaster, necessitating careful planning and consideration for all involved.

As discussed in chapter 2, a growing number of resources target caregivers to help people with dementia better prepare for disasters. But the emergency management profession, as well, must more proactively plan and consider the needs of people with dementia and their caregivers. The Alzheimer's Association paired with Healthcare Ready and the CDC to develop guidance for public health professionals to more effectively plan for people with dementia in times of disaster, largely accounting for the need for caregivers to remain with their loved ones at shelters. Specialized training for emergency responders can help them better recognize signs of dementia, which might otherwise be mistaken as forgetfulness, stubbornness, or agreement to take action that is soon forgotten. Further, emergency management plans should integrate technology designed to address wandering—such as the MedicAlert Foundation's 24/7 Wandering Support program—into standard emergency preparedness education, notification systems, and training.

Clearly, the range of approaches needed to build true community resilience in ways that better account for the needs of an aging population transcend any one sector or any one level of government. The strategies in this chapter paint a picture for an "all of the above" approach that engages public, private, and nonprofit sectors in the delivery of energy, housing, transportation, health, social infrastructure, and emergency management services. They speak to the need to construct new spaces (such as resilience hubs), implement new protocols (such as better communication regarding utility blackouts), make different land use decisions (such as more transit-oriented development and smaller, denser housing), engage new partners (such as those possible through age-friendly efforts)—and much more—in order to bolster community resilience in ways that will better meet the needs of an aging nation and respond to the unique needs of older adults in the face of a changing climate.

To date, few places in our country have embraced the challenge—and arguably none can be affirmatively named as true leaders in building community resilience for older adults. But it is worthwhile to review how states and communities are approaching the task and where they are showing the way to success in order to inform future action, as chapter 5 endeavors to do.

05 COMMUNITY RESILIENCE FOR ALL AGES IN ACTION

—

Given the complexity of the task of preparing a nation for an aging future in the face of growing climate challenges, it is unfair to imagine that any one community or state has figured it out. Climate change is accelerating, presenting new challenges that upend even the best-laid plans and exposing new weaknesses in the systems that have been created to protect our nation, communities, and people. Nevertheless, important lessons can be drawn from the experiences of different communities at the state, county, and local levels. This chapter explores the experience of three places—the State of New York, the City of Portland and Multnomah County, Oregon, and the City of New Orleans—to understand how their current approaches to resilience are shaped by past experiences and, in some cases, by their affirmative commitment to better center the needs of older adults. All of these entities have experienced tragedy resulting from climate change in recent years, in which their ability to protect older adults was tested. Their experiences are helpful in assessing how to best craft approaches that integrate new frameworks for planning (see chapter 3) and function to bring together disparate sectors and solutions (see chapter 4). Individually and collectively, they offer lessons in how to work toward better community-scale resilience in the places where we live now and hope to age in the future.

State of New York

New York is one of the most populous US states for older adults (the fourth highest in terms of sixty-five-plus population)—in 2021, 3.9 million older adults lived in the state, representing nearly 18 percent of all New Yorkers. Between 2010 and 2020, the number of older adults grew by nearly 30 percent. Today, more than one in every ten older New Yorkers live at or below the poverty line.[1] Recognizing these trends, in 2017 Governor Andrew Cuomo enrolled New York in the AARP Network of Age-Friendly States and Communities—it was the first state to join. That commitment has been affirmed and accelerated by the current governor, Kathy Hochul.

New York is also a state that has experienced a number of natural disasters, perhaps most famously Hurricane Sandy in 2012, in which the median age of people who died was sixty-five.[2] Hurricane Ida then hit in 2021, and record-setting winter storms in 2022 affected Erie County—a place not unaccustomed to harsh winters and freezing temperatures. In all of these events, older adults were among the fatalities, in most cases disproportionately so.

As part of its commitment to becoming an age-friendly state, New York has demonstrated its intention to better center decision-making on the needs of older adults, particularly through a lens of healthy aging.[3] Cuomo's Executive Order No. 190, issued in 2018, sought to rewire the way state agencies work together, tasking state departments with better integrating the needs of older adults into programs and policies.[4] To date, the New York State Office for the Aging (in collaboration with philanthropic partners) has awarded more than $1 million in incentive grants to localities to create more age-friendly environments, and it has leveraged $600 million in economic development investment across ten New York regions to encourage greater adoption of age-friendly considerations, such as policies that support Complete Streets approaches, create housing that serves various ages and abilities, or otherwise align with the AARP age-friendly program goals.[5] Leadership from the New York Department of State means that, without using the words "climate change," the state's age-friendly commitments have thoughtfully integrated smart growth approaches that can deliver better environmental outcomes by reducing emissions and improving the built environment to promote better health and wellness across the ages. Investments such as more walkable communities and more dense, mixed-use downtowns are all encouraged—including in the smaller rural places so common across the state—because they respond as much, if not more, to the social environment that shapes people's lives.[6]

Perhaps even more important, these types of commitments were made in collaboration across state agencies as well as with key philanthropic and nonprofit partners—particularly the New York Academy of Medicine (NYAM) and the Health Foundation for Western and Central New York. These organizations are equally invested in the state's age-friendly effort (also referred to as Health and Age Across All Policies), helping to create and support regional Centers of Excellence and Learning Collaboratives among grantees that provide critical capacity-building support to communities seeking to develop their own age-friendly plans. As a result, the state's age-friendly aspirations have resulted in local-level age-friendly actions, with thirty-two cities, towns, and counties making their own age-friendly commitments.[7] Glen Cove, New York, is among them, having celebrated in December 2022 its status as one of several statewide Age-Friendly Centers of Excellence, pointing to the New York State leadership as catalytic in its adoption of new health- and transportation-related programs that aim to better serve older adults. To date, its focus has been on expanding older adults' access to health information and social connection; future efforts will aim to make sidewalks more accessible and expand transportation options.[8]

As a result of these efforts, New York has great potential to better integrate aging considerations into resilience planning efforts, although implementation challenges remain. In 2014, following Hurricane Sandy, NYAM issued a report based on a robust engagement and research process drawing on the lived experiences of older adults in the region to document lessons learned and to craft recommendations to guide policymakers in New York City and the state. The report, "Resilient Communities: Empowering Older Adults in Disasters and Daily Life," laid out a framework for action that includes many of the same core messages that this book does, including the following key findings:

- Formal and informal social networks influenced decisions [by older adults] and facilitated access to information and assistance.
- Because older people had not been engaged in emergency planning, emergency services were often inadequate, inappropriate, or inaccessible to older people, and their basic and healthcare needs went unmet.

- Older adults actively supported their communities before, during, and after Hurricane Sandy.
- The local neighborhood infrastructure was effective in meeting the needs of older people.[9]

Twelve recommendations were offered (see table 5-1) for action by the city and by New York State—including requirements that owners of multifamily buildings with a high prevalence of older residents be trained in disaster preparedness, encouragement of community resilience hubs to foster communal planning and service delivery, and greater efforts by localities and academia to measure the ways in which vulnerable populations are affected by disasters. The report is among the most comprehensive and thoughtful resources to date in exploring how older adults experience disaster and how communities can better respond. There was not, however, a permanent accountability structure created to accompany the report, nor does NYAM have the authority to monitor adoption of the recommendations by the state or city (as the US Government Accountability Office does with the Federal Emergency Management Agency, for example; see table 3-2). But one of the report's authors indicated in 2022 that "localities have been implementing some of the recommendations locally."[10]

There is evidence of that indeed. Beginning in March 2020, NYAM led, on behalf of state agency partners, a Learning Collaborative for age-friendly leaders across the state with the dual objectives of encouraging better collaboration across health, aging, and planning at local levels and fostering learning among age-friendly communities.[11] NYAM conveners shared content from the 2014 report—specifically the age-centered resilience framework developed by RAND Corporation (discussed in chapter 3)—and asked age-friendly leaders to share their own progress in advancing emergency response and planning at a May 2020 meeting.

Given the timing of the event during the early months of the pandemic, many participants focused on how their age-friendly efforts were able to quickly pivot to meet new challenges related to COVID-19, including delivering food, ensuring social connection, and strengthening communication with older adults. But some participants shared efforts underway to better integrate broader disaster

Table 5-1: NYAM Recommendations for Resilient Communities in New York

Recommendation

1. Older adults in underserved neighborhoods should be trained to identify and link vulnerable people with community assets (e.g., healthcare, social services, benefits, food) under routine conditions and during emergencies.

2. Older adults and informal caregivers should be provided with access to and training in multiple forms of communication and technology.

3. Landlords with large concentrations of older adults and mobility-impaired people should be supported in developing plans to meet the needs of these populations during disasters.

4. Employees of city services, local businesses, cultural institutions, and others who routinely interact with older adults should be trained in identifying and providing appropriate local health and human service referrals to those who may be in need of assistance before, during, after, and outside of an emergency.

5. Communities should be assisted in organizing community resilience hubs housed at the most appropriate and accessible institutions within each neighborhood to facilitate communal planning and multisectoral partnerships and to serve as a central repository for information and supplies during an emergency.

6. Providers of essential services to older adults should develop contingency plans to ensure that the needs of their patients and clients will be met during disasters and emergencies. The city should extend memorandums of understanding and set funding policies in advance to enable providers to expand their reach during disasters.

7. Mental health support, spiritual care, and psychological first aid should be systematically colocated and coordinated with nonstigmatized disaster response and recovery services.

8. Academia, city agencies, and community-based organizations should develop and implement appropriate metrics to indicate how vulnerable populations are affected by and assisted during disasters.

9. The city should consult older people, caregivers, and service providers about their experiences with and perceptions of the public shelter system.

10. Training for professional and volunteer first responders should include information about the needs of older adults during disasters as well as the cultural, linguistic, and developmental competencies that may be required to meet those needs.

11. New York State should enact a disaster pharmacy law to provide a regulatory framework for pharmacists and pharmacies to dispense medication when a state of emergency is declared.

(table continues)

Table 5-1 *(continued)*

12. New York State should enact bill S.4719/A.6530, which will require counties and cities to consult with home healthcare and hospice providers on emergency plans and to include provisions in those plans for the deployment of home healthcare and hospice personnel.

Source: Adapted from Lindsay Goldman et al., "Resilient Communities: Empowering Older Adults in Disasters and Daily Life," New York Academy of Medicine, July 2014, https://media.nyam.org/filer_public/64/b2/64b2da62-f4e7-4e04-b5d1-e0e52b2a5614/resilient_communities_report_final.pdf.

planning and age-friendly efforts: Glen Cove was considering a dedicated domain on emergency response and disaster planning in its updated action plan; Rockland County was delivering cross-agency training to better integrate aging and emergency response, leading to implementation of a Special Needs Registry; and Erie County, after learning that "the segment of County government that provides human services [had] not traditionally worked with local emergency planning efforts," planned to "address this oversight and strengthen the relationship we have with emergency planning officials."[12]

Tompkins County, in the southwest of the state, shared its disaster-related efforts to combat social isolation and ensure effective communication, particularly among rural residents and those without in-home internet service. For example, the partnership between the county's Office for the Aging and its health and communications departments that had been cultivated through their age-friendly efforts[13] allowed the county to rapidly activate local Board of Elections mailing lists to send mailers out to every household with a resident aged sixty-five or older that included up-to-date information about new vaccine eligibility and availability.[14] Over time, training and education in emergency preparedness has shifted to climate-related events, with the Human Services Coalition of Tompkins County recently hosting a workshop on climate change and what it means for older adults.[15] One workshop participant—an age-friendly volunteer in Caroline, New York (population 3,500)—was seeking to implement the coalition's recommendation to establish neighborhood emergency preparedness groups that would assist with basic training and preparedness and to foster groups of six to twelve households to get acquainted with one another "so that they know about people's disabilities, pets, farm animals, or any other special conditions that local emergency teams would benefit from knowing"[16] during disaster response efforts.

The statewide commitment has also delivered a stronger infrastructure for collaboration among state agencies,[17] such as that between the New York State Office for the Aging (NYSOFA) and the New York State Energy and Research Development Authority (NYSERDA), which collaborated to bring energy efficiency retrofits to nursing homes and encourage older adults to make similar investments in their homes.[18] The partnership between NYSOFA and the New York Department of State has been a particularly robust one, leveraging the aforementioned programs (including $600 million in economic development resources) and also partnering to ensure that older adults' experiences are included in statewide interagency efforts to explore how urban heat island effects are affecting vulnerable and disadvantaged communities.[19] Nevertheless, the director of NYSOFA acknowledged that "we probably missed a couple windows" to formalize aging as part of the state's climate-related efforts and to build in a stronger structure for more routine cross-agency collaboration.[20] When disasters strike, NYSOFA is called upon as an expert by state agencies and localities to help them reach older adults—and they do so effectively, having cultivated a strong network of Area Agencies on Aging (AAAs) and community-based partners tasked with taking action in advance of approaching storms to "reach out to every client to let them know that there is a storm coming, and to have food and medications on hand. It's now standard practice."[21] However, only a relatively small share of older New Yorkers are connected with AAAs.[22] A better way would have been to build the capacity within each state agency and across localities to better acknowledge the needs of older adults, consider their communication and service needs, and incorporate these into all community-serving efforts.

Perhaps the greatest opportunity to do just that still lies ahead. In November 2022, Governor Hochul issued an executive order[23] tasking the state with developing a Master Plan for Aging (MPA). This statewide plan will likely follow the model created by the State of California with its Master Plan for Aging[24] (released in 2021), which sets clear priorities for state action and a dashboard to track progress. In 2023, California released an updated set of strategies and initiatives that explicitly focus on emergency preparedness and response and climate-friendly aging.[25] Such an approach could, if replicated in New York, create stronger and more direct ties between age-friendly efforts and the state's climate goals as articulated in the 2022 New York State Climate Action Council Scoping Plan, which include, for example, goals to incentivize energy efficiency upgrades for disadvantaged communities (including the elderly).[26] The charge to create the MPA (which may ultimately be known as the Multisector Plan for Aging) resides with both the New York State Department of Health and NYSOFA. The director of NYSOFA stated, "There will be a serious effort to bring [climate resilience] to the table. It is already listed as an example of the kinds of things that the MPA can show that will deliver improved air quality, lower fuel cost while balancing choice [in home heating and cooling], and more."[27] NYSOFA intends for the MPA to start with the many disparate efforts already in progress across agencies to serve the needs of older adults in the face of a changing climate to identify gaps and new solutions and aggregate the work and connect the efforts together. The state director of smart growth shares the view, likening the plan to a loom, allowing for the state to "tie the pieces together and ensure that we don't miss the big pieces."[28]

In the meantime, NYAM is updating its 2014 report at the urging of Carolyn Stem, a part-time employee of NYAM who is in her late seventies. The updated report will focus on lessons learned from pandemic emergency response efforts in New York City, specifically, and include an updated literature review to see how community resilience frameworks have changed over the years.[29]

The NYAM report's conclusion that "the best predictor of how a neighborhood will respond to and recover from a disaster is how it functioned prior to the disaster"[30] appears to hold true. The age-friendly efforts across the state—both between state agencies and within and among localities—demonstrate the value of strengthening relationships across silos, engaging older adults in planning and response, and fostering a community-led structure that serves the needs of older adults. The MPA could help propel the state to an even stronger and more resilient future for all.

City of Portland and Multnomah County, Oregon

Portland, Oregon, has long been a leader in promoting age-friendly approaches, joining the World Health Organization's age-friendly program in 2006—the first US city to do so. AARP Oregon has been a long-standing advocate for making the connection between older adults and disaster risks, leading up to and including a 2005 state-wide conference it co-convened on how older adults and people with disabilities are affected by disasters to address the looming threat of a Cascadia earthquake.[31] It is not surprising, therefore, that the City of Portland incorporated a focus on preparing for natural disasters in its 2013 Action Plan for an Age-Friendly Portland, addressing the need to improve coordination within Portland's response systems to better meet the needs of vulnerable populations, improve emergency responders' understanding of mental health issues, and engage older adults and people with disabilities in emergency preparedness training.[32] When Multnomah County joined in 2014, it affirmed its commitment to partner with Portland on all age-friendly subcommittees, including the one focusing on preparedness.[33] This city-county alignment proved to be a critical element in building resilience for the area's older population when the pandemic struck in 2020 and again when extreme heat blanketed the region in 2021 and 2022. It is impossible to know whether age-friendly efforts in any way blunted the effects of the deadly heat event in 2021, which took the lives of 116 people, including many older adults (see chapter 2), or the 2022 heat wave, which was responsible for fifteen deaths.[34] But it is clear that the region's response to the unexpected catastrophes of both the pandemic and extreme heat reveal some important contributions to resilience that are worth replicating, including its practice of cross-agency collaboration, its integration of deeply rooted community-based organizations (CBOs), and its commitment to continuous improvement.

The early commitments by the City of Portland to improve preparedness for older adults and people with disabilities found greater success when Multnomah County joined the age-friendly effort in 2014 because the county houses two critical functions: the Area Agency on Aging, responsible for many of the services that support the ability of older adults to age in place, and the emergency management function. As a result, responsibility for mass care and sheltering during emergencies (as determined by the National Response Framework; see chapter 4) resides in the same county department that oversees implementation of Older Americans Act programs and non-Medicaid and safety net programs for older adults and people with disabilities.[35] The location of these two functions in the same unit of government facilitated integration within the county and also between the county and city. The county was able to bring an awareness of the needs of older adults, where they live, and how best to communicate with them to the task of emergency management, and the city was better able to strategically integrate its own efforts to build communication systems, foster a network of trusted and culturally relevant CBOs, and leverage volunteers through Neighborhood Emergency Teams[36] (which include many older volunteers) and other means to support the county's emergency response approach.[37]

The value of collaboration is well illustrated in the pandemic-era example of the Joint Volunteer Information Center (JVIC), led by the Portland Bureau of Emergency Management (PBEM) and implemented by the county. The JVIC was "established to distribute essential resources during the pandemic and to support emerging and grassroots organizations and leaders in communities that are typically underserved by government."[38] The intent of the JVIC was to ensure that high-risk and historically underserved communities—including communities of color, people with disabilities, the unhoused, and older adults—remained a focus of pandemic response by strengthening the capacity of CBOs to serve their needs. What that means in real terms is that food, information, personal protective equipment, cleaning supplies, and toiletries (such as adult diapers and culturally specific hair products) were delivered by trusted, familiar community organizations directly to often-overlooked residents as a result of JVIC funding and coordination. The JVIC was not without challenges, including supply and storage limitations and confusion about processes, but it was effective in providing meaningful service and relief. PBEM reported that the JVIC had leveraged ninety-one CBOs across the region, each with an established background among the communities it serves, and helped 792 coordinators deliver tens of thousands of units of care, hygiene, and cleaning supplies.[39]

Funded by the 2020 Coronavirus Aid, Relief, and Economic Security Act (CARES Act), the JVIC was decommissioned in 2022 when it was not approved for future funding by the city, but it nevertheless offers lessons to inform other emergency response and age-friendly efforts about the value of empowering CBOs to strengthen resilience. The city's chief resilience officer hailed the JVIC and the systems it created as helpful in better integrating age into climate resilience, stating, "It represents a foundational part of emergency management planning—building the relationships, ensuring that people know where to get information and how to use technology [e.g., satellite radios, if distributed as part of planning efforts], well in advance of the disaster."[40] Some of the relationships and functionality fostered by the JVIC may well outlive the formal funding and position the region to better respond as new crises emerge.

But the JVIC is not the only evidence of the value of working across department or government lines in times of crisis. When the first heat dome blanketed the region in 2021, daily meetings were held that brought county and city staff together with representatives from utilities, healthcare systems, and the regional transit authority (TriMet) to quickly tackle emergent issues. As a result, the county was able to offset capacity challenges in Ride Connection—the paratransit service, which was still hindered by staff shortages following the pandemic—by offering free taxi vouchers for rides to cooling centers and medical appointments. The county was able to deploy its Aging and Disability Resource Connection (ADRC) staff to proactively reach out to older adults with electrolyte packets, information about warning signs to look out for regarding exposure to extreme heat, and links to a Multnomah County website with updates that mirrored real-time weather conditions. And ADRC staff were able to track where shelter beds were available so they could direct people to locations with availability and manage transportation connections. The multidepartment meetings were also a means to resolve contractual barriers that caused the 211 service staffing to fall short during a weekend of peak heat (see chapter 4).[41]

The participation of the utilities was critical, given the importance of cooling, especially for older adults, during extreme heat, and addressing power outages. Representatives from Portland General Electric and Pacific Power participated in daily calls, reported on where crews were and how they were responding, and suspended shutoffs for nonpayment during times of crisis. In the summer of 2022, the looming threat of wildfires led to rolling power outages in the Portland metropolitan area. Utilities publicized the times and locations of planned blackouts, provided information about centers where people could go if their power was going to be shut off, and offered drop-in spaces for people to charge phones and cool off.[42]

Inherent to the city and county's approach is a process of continual improvement and an ethos of accountability in which lessons learned, including failures or shortcomings, are used to inform new structures, processes, and approaches—particularly since climate change brings new conditions and needs. Between the 2021 and 2022 heat waves, the city and county sought to strengthen their response to extreme heat by improving communication about risk, utilizing smaller and more decentralized cooling centers (rather than larger centralized ones), and offering free transit rides to cooling centers.[43] Other partners played a role in the response, such as the Portland Clean Energy Community Benefits Fund (PCEF), which mobilized quickly after 2021 to distribute ductless portable heat pumps to cool people's homes in advance of the following summer. Informed by discussions between PCEF and staff of Portland's Bureau of Planning and Sustainability (which houses Portland's Age-Friendly City program),[44] the PCEF Heat Response Program prioritized installation for low-income people who were sixty years of age or older, who were living alone, who had underlying health conditions, or all of these.[45] The fund leaned on a network of CBOs, many of which had previously served residents through the JVIC, thereby leveraging the city's prior investment in that structure. Trusted organizations—such as the Asian Pacific American Network of Oregon and Hacienda CDC, serving the Latino community—helped to promote the program, expedite distribution, and facilitate installation to ensure that residents would be better protected during future heat events.[46]

In the vein of continuous improvement, a 2021 audit of the city's pandemic response brought attention to shortcomings in the ways in which people with disabilities were served, several of which have since been addressed. The report recommended that the city evaluate whether its Additional Needs Registry should be discontinued, formalize the inclusion of a disability advisor in the Emergency

Coordination Center command structure and operating procedures, and take responsibility for coordinating emergency preparedness outreach to people with disabilities.[47] Key staff point to the audit as an important practice, and a welcome moment for improvement, with one emergency management staff member noting, "We should always look at how we're doing, how we responded, and how we can do better."[48] Staff point to the audit as creating pathways for still stronger communication and engagement across agencies and levels of government, including a greater focus on assessing the needs of vulnerable populations early and often, and more proactively pushing information and messaging out into the community about where to seek help and support (which led to the ADRC effort described earlier).

An emergency management staff member said of the effort:

> Meaningful and impactful change happens at the local and community level. That's where the people are. When they come together, we can better see how the various puzzle pieces fit and allow us to see the whole picture. National structures [that aim to build resilience and protect communities] should figure out how to get the money to the local and community levels. City governments working closely with CBOs help get to the best impacts possible because these groups represent the lived experiences of people who are most impacted.[49]

The community-led approach upon which the city's and county's age-friendly efforts rely proved to be essential to enhancing community resilience.

City of New Orleans, Louisiana

Hurricane Katrina, which hit New Orleans in 2005, looms for many Americans as one of the most powerful illustrations of what can occur when systems break down in the face of unprecedented disaster. Many people can recall images from the Louisiana Superdome that painfully revealed the challenges of sheltering tens of thousands of people (who in this case were predominately Black and poor) who could not evacuate or tragic stories about elderly people trapped in nursing homes and submerged in floodwater. Hurricane Katrina remains one of the deadliest disasters for older adults in the United States, with 63 percent of the deaths occurring among people over sixty-five (608 deaths out of 971 total). Researchers have concluded that there were two principal explanations for the widely disproportionate fatality rate: the unwillingness or inability of older adults to evacuate and their greater risk of drowning and injury as a result of comorbidities that added to their vulnerability.[50] Thirty-six percent of people who died were found in their residence, and nearly that many died in hospitals and nursing homes (22 percent and 12 percent, respectively), where transportation challenges impeded the evacuation of patients and access to food, supplies, and clean water.

Louisiana leaders now point to Katrina as a turning point in their way of thinking about disasters from emergency preparedness to community resilience, as well as the beginning of more intentional planning for older adults.[51] New Orleans is not a member of the AARP Network of Age-Friendly States and Communities (as was the case with the other two case studies in this chapter), but the New Orleans Council on Aging (NOCOA) serves as a critical leader, collaborating with other groups to ensure that the needs of older adults are considered and met. In the years following Katrina, NOCOA was approached by disaster management officials to help prepare a better evacuation plan for Orleans Parish, which resulted in the use of pickup points at senior centers during subsequent disasters. Since then, NOCOA has worked to inform those over sixty years of age about the designated pickup spots in the event of evacuation and also to ensure that vehicles used by the regional transit authority to transport people with disabilities have the capacity to carry motorized wheelchairs, which have grown larger over time and exceed the weight limitations of the lifts used in older vans.[52] NOCOA encourages older residents to sign up for the City's Critical Care List and the new Smart911 service (see the discussion of special needs registries in chapter 4) and provides utility assistance to help people aged sixty and over with past-due bills. NOCOA has also encouraged the utility, Entergy, to draw on the agency's information about older adults who rely on in-home assistive devices so that the utility can prioritize them when reconnecting power after blackouts.[53]

A virtual cottage industry of post-Katrina books and studies has grown since 2005 that explore the failures, missteps, and outright racism that made Katrina such a deadly event then and that continue to plague many neighborhoods nearly twenty years later. The disaster continues to loom large in the minds of state, parish,[54] and city officials as well. Yet, tragically, many of the weaknesses that became evident in Katrina (plus Hurricane Rita, which struck just three weeks later)—such as challenges in ensuring safe and secure housing for those unable to evacuate—were as yet unresolved by the time Hurricane Ida struck the region in August 2021.

The events were different in important ways. Whereas Katrina was largely a water event characterized by rain, storm surge, and breached levees leading to flooding, Ida was characterized more by its fast-changing nature, its strong winds, and the resulting damage to the electric power grid, leading to extended power outages. Homes in high-rise buildings—where many older adults and people with disabilities lived—were ill-suited to the weeks-long power outages that followed Hurricane Ida, leaving people who could not walk down the stairs stranded and unable to call for help or utilize oxygen devices. Because these buildings were privately owned, they were not subject to the same requirements as nursing homes and congregate living facilities (see the CMS Emergency Preparedness Rule discussions in chapters 2 and 4), and as a result they lacked clear emergency plans and backup power supplies. The city's director of health attributed seven deaths to the conditions,[55] prompting the city to adopt an ordinance to require all buildings with six or more units housing older adults or people with disabilities to develop an emergency management plan and identify whether there is backup power on-site.[56] Hurricane Ida also revealed the weakness of state and local agencies in ensuring that congregate living facilities governed by the CMS Emergency Preparedness Rule have suitable emergency shelter plans in place. In the most tragic failure of the rule, at least fifteen older adults died after being moved from nursing homes owned by a single owner to a warehouse, following a plan that met the federal CMS requirements (see chapter 2).[57] People relocated to the warehouse were subjected to conditions ill-suited to any person, much less medically fragile people, including wet mattresses and poor access to food and basic hygiene. Combined, these failures—the deaths among residents in facilities covered by CMS and the dangerous conditions in privately owned multifamily buildings—dramatically increased the death toll attributable to the hurricane. They could have been largely avoided with better planning. They brought the needs of older adults during disasters to the attention of elected leaders again, resulting in calls to NOCOA from the mayor, the governor, and congressional representatives—a first in the experience of NOCOA's longtime executive director.[58]

NOLA Ready—the city's emergency preparedness campaign managed by the New Orleans Office of Homeland Security and Emergency Preparedness, formed in response to the pandemic—points to other efforts being made to better integrate the needs of older adults and people with disabilities.[59] The new Smart911 system supports a more data-driven emergency response based on the needs of people who register, particularly now that fixes have been implemented that allow for phone-in registration (bypassing an online interface that was confusing for some and wholly unreachable for those without an internet connection) and that eliminate the need for registrants to reaffirm their data every six months. Emergency Resource Centers—such as the cooling centers implemented in response to Hurricane Ida and warming centers in response to a 2022 December hard freeze—are now opened more routinely by the New Orleans Recreation Development Commission in city-owned recreational facilities, which often are already accessible for people with disabilities.

In partnership with the city and leveraging federal, philanthropic, and other funding, Together New Orleans has constructed three Community Lighthouses (see figures 5-1a, 5-1b, and 5-1c) as part of a project that will ultimately include sixteen solar- and battery-powered resilience hubs at churches and community centers across New Orleans, coupled with a ground game of volunteers to conduct direct outreach to residents in need.[60] The effort was formed by the group—a coalition of community- and faith-based groups—in direct response to Hurricane Ida and the two primary needs identified then by its members: access to power during extended blackouts and a stronger disaster response approach that better serves residents, many of whom are older adults (see chapter 6). The project organizer described their disaster response approach:

The Lighthouses will have teams in place who are responsible for going out into neighborhoods to make connections with neighbors and assess needs before disaster strikes: to find out, who can walk to the Lighthouse? Who has vulnerabilities? In

Figure 5-1a: Three Community Lighthouses have been constructed to date by Together New Orleans, this one at Broadmoor Community Church.

Figure 5-1b: CrescentCare Community Health Center is one of the few planned Community Lighthouse locations that is not a house of worship.

Figure 5-1c: Bethlehem Lutheran Church is home to a Community Lighthouse. (Photos courtesy of Together New Orleans)

that way, we know that Mrs. Johnson can walk to the location—or that she needs help getting there. It's also so that the team knows that we need to check in on her within twenty-four hours. And when we do, we will already have established the trust that will help her get the support she needs.[61]

Two other projects, also implemented in collaboration with the city, aim to bring critical energy sources to people most in need during events. UNITY of Greater New Orleans, the city's Continuum of Care Program provider delivering housing and support services, seeks to install solar powered backup generators in three multifamily properties serving low-income and formerly unhoused residents. The Footprint Project delivers mobile solar-powered stations to support responders and residents in times of crisis and prioritizes the delivery of solar batteries directly to the homes of people with disabilities.[62]

Yet even with these new efforts, the legacy of such deeply traumatic events and the long tail of recovery for many New Orleanians continues to inform the broader understanding of what disaster means for older adults, particularly for people of color and those who are poor. In one respect, the solutions described here illustrate the challenge of "serving the most people rather than serving those with the most needs," as articulated by one disability advocate.[63] In another way, the evolution of New Orleans's recovery highlights the disproportionate impact of climate-related disasters on the poor, communities of color, and people living with mental or physical challenges. Pam Jenkins, a New Orleans–based researcher who has published several books and articles on the intersections of age, race, and disaster since Katrina, said:

> Before Katrina, people who were older and had disabilities found ways to make their lives work; they could manage their day-to-day life. Katrina destroyed that. We interviewed people who went to Houston. I recall a story of a family with an elderly father who had dementia; he was okay here, but he had to be put in nursing homes in Baton Rouge because the social network didn't exist. Around New Orleans, you can get around on the bus system, or get rides from neighbors and families. That wasn't the case in Houston, especially for people who were relocated there. That dislocation is very powerful. You've got people who evacuated to Houston who wanted to come back home to die; they wanted to die *here*. They wanted to die where it was familiar. We lost 1,800 people from Katrina across the coast, but we don't count the people who died later. Katrina shortened our lives because of the stress. If you were poor and old, Katrina was a terminal event for you. That's who died: people over sixty.[64]

The long-term physical, emotional, mental, and financial stress of disasters has not yet been fully integrated into most disaster planning efforts, including those in New Orleans. Despite some efforts by FEMA, for example, to improve disaster assistance to better serve older adults and people with disabilities (see table 3-2), navigating the long process of recovery is difficult and stressful for many older adults. Jenkins recalled a scene during her own experience navigating the Road Home program,[65] which compensated owners for the loss of their homes or helped them rebuild. The program required going to the Road Home offices as part of the inspection process. She and her husband arrived with file folders, already beleaguered, and saw "so many others with paper bags holding their belongings, just waiting to talk to someone." People who could not manage the bureaucracy—understanding the process, completing the required steps, and advocating for themselves in the face of delays—ended up with even greater long-term setbacks. "That's why funding should go to local groups that work with marginalized people to have advocates help with recovery, who understand the process and can do that. Those challenges and the ongoing stress in the aftermath of the disaster is what [also] shortened the lives of people."[66]

After Ida, some homes were left without power for weeks, placing an incredible strain on older people with no access to goods and services. People had become accustomed to one or two days without power or had a backup generator, but living safely and securely without power for weeks was something altogether different. The conditions served as a "big wake-up call" for the New Orleans community, a realization that resilience isn't just about evacuating people but is also about planning for the dimensions of what it means to survive.[67]

Increasingly, disasters are recognized not as onetime events but as cascading events in which people are tasked with both weathering the proverbial storm and dealing with what happens afterward. In the short term, this can mean securing access to power, housing, food, medicine, and healthcare. In the medium to long term, it means that people must rebuild their lives to overcome the challenges that disasters leave in their wake, while also preparing for the next one.

06 LESSONS LEARNED AND HOW TO MOVE FORWARD

—

Time is limited for us to make the kinds of changes needed in our communities to make them safer for older adults. Each year seems to bring new climate challenges that test the ability of individuals to prepare and of communities to plan. And yet, there has never been a better time than today to make the commitment to a more age-friendly, resilient, and equitable future given what we now know.

The challenges described throughout this book, the proposed frameworks and strategies to address them, and the experience of communities across the country (particularly those featured in chapter 5) lead to several broad lessons that can and must inform action going forward.

Actively Engage Older Adults and Their Advocates at the Planning Table

Older adults can be critical contributors to community resilience as a result of their volunteer efforts and their lifetime of expertise and insights. Create space at the table for older adults and their advocates and actively engage them to identify solutions, thereby realizing the maxim "No about us without us." This can be encouraged by ensuring that aging considerations are a requirement of any policy or program that affects community design, emergency preparedness, or resilience.

For any long-term resilience plans that seek to wholly relocate communities at greatest risk of climate-related impacts and disasters (such as low-lying coastal areas, barrier islands, or areas experiencing subsidence), it is essential to engage older adults in the planning effort at the outset and throughout the process. For older adults in these communities, it is critical to acknowledge and honor the importance and life-giving nature of social connections that exist and people's historical and personal connection to the land and its natural resources.

Older adults can also be enlisted as volunteers and participants in community resilience efforts, such as helping people to enroll in home energy assistance programs or installing home energy use monitors, or in designing evacuation and sheltering plans that account for the needs of older adults. Older adults can foster relationships and connections among those at greatest risk of isolation. Formal mechanisms—such as Voluntary Organizations Active in Disasters (VOADs) and age-friendly efforts (chapter 3)—can serve as a bridge to engage older adults in emergency, disaster, and community planning efforts.

The chief resilience officer for the City of Portland, Oregon, notes that the city takes a universal design approach in its emergency preparedness and program design efforts: "If you design a program with the needs of people with disabilities at the outset, they will be better served. By designing a heat response plan that assumes people are hard of hearing, have mobility impairments, and lack transportation, we can create a plan that better serves everyone."[1] That work is intentional: 10 percent of volunteers with the Portland Bureau of Emergency Management identify as people with disabilities; many more than that are people who are older. She also argues:

> Resilience programs that are more inclusive (including those focusing on older adults) will be the longer-lasting ones; they'll show more value because they make a difference in people's lives every day—more so than just by building a sea wall. If there is a focus on creating ways for people to contribute throughout the entirety of their lives, then that is a program that is going to live on.[2]

Plan for Older Adults' Limitations in Mobility and Ability (Physical, Financial, Cognitive)

Plans and projects that rely upon the ability of individuals to mobilize to relocate out of harm's way, for either the short or the long term, fail to account for the fact that many older adults do not drive, may live alone with little access to on-demand personal transportation, or lack the physical or cognitive ability to easily accommodate new routines in a new environment. Given the precarious financial status of many older adults, plans must better account for older adults who lack the resources to hire a taxi (if available), move to a hotel (if accessible), or otherwise temporarily relocate in the face of a disaster. More age-friendly resilience planning would provide ample time for older adults to weigh their evacuation options, ensuring that sufficient information in a variety of means is available about where the shelter is located, what to expect at the shelter, and options for how to get there.

Even preparedness activities that aim to help older adults shelter in place must acknowledge that some older adults will struggle to carry large jugs of water or bags of pet food or will be unable to afford the cost of stockpiling food and prescriptions—much less cover the cost of enhanced hazard insurance or upgrades to enable their home to better withstand disasters.

Use Communication Systems That Match the Habits, Abilities, and Preferences of Older Adults

Plans that rely upon social media, text messaging, or web-based transmission of timely information to aid individual decision-making fail to acknowledge that there are individuals for whom those channels simply do not work. There are many people—particularly among those most vulnerable—who rely upon print media, local news, and personal and direct outreach from trusted community members, especially those who share the same language and cultural traditions. Information that is needed for time-sensitive decision-making— such as whether to evacuate or how to reach a cooling center—is especially important to have in readily available print form, accessible by telephone, or both in order to minimize any delay associated with technology.

Engage a diversity of partner organizations in the communication and education campaign, including those who can reach non-English-speaking individuals, recent arrivals, people with disabilities, those with cognitive impairments—and those who care for them. Be mindful that even with the use of adaptive technology, people with disabilities may be unable to receive or process alerts that are meant to reach the community as a whole—such as alerts posted on highway signs, audio alert signals, or door hang tags.

Recognize That the Majority of Older Adults Live Outside of Congregate Settings and Often Live Alone

To the degree that older adults are explicitly considered in formal emergency and evacuation plans, for the most part they are considered as residents of congregate living facilities, such as assisted living facilities, nursing homes, or care facilities. While the needs of these residents certainly represent a critical requirement in terms of planning and preparation, emergency managers may wrongly believe that planning for them fulfills their responsibility to consider the needs of all older adults.

More than 90 percent of older adults live in their homes, often alone. They live in urban centers, suburban communities, and rural (or even frontier) places. They may be isolated physically, socially, and emotionally, making them more difficult to reach and plan for than those in congregate facilities—and therefore perhaps even more in need of targeted support and planning. Emergency and evacuation plans must account for the needs of residents of congregate living facilities—and of facilities not governed by the Centers for Medicare and Medicaid Services (CMS) Emergency Preparedness Rule, such as adult day centers and respite care facilities—as well as those who live on their own. In San Francisco, the Resiliency and Emergency Preparedness domain of its age-friendly action plan acknowledges this and seeks to ensure that there is a strategy in place in multistory buildings for evacuating people with mobility challenges, for example. The plan further recommends "policies and procedures that account for and are prepared to respond promptly to seniors and people with disabilities, prioritizing those who require additional support or are unable to shelter in place for 72 hours."[3]

Plan for Family and Nonfamily Caregivers (as Both Providers and Recipients)

Evacuation plans must consider the role of caregivers—both older adults providing care to others and those receiving care—and home health aides as essential parts of the decision-making process for older adults contemplating relocation or being asked to relocate. An older adult caregiver who is responsible for a frail spouse or an adult child with a disability will weigh the task of disaster preparation or evacuation with a much more complex set of requirements and considerations than one who is responsible for herself alone. Further, older adults who are receiving regular care—either to treat a medical condition or to assist with activities of daily living—from a home health aide or family member may be ill-equipped to make decisions about how to withstand disaster without first understanding how they will continue to receive the help that they require. Even the task of caring for pets—which for many older adults living alone represent their closest family—can be a complicating factor in disaster response efforts.

Enlist organizations and individuals who deliver care in the home and who are trusted sources of information for older adults as partners in planning efforts. This backbone industry of in-home care—which has endured so much strain as a result of the COVID-19 pandemic—must be elevated in the task of ensuring that older adults are better equipped to prepare for and withstand climate change. Often, they already serve as lifelines, ensuring that the health and well-being of older adults is tended to during more acute climate-enhanced conditions.

Acknowledge the Medical and Health Requirements of Older Adults during Disaster Response and Recovery

Plans to protect older adults during disasters must intentionally account for essential medical and health resources—such as regular dialysis treatments or access to prescription drugs—that older adults rely upon. In Montana, for example, the state encourages people with medical and functional needs to complete an Emergency Medical Information Kit—which includes questions about medical therapies and equipment, prescriptions, and other critical information—and post it in a plastic bag on a magnetic hook on their refrigerator to aid emergency response personnel.[4]

Resilience for older adults—as well as others who require ongoing medical treatment—can be achieved only when there is sufficient acknowledgment of and planning for the many component parts that make needed care possible. In addition to ensuring the availability of medical care, improved resilience planning would ensure legal authority to administer care and benefits across jurisdictional lines; ready access to medical records; safe, hygienic, and private facilities; portability of Medicaid eligibility; and adequate translation services and cultural competencies among medical staff. Without such assurances, older adults are challenged to make informed decisions about how to respond to disasters, and the medical risks to older adults as a result of the disaster are compounded.

Established practices that prioritize critical facilities—such as hospitals, shelters, and nursing homes—when restoring power after a blackout are helpful but again fail to account for the needs of older adults who live independently and require access to reliable power for in-home medical support devices. Clear-eyed understanding of the medical needs of all older adults can and should more broadly inform efforts to ensure a reliable power supply during and after disasters, including increased redundancy in the form of in-home generators, solar battery storage, or other common-area solutions.

Build the Capacity of Community-Based Organizations with Training and Resources

Those closest to older adults are the best equipped to recognize their needs, tailor solutions that work best, and leverage existing readily available resources (such as friends, neighbors, nearby community amenities) to address challenges. CBOs can create and formalize partnership agreements to share space, resources (transportation, delivery networks, home-based care providers), and information to quickly deploy essential services in times of disaster. The Community Lighthouses in New Orleans are an exemplar of this, with agreements in place with eighty-five congregations and community institutions across the state that will, when completed, provide backup power during disasters in central locations so that all residents are within a fifteen-minute walk of a Lighthouse facility.[5] Three Lighthouses have been constructed so far: two in existing church facilities and one in an existing health center (see figures 5-1a, 5-1b, and 5-1c).

Seek out and build the capacity of organizations that speak to the unique needs of older adults (such as villages; see chapter 3) as well as those that represent the many dimensions of what makes individuals unique beyond age: language, ability, race, ethnicity, immigrant status, faith. Foster connections among these groups, and engage them, too, in disaster planning—and then resource them adequately to enable them to play their critical role in building community resilience for all ages.

Build Accountability Structures and Feedback Loops to Continually Improve

Plans are only as good as their implementation. Well-intentioned, community-driven, and thoughtful efforts can sit on the shelf as crises unfold—which not only fails to capitalize on the wisdom and contributions of those who helped create the plans but also risks fostering cynicism and disengagement over time. The nature of climate change is that new risks and vulnerabilities are unfolding before our very eyes. It is only by holding people accountable for implementing and testing new approaches—such as rolling out new communication modes, or deploying more dynamic transportation solutions, or working collaboratively across silos—that we ensure that the necessary feedback loop is in place to teach us what worked and what didn't.

Certainly, the field of planning has reckoned in recent years with the consequences of decades of racist land use policy, which left some more vulnerable than others to disasters and economic distress. So too have federal agencies been taken to task for failures to sufficiently ensure equitable access to disaster assistance and protections. This accountability is necessary and should be encouraged, for it is only in learning from past failures that communities can deliver safer and more resilient places for all.

There Is a Role for Each of Us

Effecting the kind of change that is needed to put these lessons learned into practice will require people throughout the public, private, philanthropic, and nonprofit sectors, and across industries to commit to examining climate change through the lens of older adults. It is not an impossible task, and—as this book has argued—it does not benefit only older adults. It helps their families and caregivers, gives voice to those who are traditionally marginalized or overlooked, and leads to safer communities for all.

Part of the reason there is a role for every person in creating more resilient communities is that the cost of inaction is simply too high. Anything less than a surround-sound call for action to better protect older adults in the face of climate change risks confusion, inertia, and inaction. There is no longer the time or opportunity to debate about how or if climate change is affecting our nation's oldest residents. The evidence is clearly visible for anyone who chooses to see it. And for every elected official or national organization or federal agency that equivocates on the importance of the issue, another minute is wasted that could be spent creating safer communities for all. It is only through widespread, accelerated, and informed calls for action that those who seek to demur and deflect will instead be compelled to change.

The American Society on Aging (ASA) seems to have unlocked a pathway to make its membership of aging advocates better understand the urgency of connecting their work to climate change by focusing on education and engagement. ASA's president and chief executive officer, Peter Kaldes, says, "When you connect the dots for people, they understand why we are talking about climate."[6]

Longtime environmental advocate Bill McKibben shares that view and believes that older adults play a particularly important role in calling for change:

> Older adults that are now coming to climate action are doing it less because of the impact of climate change on themselves and more because they're afraid they're leaving a poisoned legacy behind to their grandkids. Older people are uniquely able to recognize that because the world has changed so much in our sixty, seventy years. If you're twenty, you don't see the change so much.[7]

Through his organization, Third Act, McKibben is committed to engaging people sixty and older in advocating for climate mitigation and in bringing awareness of the impacts of climate change to policymakers, business leaders, and the general public. He is not alone. Other groups taking similar or even more strident steps—by actively putting themselves on the front lines of intergenerational protests calling for climate action—include 1000 Grandmothers for Future Generations, Elders Climate Action, Climate Action Now, and Gray is Green. In the words of one advocate, "We can afford to risk our lives for this. Younger generations shouldn't have to."[8]

AFTERWORD

—

As I write the final words in mid-February 2023, it's hard to believe that one year ago, this book was barely a glimmer of an idea. At the time, I had begun to see the mounting pile of evidence of how and why the climate crisis was affecting older adults, largely in the form of repeat news stories with the all-too-common data point about the toll that disasters—nearly any disaster—have on people over sixty-five. It was and is a sad realization to note that the proportional share of older adults who died in Hurricane Katrina in 2005 (two-thirds) is nearly the same as those who died in the winter storms in 2022 in Buffalo, showing in stark relief that we have not yet made older adults' safety a priority. I know that I felt increasingly compelled to show others what I was seeing and point out for them this pattern of more older adults dying, as a call to action. I recall saying once to a colleague who was working on climate resilience, "Once you see it [the pattern], you can't unsee it."

But over the course of writing this book, it has become clear to me—and now I hope to you—that confronting the reality of how climate change affects older adults is equally urgent for all the days in between disasters. Increasingly, climate change is routinely leaving its mark in the form of job disruptions and property damage that lead to financial instability; extreme temperatures and more pollutants that exacerbate health challenges; and strained energy, transportation, and healthcare systems that affect everyone's quality of life—but can be the difference between life and death for some older adults. For all of these reasons and more, I firmly believe that we need to address climate change and its effects with clarity and conviction and re-center our adaptation efforts with older adults in mind. That means augmenting our focus on individual preparedness by creating more community-scale resilience that helps people of all ages and abilities to survive, or better yet, thrive.

I have had the good fortune to learn so much from so many in the course of writing this book, but it was my serendipitous final interview with Asia Ognibene, project organizer for Together New Orleans, that gives me the most hope. She inspired me with her story of how she is helping her community to grow into a more resilient future by learning from the past. Project leaders are listening to their residents, working with diverse partners, and together forging an ambitious but achievable plan to build connections and reduce risk for older residents. It felt like a very full-circle moment to meet someone and hear about an effort that so beautifully encapsulates the ethos that underpins this book. Asia and Together New Orleans show that resilience can best be achieved when solutions are grounded in respect for older adults, in care for community, and in a commitment to honestly assess risks—all of which ultimately harness people to drive action. She sees the pattern, and she is working to change it.

Which brings me back to where I began. Over the twenty-five-plus years of my career, I have witnessed that better environmental, economic, and equity outcomes can flow to people when we are more intentional in our planning. I've seen that the greatest accelerators of that shift are collaboration across sectors, a bias toward innovation and adaptation, and a shared commitment to a common goal of creating better communities. That has been my life's work, but it continues to evolve. I now know that the smartest type of growth to create the most livable communities for all must ensure that they are *safe, secure, and affordable for people of all ages and all abilities in the face of a changing climate.* Failure to do so only perpetuates inequitable outcomes for those who are most often overlooked. The task is ever more urgent given how quickly our demographics are shifting: with every passing year, more of our population will be composed of older adults. We owe it to this complex, diverse, and hard-to-define group of older adults to plan for a future that supports their ability to age well. We owe it to the older adults we love for whom we seek more comfort and safety in the face of a changing climate. And finally, we also owe it to ourselves as individuals to create communities that will ensure we benefit from the privilege of aging—and maybe even thrive as we do so.

Let's get to work.

ABOUT THE AUTHOR

—

Danielle Arigoni is a policy and program expert in the fields of livable communities, affordable housing, and climate resilience. With degrees in urban planning from the University of Oregon and Cornell University, she has worked for more than twenty-five years in the federal government and nonprofit sectors in pursuit of more equitable, sustainable, and resilient places. She

Shelly Han Photography

began her career as a Peace Corps volunteer in Kenya and has since led influential and innovative teams at the US Agency for International Development, the US Environmental Protection Agency, the US Department of Housing and Urban Development, and AARP. She is currently serving as managing director of policy and solutions at National Housing Trust. She is a member of the boards of Smart Growth America and the League of American Bicyclists. Danielle presently lives in the Washington, DC, area but maintains that she is and always will be a Californian.

Learn more and get in touch at www.resilienceforanagingnation .com.

NOTES

—

Introduction: Why It's Essential to Approach Resilience through a Lens of Aging

1. US Environmental Protection Agency, "Climate Change and Social Vulnerability in the United States: A Focus on Six Impacts," EPA 430-R-21-003, September 2021, 6, http://www.epa.gov/cira/social -vulnerability-report.
2. US Department of Health and Human Services, Administration for Community Living (ACL), "2021 Profile of Older Americans," November 2022, 4, https://acl.gov/sites/default/files/Profile%20of% 20OA/2021%20Profile%20of%20OA/2021ProfileOlderAmericans _508.pdf.
3. AAA, "Senior Driver Safety and Mobility," accessed December 30, 2022, https://exchange.aaa.com/safety/senior-driver-safety-mobility/.
4. AARP and National Building Museum, "Making Room: Housing for a Changing America," 2019, 8–9, https://www.aarp.org/livable-com munities/housing/info-2018/making-room-housing-for-a-changing -america.html.
5. ACL, "2021 Profile of Older Americans," 6.
6. Jennifer Molinsky, "Ten Insights about Older Households from the 2020 State of the Nation's Housing Report," Joint Center for Housing Studies of Harvard University, blog post, December 17, 2020, https:// www.jchs.harvard.edu/blog/ten-insights-about-older-households -2020-state-nations-housing-report.
7. The number of older adult households experiencing severe housing problems has steadily climbed over the past decade. During 2019, 2.24 million older adult renters had worst-case needs, an increase of 607,000 since 2017, even as 73,000 more of these households reported receiving rental assistance in 2019. The increase is largely attributable to the growing population of older adult very low-income (VLI) renter households. US Department of Housing and Urban Development, Office of Policy Development and Research, "Worst Case Housing Needs: 2021 Report to Congress," July 2021, https://

www.huduser.gov/portal/sites/default/files/pdf/Worst-Case-Housing
-Needs-2021.pdf.

8. Center for Disaster Philanthropy (CDP), "Older Individuals,"
   accessed August 30, 2022, https://disasterphilanthropy.org/resources
   /older-individuals/.

9. CDP, "Older Individuals."

10. Roz Brown, "TX Power Reform Triggered by Winter Storm Uri
    Needs Public Input," Public News Service, January 19, 2022, https://
    www.publicnewsservice.org/2022-01-19/senior/tx-power-reform
    -triggered-by-winter-storm-uri-needs-public-input/a77418-1%7C5
    -1-a1,5-1-a2.

11. Meghan Stromberg, "Planning for the Needs of an Aging Population,"
    Planning, Winter 2021, https://www.planning.org/planning/2021
    /winter/planning-for-the-needs-of-an-aging-population/.

12. Judith Rodin's book *The Resilience Dividend: Being Strong in a World
    Where Things Go Wrong* (New York: PublicAffairs, 2014) is one of the
    most well-respected books on the topic of community resilience.

13. US Environmental Protection Agency, "Climate Adaptation and
    EPA's Role," accessed January 22, 2023, https://www.epa.gov/climate
    -adaptation/climate-adaptation-and-epas-role.

Chapter 1: Who Are Older Adults?

1. Erica Evans, "When Disaster Strikes, the Elderly Die: What Can Be
   Done to Help?," *Deseret News*, December 14, 2017, https://www
   .deseret.com/2017/12/14/20637155/when-disaster-strikes-the
   -elderly-die-what-can-be-done-to-help.

2. Michael Dimock, "Defining Generations: Where Millennials End
   and Generation Z Begins," Pew Research Center, January 17, 2019,
   https://www.pewresearch.org/fact-tank/2019/01/17/where-millennials
   -end-and-generation-z-begins/.

3. US Department of Commerce, US Census Bureau, "Older People
   Projected to Outnumber Children for First Time in U.S. History,"
   press release no. CB18-41, March 13, 2018, https://www.census.gov
   /newsroom/press-releases/2018/cb18-41-population-projections.html.

4. US Department of Health and Human Services, Administration
   for Community Living (ACL), "2021 Profile of Older Americans,"
   November 2022, 4, https://acl.gov/sites/default/files/Profile%20
   of%20OA/2021%20Profile%20of%20OA/2021ProfileOlderAmeri
   cans_508.pdf.

5. US Department of Commerce, US Census Bureau, "Older People

Projected to Outnumber Children."

6. ACL, "2021 Profile of Older Americans," 5.

7. ACL, "2021 Profile of Older Americans," 5.

8. Jason Horowitz, "Pope Francis, Slowed by Aging, Finds Lessons in Frailty," *New York Times*, July 28, 2022, https://www.nytimes.com /2022/07/28/world/americas/pope-francis-canada-elderly.html?smid =url-share.

9. ACL, "2021 Profile of Older Americans," 5.

10. Yuki Noguchi, "American Life Expectancy Is Now at Its Lowest in Nearly Two Decades," NPR, December 22, 2022, https://www.npr .org/sections/health-shots/2022/12/22/1144864971/american-life -expectancy-is-now-at-its-lowest-in-nearly-two-decades.

11. Lauren D. Medina, Shannon Sabo, and Jonathan Vespa, "Living Longer: Historical and Projected Life Expectancy in the United States, 1960 to 2060," US Department of Commerce, US Census Bureau, *Current Population Reports*, P25-1145 (February 2020), 3–5, https:// www.census.gov/content/dam/Census/library/publications/2020 /demo/p25-1145.pdf.

12. Medina, Sabo, and Vespa, "Living Longer," 6.

13. ACL, "2021 Profile of Older Americans," 5.

14. ACL, "2021 Profile of Older Americans," 5.

15. Mara Siegler, "NYC Marathon's Oldest Runner Was Adventurous Mogul Alan Patricof, 88," Page Six, November 7, 2022, https://page six.com/2022/11/07/venture-capitalist-alan-patricof-88-finishes-nyc -marathon/.

16. US Department of Labor, Bureau of Labor Statistics, "Number of People 75 and Older in the Labor Force Is Expected to Grow 96.5 Percent by 2030," *TED: The Economics Daily*, November 4, 2021, https://www.bls.gov/opub/ted/2021/number-of-people-75-and-older -in-the-labor-force-is-expected-to-grow-96-5-percent-by-2030.htm.

17. SeniorLiving.org, "2022 Workplace Age Discrimination Statistics," accessed December 30, 2022, https://www.seniorliving.org/research /age-discrimination-statistics-facts/.

18. ACL, "2021 Profile of Older Americans," 12.

19. Brittany King, "Women More Likely than Men to Have No Retire-ment Savings," US Department of Commerce, US Census Bureau, January 13, 2022, https://www.census.gov/library/stories/2022/01 /women-more-likely-than-men-to-have-no-retirement-savings.html.

20. ACL, "2021 Profile of Older Americans," 13.

21. Karen Bennett, "Survey: Majority of US Households Uneasy with Level of Emergency Savings," Bankrate, June 23, 2022, https://www

.bankrate.com/banking/savings/financial-security-emergency-savings
-june-2022/.

22. Alain Sherter, "Less than Half of Americans Can Cover a Surprise
$1,000 Expense, Survey Finds," CBS News, January 19, 2022,
https://www.cbsnews.com/news/bankrate-less-than-half-americans
-can-cover-surprise-1000-expense/.

23. ACL, "2021 Profile of Older Americans," 7.

24. ACL, "2021 Profile of Older Americans," 6.

25. US Department of Commerce, US Census Bureau, "First-Ever Census Bureau Report Highlights Growing Childless Older Adult Population," press release no. CB21-TPS.99, August 31, 2021, https://www
.census.gov/newsroom/press-releases/2021/childless-older-adult
-population.html.

26. ACL, "2021 Profile of Older Americans," 14.

27. Joanne Binette, "Where We Live, Where We Age: Trends in Home
and Community Preferences," AARP Research, November 2021,
https://www.aarp.org/research/topics/community/info-2021/2021
-home-community-preferences.html.

28. ACL, "2021 Profile of Older Americans," 14.

29. Jennifer Molinsky, "Ten Insights about Older Households from the
2020 State of the Nation's Housing Report," Joint Center for Housing
Studies of Harvard University, blog post, December 17, 2020, https://
www.jchs.harvard.edu/blog/ten-insights-about-older-households
-2020-state-nations-housing-report.

30. Joint Center for Housing Studies of Harvard University, "America's
Rental Housing 2022," 22, https://www.jchs.harvard.edu/sites
/default/files/reports/files/Harvard_JCHS_Americas_Rental_Housing
_2022.pdf.

31. *Affordability and Accessibility: Addressing the Housing Needs of America's
Seniors: Hearing before the US Senate Committee on Banking, Housing,
and Urban Affairs*, 117th Cong. (March 31, 2022) (statement of
Shannon Guzman, MCP, senior strategic policy advisor, AARP Public
Policy Institute), 9, https://www.aarp.org/content/dam/aarp/politics
/advocacy/2022/03/sen-banking-hearing-testimony-3-31-22.pdf.

32. *Affordability and Accessibility: Hearing before the US Senate*, statement
of Shannon Guzman, 9.

33. US Department of Housing and Urban Development, Office of
Community Planning and Development, "The 2017 Annual Homeless Assessment Report (AHAR) to Congress, Part 2: Estimates of
Homelessness in the United States," October 2018, 2–8, https://www
.huduser.gov/portal/sites/default/files/pdf/2017-AHAR-Part-2.pdf.

34. *Affordability and Accessibility: Hearing before the US Senate*, statement of Shannon Guzman, 9.

35. Consumer Financial Protection Bureau, "Data Spotlight: Profiles of Older Adults Living in Mobile Homes," May 10, 2022, https://www.consumerfinance.gov/consumer-tools/educator-tools/resources-for-older-adults/data-spotlight-profiles-of-older-adults-living-in-mobile-homes/.

36. Consumer Financial Protection Bureau, "Older Adults Living in Mobile Homes."

37. ACL, "2021 Profile of Older Americans," 19.

38. *Affordability and Accessibility: Hearing before the US Senate*, statement of Shannon Guzman, 2.

39. *Affordability and Accessibility: Hearing before the US Senate*, statement of Shannon Guzman, 7.

40. Smart Growth America, "Dangerous by Design 2022," accessed December 30, 2022, https://smartgrowthamerica.org/dangerous-by-design/. Furthermore, the book *Right of Way: Race, Class, and the Silent Epidemic of Pedestrian Deaths in America* by Angie Schmitt (Washington, DC: Island Press, 2020) provides a useful in-depth analysis of the impacts of policies, enforcement, and design of cars and the built environment on pedestrians that have led to disproportionate deaths among low-income people and older adults.

41. US Department of Health and Human Services, Centers for Disease Control and Prevention, Transportation Safety, "Bicycle Safety," accessed December 30, 2022, https://www.cdc.gov/transportationsafety/bicycle/index.html.

42. John Cromartie, "Rural Aging Occurs in Different Places for Very Different Reasons," US Department of Agriculture, blog post, July 30, 2021, https://www.usda.gov/media/blog/2018/12/20/rural-aging-occurs-different-places-very-different-reasons.

43. Cromartie, "Rural Aging."

44. ACL, "2021 Profile of Older Americans," 8.

45. ACL, "2021 Profile of Older Americans," 8.

46. ACL, "2021 Profile of Older Americans," 8.

47. ACL, "2021 Profile of Older Americans," 17.

48. ACL, "2021 Profile of Older Americans," 17.

49. ACL, "2021 Profile of Older Americans," 17.

50. Mayo Clinic, "High Blood Pressure Dangers: Hypertension's Effects on Your Body," https://www.mayoclinic.org/diseases-conditions/high-blood-pressure/in-depth/high-blood-pressure/art-20045868.

51. Alzheimer's Association, "2022 Alzheimer's Disease Facts and

Figures," *Alzheimer's & Dementia* 18, no. 4 (April 2022): 700–789, https://doi.org/10.1002/alz.12638.

52. ACL, "2021 Profile of Older Americans," 18–19.

53. US Department of Health and Human Services, Administration for Community Living (ACL), "2020 Profile of Older Americans," May 2021, 20, https://acl.gov/sites/default/files/Profile%20of%20OA /2020ProfileOlderAmericans_RevisedFinal.pdf.

54. Cheryl L. Lampkin, "Healthy Living: How Older Adults Are Managing Their Emotional and Mental Well-Being," AARP Research, May 2022, https://doi.org/10.26419/res.00533.001.

55. Lampkin, "Healthy Living."

56. Pew Research Center, "Internet/Broadband Fact Sheet," April 7, 2021, https://www.pewresearch.org/internet/fact-sheet/internet-broadband/.

57. Pew Research Center, "Internet/Broadband Fact Sheet."

Chapter 2: Climate-Enhanced Disasters Look (and Feel) Different Based on Age and Other Vulnerabilities

1. Eliza Fawcett et al., "Vulnerable and Trapped: A Look at Those Lost in Hurricane Ian," *New York Times*, October 21, 2022, https://www .nytimes.com/2022/10/21/us/hurricane-ian-victims.html.

2. Fawcett et al., "Vulnerable and Trapped."

3. Reis Thebault, "California's Winter Storms Have Been Deadlier than Any Wildfire since 2018," *Washington Post*, January 14, 2023, https:// www.washingtonpost.com/nation/2023/01/14/california-winter-rain -storms-death-toll/.

4. In an email to the author on January 13, 2023, the Erie County Public Information Office shared the following: "From 12/23/2022– 1/4/2023, the Erie County Medical Examiner's Office confirmed 43 storm-related deaths. Countywide, 7 were under age 50; 9 were between ages 50–59; 14 were between ages 60–69; 8 were ages 70–79, and 5 were over age 80."

5. JoNel Aleccia, "Confusion in the Storm: Alzheimer's Patient Refused to Evacuate," NBC News, October 31, 2012, https://www.nbcnews .com/health/health-news/confusion-storm-alzheimers-patient-refused -evacuate-flna1c6781253.

6. US Global Change Research Program (USGCRP), "Summary Findings," in *Impacts, Risks, and Adaptation in the United States: Fourth National Climate Assessment, Volume II*, ed. D. R. Reidmiller et al. (Washington, DC: USGCRP, 2018), 25, https://nca2018.global change.gov/downloads/NCA4_Ch01_Summary-Findings.pdf.

7. US Global Change Research Program (USGCRP), "Human Health," chap. 14 in *Impacts, Risks, and Adaptation in the United States: Fourth National Climate Assessment, Volume II*, ed. D. R. Reidmiller et al. (Washington, DC: USGCRP, 2018), 544, https://nca2018.global change.gov/downloads/NCA4_Ch14_Human-Health_Full.pdf.

8. US Global Change Research Program (USGCRP), "Built Environment, Urban Systems, and Cities," chap. 11 in *Impacts, Risks, and Adaptation in the United States: Fourth National Climate Assessment, Volume II*, ed. D. R. Reidmiller et al. (Washington, DC: USGCRP, 2018), 456, https://nca2018.globalchange.gov/downloads/NCA4 _Ch11_Built-Environment_Full.pdf.

9. USGCRP, "Built Environment, Urban Systems, and Cities," 447.

10. Intergovernmental Panel on Climate Change, "Summary for Policymakers," in *Climate Change 2022: Mitigation of Climate Change. Contribution of Working Group III to the Sixth Assessment Report of the Intergovernmental Panel on Climate Change*, ed. P. R. Shukla et al. (Cambridge: Cambridge University Press, 2022), https://doi.org /10.1017/9781009157926.001.

11. NOAA reported that the 1980–2022 annual average was 7.9 events (CPI adjusted), whereas the annual average for the most recent five years (2018–2022) was 17.8 events (CPI adjusted). National Oceanic and Atmospheric Administration, National Centers for Environmental Information (NCEI), "Billion-Dollar Weather and Climate Disasters," accessed January 22, 2023, https://www.ncei.noaa.gov /access/billions/.

12. NCEI, "Billion-Dollar Weather and Climate Disasters."

13. US Global Change Research Program (USGCRP), "Agriculture and Rural Communities," chap. 10 in *Impacts, Risks, and Adaptation in the United States: Fourth National Climate Assessment, Volume II*, ed. D. R. Reidmiller et al. (Washington, DC: USGCRP, 2018), 392–411, https://nca2018.globalchange.gov/chapter/10/.

14. US Environmental Protection Agency (EPA), "Climate Change and Social Vulnerability in the United States: A Focus on Six Impacts," EPA 430-R-21-003, September 2021, 6, http://www.epa.gov/cira /social-vulnerability-report, https://www.epa.gov/system/files/docu ments/2021-09/climate-vulnerability_september-2021_508.pdf. On page 8 of the report, EPA acknowledges explicitly that its analysis did not estimate asthma impacts for people sixty-five and older.

15. EPA, "Climate Change and Social Vulnerability." EPA uses the terms "Hispanic," "Latino," and "minority" in its report; it explains its use of the term "minority" on pages 16 and 17.

16. EPA, "Climate Change and Social Vulnerability," 6.

17. EPA, "Climate Change and Social Vulnerability," 7.

18. EPA, "Climate Change and Social Vulnerability," 82–88.

19. Shalanda Young, Brenda Mallory, and Gina McCarthy, "The Path to Achieving Justice40," White House Office of Management and Budget Briefing Room, blog post, July 20, 2021, https://www.whitehouse .gov/omb/briefing-room/2021/07/20/the-path-to-achieving-justice40/.

20. David Dosa et al., "To Evacuate or Shelter in Place: Implications of Universal Hurricane Evacuation Policies on Nursing Home Residents," *JAMDA* Online Original Study, *JAMDA* 13, no. 2 (February 1, 2012): P190.E1–190.E7, https://doi.org/10.1016/j.jamda.2011.07 .011.

21. Healthcare Ready, "2022 National Preparedness Poll: July 18, 2022 Analysis," 10–13, https://healthcareready.org/wp-content/uploads /2022/07/July-Analysis_HcR-2022-Domestic-Preparedness-Poll -Summary_Final-7-18.pdf.

22. AARP Research, "Vital Voices: Issues That Impact Florida Adults Age 45 and Older," 2020, 19–28, https://www.aarp.org/content/dam /aarp/research/surveys_statistics/life-leisure/2020/vital-voices-chart book-florida.doi.10.26419-2Fres.00351.005.pdf.

23. Sue Anne Bell, "Hurricane Ian: Older Adults Have Many Reasons for Not Evacuating—Here's Why It's Important to Check on Aging Neighbors," The Conversation, September 27, 2022, https://thecon versation.com/hurricane-ian-older-adults-have-many-reasons-for-not -evacuating-heres-why-its-important-to-check-on-aging-neighbors -191425.

24. Luis Andres Henao, "Climate Migration: How One Alaska Village Resists Despite Threats," Associated Press, *Anchorage Daily News*, October 30, 2022, https://www.adn.com/alaska-news/rural-/2022 /10/30/climate-migration-how-one-alaska-village-resists-despite -threats/.

25. US Department of Commerce, US Census Bureau, "QuickFacts: Mora County, New Mexico," accessed September 4, 2022, https:// www.census.gov/quickfacts/fact/table/moracountynewmexico/PST 045221.

26. Reuters, "Thousands Refuse to Evacuate Largest U.S. Wildfire in New Mexico," NBC News, May 6, 2022, https://www.nbcnews.com/news /us-news/thousands-refuse-evacuate-largest-us-wildfire-new-mexico -rcna27612.

27. Climate Central, "Coming Storms: Climate Change and the Rising Threat to America's Coastal Seniors; Part 1: Senior Facilities at Risk,"

March 3, 2021, 3, https://assets.ctfassets.net/cxgxgstp8r5d/2uTS
DDYYYsskJ3HTAoggSo/ea1cde8e4320b4dfe695bb43a273b080
/Seniors_and_SLR_-_Full.pdf.

28. Climate Central, "Coming Storms," 5.

29. David Dosa et al., "Effects of Hurricane Katrina on Nursing Facility
Resident Mortality, Hospitalization, and Functional Decline," *Disaster
Medicine and Public Health Preparedness* 4, no. S1 (September 2010):
S28–S32, https://doi.org/10.1001/dmp.2010.11.

30. AARP and US Department of Homeland Security, Federal Emergency Management Agency, "Disaster Resilience Tool Kit: A Guide
for How Local Leaders Can Reduce Risks and Better Protect Older
Adults," 2022, 2, https://www.aarp.org/content/dam/aarp/livable
-communities/tool-kits-resources/2022/AARP%20Disaster%20
Resilience%20Tool%20Kit-singles-060122-.pdf.

31. Patrick Connole, "Long Term Care Providers Tackle Disaster Preparedness in a Post-Katrina World," *Provider Magazine*, February 1,
2011, https://www.providermagazine.com/Issues/2011/Pages/0211
/Disaster-Preparedness-In-A-Post-Katrina-World.aspx.

32. US Department of Health and Human Services, Centers for Medicare and Medicaid Services, "Final Rule: Medicare and Medicaid
Programs; Emergency Preparedness Requirements for Medicare and
Medicaid Participating Providers and Suppliers," *Federal Register*, 81
FR 63859 (September 16, 2016), https://www.federalregister.gov
/documents/2016/09/16/2016-21404/medicare-and-medicaid
-programs-emergency-preparedness-requirements-for-medicare-and
-medicaid.

33. US Department of Health and Human Services, Centers for Medicare
and Medicaid Services, "CMS Emergency Preparedness Rule: What's
New Based on the Medicare and Medicaid Programs; Regulatory
Provisions to Promote Program Efficiency, Transparency, and Burden
Reduction Final Rule," accessed January 22, 2023, https://www.cms
.gov/Medicare/Provider-Enrollment-and-Certification/SurveyCert
EmergPrep/Downloads/CMS-Understanding-the-EP-Final-Rule-Up
date-BRIII-2019.pdf.

34. Suzy Khimm and Laura Strickler, "U.S. Scrutinizes Nursing Home
Evacuation Rules after Hurricane Ida Deaths," NBC News, September 30, 2021, https://www.nbcnews.com/news/us-news/u-s-scrutin
izes-nursing-home-evacuation-rules-after-hurricane-ida-n1280492.

35. Tom Scherberger, "Are Florida Long-Term Care Facilities Prepared for
Natural Disasters?," AARP, May 1, 2022, https://states.aarp.org
/florida/aarp-florida-disaster-preparedness-long-term-care-facility.

36. Mark Hollis, "AARP Texas Letter to Legislators Regarding Joint Hearing on Electrical Blackouts," AARP, February 19, 2021, https://states.aarp.org/texas/aarp-texas-letter-to-legislators-regarding-joint-hearing-on-electrical-blackouts.

37. US Department of Homeland Security, Federal Emergency Management Agency, "Older Adults," accessed January 1, 2023, https://www.ready.gov/seniors.

38. American Red Cross, "Emergency Preparedness for Older Adults," accessed January 1, 2023, https://www.redcross.org/get-help/how-to-prepare-for-emergencies/older-adults.html.

39. Brian Barth, "Backup Generators Can Give Your House Some Juice," AARP, October 7, 2021, https://www.aarp.org/home-family/your-home/info-2021/backup-generators.html.

40. Stacey Colino, "Caring for Loved Ones in Cases of Emergency," AARP, May 20, 2019, https://www.aarp.org/caregiving/basics/info-2019/preparing-for-emergency.html.

41. US Department of Health and Human Services, National Institutes of Health, National Institute on Aging, "Disaster Preparedness and Recovery for Older Adults," accessed April 24, 2023, https://www.nia.nih.gov/health/disaster-preparedness-and-recovery-older-adults.

42. Healthcare Ready, "2022 National Preparedness Poll," 59.

43. Keren Landman, "The Surprising Link between Covid-19 Deaths and . . . Internet Access," Vox, March 16, 2022, https://www.vox.com/22979086/covid-pandemic-deaths-mortality-broadband-internet-access.

44. Tornadoes remain the subject of some dispute as to the ways in which they are accelerated, made more frequent, or made more intense by climate change, particularly as a result of warmer temperatures. There is little debate that they pose a threat to well-being, health, and property in the areas they affect, although it is not clear at this time that the impacts disproportionately affect older adults in ways that make tornadoes unique—beyond the risks depicted elsewhere related to challenges associated with preparedness, evacuation, communication, and rebuilding.

45. US Department of Agriculture (USDA), Forest Service, "Rx for Hot Cities: Urban Greening and Cooling to Reduce Heat-Related Mortality in Los Angeles and Beyond," webinar, July 8, 2020, https://www.fs.usda.gov/research/products/multimedia/webinars/rx-hot-cities-urban-greening-and-cooling-reduce-heat-related-mortality.

46. Climate Central, "Seniors at Risk: Heat and Climate Change," research brief, June 24, 2020, 2, https://ccimgs-2020.s3.amazonaws

.com/2020HeatAndSeniors/2020HeatAndSeniors_Final0623.pdf.

47. USDA, Forest Service, "Rx for Hot Cities."

48. EPA, "Climate Change and Social Vulnerability," 34.

49. Stephanie Dutchen, "The Effects of Heat on Older Adults," *Harvard Medicine: The Magazine of Harvard Medical School*, Autumn 2021, https://hms.harvard.edu/magazine/aging/effects-heat-older-adults.

50. Ardeshir Tabrizian, "Oregon's Heat Wave Death Toll Grows to 116," *The Oregonian*, December 1, 2021, https://www.oregonlive.com/data/2021/07/oregons-heat-wave-death-toll-grows-to-116.html.

51. Dutchen, "Effects of Heat on Older Adults."

52. Copernicus Climate Change Service, "Copernicus: Summer 2022 Europe's Hottest on Record," press release, September 8, 2022, https://climate.copernicus.eu/copernicus-summer-2022-europes-hottest-record.

53. Jason Samenow, "No September on Record in the West Has Seen a Heat Wave Like This," *Washington Post*, September 9, 2022, https://www.washingtonpost.com/climate-environment/2022/09/08/western-heatwave-records-california-climate/.

54. Eric Klinenberg, "Want to Survive Climate Change? You'll Need a Good Community," Wired, October 25, 2016, https://www.wired.com/2016/10/klinenberg-transforming-communities-to-survive-climate-change/.

55. Chelsea Harvey, "Urban Heat Islands Mean Warming Will Be Worse in Cities," *Scientific American*, November 21, 2019, https://www.scientificamerican.com/article/urban-heat-islands-mean-warming-will-be-worse-in-cities/.

56. Linda Searing, "Heart Failure Mortality Surges by 37 Percent in Extremely Cold Weather," *Washington Post*, January 3, 2023, https://www.washingtonpost.com/wellness/2023/01/03/cardiac-deaths-rise-extreme-cold/.

57. Searing, "Heart Failure Mortality."

58. US Department of Homeland Security, Federal Emergency Management Agency, "Fact Sheet: Flooding—Our Nation's Most Frequent and Costly Disaster," March 2010, https://www.fbiic.gov/public/2010/mar/FloodingHistoryandCausesFS.PDF.

59. National Center for Healthy Housing, "Mold in the Home," accessed September 24, 2022, https://nchh.org/information-and-evidence/learn-about-healthy-housing/health-hazards-prevention-and-solutions/mold/.

60. US Department of Health and Human Services, Centers for Disease Control and Prevention, "Mold after a Disaster," accessed September

24, 2022, https://www.cdc.gov/disasters/mold/index.html.

61. EPA, "Climate Change and Social Vulnerability," 53–77.

62. Janet L. Gamble et al., "Populations of Concern," chap. 9 in *The Impacts of Climate Change on Human Health in the United States: A Scientific Assessment* (Washington, DC: US Global Change Research Program, 2016), 257, https://health2016.globalchange.gov/low /ClimateHealth2016_09_Populations_small.pdf.

63. Simon Romero, "Booming Utah's Weak Link: Surging Air Pollution," *New York Times*, September 7, 2021, https://www.nytimes.com/2021 /09/07/us/great-salt-lake-utah-air-quality.html.

64. Patricia To, Ejemai Eboreime, and Vincent I. O. Agyapong, "The Impact of Wildfires on Mental Health: A Scoping Review," *Behavioral Sciences* 11, no. 9 (September 2021): 126, http://doi.org/10.3390 /bs11090126.

65. Allison Crimmins et al., "Executive Summary," in *The Impacts of Climate Change on Human Health in the United States: A Scientific Assessment* (Washington, DC: US Global Change Research Program, 2016), 6–7, https://health2016.globalchange.gov/high/Climate Health2016_ExecSummary_Standalone.pdf.

66. Gamble et al., "Populations of Concern," 249.

67. Gamble et al., "Populations of Concern," 249.

68. Laura Bailey, "Living through Katrina Associated with Higher Death Rate among Breast Cancer Patients," University of Michigan, Michigan News, October 30, 2019, https://news.umich.edu/living -through-katrina-associated-with-higher-death-rate-among-breast -cancer-patients/.

69. *Inclusive Disaster Management: Improving Preparedness, Response, and Recovery: Hearing before the Special Committee on Aging, United States Senate*, 117th Cong., 1st sess. (November 18, 2021), 6, https://www .aging.senate.gov/imo/media/doc/SCA_11.18.21.pdf.

70. Sue Anne Bell, "Disasters Can Harm Older Adults Long after Storms Have Passed," The Conversation, August 8, 2017, https://theconver sation.com/disasters-can-harm-older-adults-long-after-storms-have -passed-81429.

71. University at Albany, School of Public Health, "Study Shows That Natural Disasters Can Impact the Mental Health of Older Adults Years Later," September 20, 2022, https://www.albany.edu/sph/news /2022-study-shows-natural-disasters-can-impact-mental-health-older -adults-years-later.

72. AARP Research, "Wildfire Recovery: Evaluating the Issues around Rebuilding after a Natural Disaster: A Survey on Wildfire Recovery

among Jackson County, Oregon Residents and Former Residents Age 45+," 2021, 2, https://www.aarp.org/content/dam/aarp/research /surveys_statistics/life-leisure/2022/2021-jackson-county-wildfire -recovery-survey-report.doi.10.26419-2Fres.00511.001.pdf.

73. American Psychiatric Association, "Climate Change and Mental Health Connections," accessed January 22, 2023, https://www.psy chiatry.org/patients-families/climate-change-and-mental-health -connections.

74. AARP Research, "Vital Voices: Issues That Impact Florida Adults Age 45 and Older, August 2022," 3, https://aarp-states.brightspotcdn.com /bd/e3/fbd9d2d04833bbb6678138c60bb1/vital-voices-c2-2022-fl -factsheet-natural-disaster-preparedness.pdf.

75. AARP Research, "Wildfire Recovery: Evaluating the Issues," 2.

76. AARP Research, "Vital Voices, August 2022," 3.

77. Jennifer A. Kingson, "Yellowstone's Historic Flooding Is an Insurance Nightmare," Axios, June 17, 2022, https://www.axios.com/2022/06 /17/montana-yellowstone-insurance-flood-flooding.

78. Christopher Flavelle, "The Cost of Insuring Expensive Waterfront Homes Is About to Skyrocket," *New York Times*, September 24, 2021, https://www.nytimes.com/2021/09/24/climate/federal-flood-insur ance-cost.html.

79. AARP Research, "Wildfire Recovery: Evaluating the Issues," 2.

80. Katherine Skiba and Christina Ianzito, "Beware of Scams after a Hurricane or Other Natural Disaster," AARP, September 29, 2022, https://www.aarp.org/money/scams-fraud/info-2020/tips-to-avoid -fraud-after-disasters.html#:~:text=6.,the%20NCDF's%20web%20 complaint%20form.

81. Gema de las Heras, "Consumer Alert: Avoid Scams in the Aftermath of Merbok, Fiona and Ian," Federal Trade Commission, September 28, 2022, https://consumer.ftc.gov/consumer-alerts/2022/09/avoid -scams-aftermath-merbok-fiona-and-ian?utm_source=govdelivery.

82. Susan B. Garland, "'Do You Really Want to Rebuild at 80?' Rethink-ing Where to Retire," *New York Times*, November 22, 2022, https:// www.nytimes.com/2022/11/18/business/where-to-retire-climate -change.html.

83. Richard Rothstein's book *The Color of Law: A Forgotten History of How Our Government Segregated America* (New York: Liveright, 2017) is perhaps the best exploration into these issues in recent years.

84. Reilly Morse, "Environmental Justice through the Eye of Hurricane Katrina," Joint Center for Political and Economic Studies, Health Policy Institute, 2008, https://inequality.stanford.edu/sites/default

/files/media/_media/pdf/key_issues/Environment_policy.pdf.

85. Abbey Interrante, "These U.S. Cities, Neighborhoods Have Lowest Life Expectancy: How Does [Yours] Stack Up?," *Newsweek*, September 18, 2018, https://www.newsweek.com/these-cities-neighborhoods -lowest-life-expectancy-how-yours-stack-1127278.

86. Sophia Wedeen, "The Threat of Environmental Hazards to the Rental Stock," Joint Center for Housing Studies of Harvard University, blog post, March 9, 2022, https://www.jchs.harvard.edu/blog/threat -environmental-hazards-rental-stock.

87. Public and Affordable Housing Research Corporation (PAHRC) and National Low Income Housing Coalition (NLIHC), "Taking Stock: Natural Hazards and Federally Assisted Housing," 2021, 3, https:// preservationdatabase.org/wp-content/uploads/2021/06/Taking-Stock .pdf.

88. PAHRC and NLIHC, "Taking Stock," 15.

89. Sarah Sax, "Black Families Passed Their Homes from One Generation to the Next. Now They May Be Lost," *Guardian*, October 6, 2021, https://www.theguardian.com/us-news/2021/oct/06/leading-cause -black-land-loss-how-climate-crisis-supercharging-dispossession.

90. Ivis Garcia, "The Lack of Proof of Ownership in Puerto Rico Is Crippling Repairs in the Aftermath of Hurricane Maria," American Bar Association, *Human Rights Magazine* 44, no. 2 (*Housing*), May 21, 2021, https://www.americanbar.org/groups/crsj/publications/human _rights_magazine_home/vol--44--no-2--housing/the-lack-of-proof -of-ownership-in-puerto-rico-is-crippling-repai/.

91. EPA, "Climate Change and Social Vulnerability."

92. EPA, "Climate Change and Social Vulnerability," 10.

Chapter 3: Moving toward Climate Resilience for All Ages

1. World Health Organization, "Global Age-Friendly Cities: A Guide," 2007, 8–10, https://extranet.who.int/agefriendlyworld/wp-content /uploads/2014/06/WHO-Global-Age-friendly-Cities-Guide.pdf.

2. World Health Organization, "About the Global Network for Age-Friendly Cities and Communities," accessed January 28, 2023, https://extranet.who.int/agefriendlyworld/who-network/.

3. World Health Organization, "About Us: What Is an Age Friendly World?," accessed January 28, 2023, https://extranet.who.int/age friendlyworld/about-us/.

4. AARP Livable Communities, "Making Plans, Taking Action," May

2020, https://www.aarp.org/livable-communities/network-age
-friendly-communities/info-2020/making-plans-taking-action.html.

5. The AARP Network of Age-Friendly States and Communities website
provides an array of case studies on success from age-friendly members:
https://www.aarp.org/livable-communities/network-age-friendly-com
munities/.

6. AARP Livable Communities, "'Age-Friendly' Responses to COVID-
19," May 2021, 4, https://www.aarp.org/livable-communities/net
work-age-friendly-communities/info-2020/age-friendly-responses-to
-COVID-19.html.

7. Results of a scan conducted by the author on October 30, 2022, at
AARP Livable Communities Map, https://livablemap.aarp.org/#
/view=map.

8. Purposeful Aging Los Angeles, "Age-Friendly Action Plan for the
Los Angeles Region 2018–2021," August 2018, 38–40, https://
www.purposefulagingla.com/sites/default/files/Age-Friendly%20
Action%20Plan%20for%20the%20Los%20Angeles%20Region%20
2018-2021-V12-compressed.pdf.

9. City and County of San Francisco, Department of Aging and Adult
Services, "An Action Plan for an Age and Disability Friendly San
Francisco 2018–2021," 2019, 50, https://www.sfhsa.org/sites/default
/files/Report_Age%20and%20DisabilityFriendly%20SF_2018-21
.pdf.

10. City of Austin, Texas, "Age-Friendly Austin: Progress Report 2021,"
accessed October 30, 2022, 4, 50–55, https://www.aarp.org/content
/dam/aarp/livable-communities/age-friendly-network/2021-progress
-reports/tx-austin-progress-report-2021.pdf.

11. City of Longwood, Florida, "City of Longwood's AARP Age-Friendly
Action Plan," August 2019, 17, https://www.aarp.org/content/dam
/aarp/livable-communities/age-friendly-network/2019/FL-Longwood
-Action-Plan-2019-Final.pdf.

12. Age-Friendly DC, "Age-Friendly DC Five Year Progress Report to
the World Health Organization," accessed January 20, 2023, 7 and
27, https://extranet.who.int/agefriendlyworld/wp-content/uploads
/2015/01/Washington-DC-Progress-Report.pdf.

13. Dementia Friendly America, "What Is DFA?," accessed January 17,
2023, https://www.dfamerica.org/what-is-dfa.

14. Read more about Tempe's commitments as a dementia-friendly and
age-friendly community at the City of Tempe's Age-Friendly Tempe
website, https://www.tempe.gov/government/education-career-and
-family-services/age-friendly-tempe.

15. Chenghao Wang et al., "Rethinking the Urban Physical Environment for Century-Long Lives: From Age-Friendly to Longevity-Ready Cities," *Nature Aging* 1 (December 10, 2021): 1088–1095, https://doi .org/10.1038/s43587-021-00140-5.

16. M. Villeneuve et al., "Disability Inclusive Disaster Risk Reduction (DIDRR) Framework and Toolkit," University of Sydney, New South Wales, Centre for Disability Research and Policy, 2019, https:// collaborating4inclusion.org/wp-content/uploads/2019/11/DIDRR _Framework_document_FINAL.pdf.

17. RAND Corporation, "Toolkit: Building Resilience in Older Adults," accessed January 20, 2023, https://www.rand.org/pubs/tools/TL282 /introduction.html.

18. Meredith Freed et al., "Deaths among Older Adults Due to COVID-19 Jumped during the Summer of 2022 before Falling Somewhat in September," Kaiser Family Foundation, October 6, 2022, https:// www.kff.org/coronavirus-covid-19/issue-brief/deaths-among-older -adults-due-to-covid-19-jumped-during-the-summer-of-2022-before -falling-somewhat-in-september/.

19. Lourdes R. Guerrero and Steven P. Wallace, "The Impact of COVID-19 on Diverse Older Adults and Health Equity in the United States," *Frontiers in Public Health* 9 (2021), https://doi.org/10.3389/fpubh .2021.661592.

20. Reginald D. Williams II et al., "The Impact of COVID-19 on Older Adults," Commonwealth Fund, September 15, 2021, https://www .commonwealthfund.org/publications/surveys/2021/sep/impact-covid -19-older-adults.

21. Bob Casey, US Senate Special Committee on Aging, "Disaster Relief Medicaid Act," accessed January 23, 2023, https://www.aging.senate .gov/imo/media/doc/DRMA%20One%20Pager%20and%20Section -by-Section.pdf.

22. Alison Hernandez and Jennifer Baker, US Senate Special Committee on Aging, interview with the author, January 12, 2023.

23. US Department Health and Human Services, Administration for Strategic Preparedness and Response, "About the National Advisory Committee on Individuals with Disabilities and Disasters," accessed October 2, 2022, https://aspr.hhs.gov/AboutASPR/Workingwith ASPR/BoardsandCommittees/Pages/NACIDD/About-Us.aspx.

24. National Advisory Committee on Individuals with Disabilities and Disasters (NACIDD), "National Advisory Committee on Individuals with Disabilities and Disasters Public Meeting Summary," April 1, 2022, https://aspr.hhs.gov/AboutASPR/WorkingwithASPR/Boards

andCommittees/Documents/NACIDD/NACIDD-Pblc-Mtg-Sum
mary-1Apr2022.pdf.

25. National Advisory Committee on Seniors and Disasters (NACSD),
"Meeting Summary," April 6, 2022, https://aspr.hhs.gov/AboutASPR
/WorkingwithASPR/BoardsandCommittees/Documents/NACSD
/NACSD-Pblc-Mtg-6Ap22-508.pdf.

26. National Advisory Committee on Seniors and Disasters (NACSD)
and National Advisory Committee on Individuals with Disabilities
and Disasters (NACIDD), "Public Meeting Summary," August 4,
2022, https://aspr.hhs.gov/AboutASPR/WorkingwithASPR/Boards
andCommittees/Documents/NACSD/NACSD-NACIDD-pblc-mtg
-summary-4Aug2022.pdf.

27. NACSD and NACIDD, "Public Meeting Summary."

28. NACSD and NACIDD, "Public Meeting Summary."

29. Peter Kaldes, "Why Aging Policy Must Include Climate Action,"
Generations, Summer 2022, https://generations.asaging.org/why-aging
-policy-must-include-climate-action.

30. American Society on Aging, *Generations*, Summer 2022. https://
generations.asaging.org/summer-2022.

31. Peter Kaldes, president and chief executive officer, American Society
on Aging, interview with the author, January 18, 2023.

32. Peter Kaldes, "Disasters Are Age-Blind: Preparation Shouldn't Be,"
The Hill, October 24, 2022, https://thehill.com/opinion/energy
-environment/3702157-disasters-are-age-blind-preparation-shouldnt
-be/.

33. American Society on Aging, "ASA Policy Priorities," April 24, 2023,
9–10, https://prod.mpxfiles.com/Uploads/Files/live/asa/e73251d1
-5bc8-4911-8d98-2c70ec1076e6.pdf?v=637949884097530000.

34. Natasha Bryant et al., "The Impact of Climate Change: Why Older
Adults Are Vulnerable," LeadingAge LTSS Center @UMass Boston,
February 2022, https://ltsscenter.org/reports/The_Impact_of_Climate
_Change_Why_Older_Adults_are_Vulnerable.pdf.

35. LeadingAge, "Emergency Preparedness Regulation Dashboard,"
accessed January 2, 2023, https://leadingage.org/emergency-prep
-dashboard/.

36. Robin Cooper, "Climate Change and Older Adults: Planning Ahead
to Protect Your Health," National Council on Aging, April 21, 2022,
https://www.ncoa.org/article/climate-change-and-older-adults-plan
ning-ahead-to-protect-your-health.

37. David Hochman et al., "What You Need to Know about Climate
Change," *AARP Bulletin*, June 1, 2021, https://www.aarp.org

/politics-society/history/info-2021/climate-change.html.

38. AARP and US Department of Homeland Security, Federal Emergency Management Agency (FEMA), "Disaster Resilience Tool Kit: A Guide for How Local Leaders Can Reduce Risks and Better Protect Older Adults," July 2022, https://www.aarp.org/content/dam/aarp /livable-communities/tool-kits-resources/2022/AARP%20Disaster% 20Resilience%20Tool%20Kit-singles-060122-.pdf. (Full disclosure: the author of this book led the effort to create the "Disaster Resilience Tool Kit" in partnership with FEMA and AARP colleagues.)

39. AARP California led a series of "Climate Chats" for its members throughout 2021 and 2022. Learn more at https://states.aarp.org /california/climatechats.

40. For more about AARP Texas's efforts, see Tim Morstad, "How to Improve Electricity Reliability for Older Texans," AARP, May 13, 2022, https://states.aarp.org/texas/how-to-improve-electricity -reliability-for-older-texans. For more about AARP Florida's advocacy efforts, see Emily Paulin, "Florida's Efforts to Protect Nursing Home Residents from Hurricane Ian May Have Worked," AARP, October 13, 2022, https://www.aarp.org/caregiving/nursing-homes/info-2022 /nursing-home-hurricane-survival.html.

41. Elissa Chudwin, "AARP to Congress: Keep Older Adults Safe during Natural Disasters," AARP, blog post, July 20, 2022, https://blog.aarp .org/fighting-for-you/older-americans-natural-disasters.

42. Author's analysis based on review of the Leadership Council of Aging Organizations' "About LCAO," "Issue Areas," and "News and Actions" landing pages on its website (https://www.lcao.org/) as of January 22, 2023.

43. Robert J. Gould, Mona Sarfaty, and Edward W. Maibach, "The Health Promise of Climate Solutions: A Report of the Medical Society Consortium on Climate and Health" (Fairfax, VA: George Mason University, May 11, 2022), https://test.ms2ch.org/wp-content /uploads/2022/10/The-Health-Promise-of-Climate-Solutions-5-22-1 .pdf; Health Care Without Harm, "Climate Resilience for Health Care and Communities: Strategies and Case Studies," January 2022, https://noharm-uscanada.org/sites/default/files/documents-files/7024 /Climate-Resilience-for-Health-Care-and-Communities-Stategies -and-Case-Studies.pdf.

44. American Public Health Association, "Center for Climate, Health and Equity," accessed January 2, 2023, https://www.apha.org/topics-and -issues/climate-change/center.

45. Regina A. Shih et al., "Improving Disaster Resilience among Older

Adults: Insights from Public Health Departments and Aging-in-Place Efforts," *RAND Health Quarterly* 8, no. 1 (August 2, 2018): 3, https://www.ncbi.nlm.nih.gov/pmc/articles/PMC6075802/.

46. US Department of Homeland Security, Federal Emergency Management Agency (FEMA) and AARP, "Guide to Expanding Mitigation: Making the Connection to Older Adults," July 2022, https://www.fema.gov/sites/default/files/documents/fema_mitigation-guide_older-adults.pdf.

47. Resilient Nation Partnership Network; US Department of Homeland Security, Federal Emergency Management Agency; and National Oceanic and Atmospheric Administration, "Building Alliances for Equitable Resilience: Advancing Equitable Resilience through Partnerships and Diverse Perspectives," April 2021, https://www.fema.gov/sites/default/files/documents/fema_rnpn_building-alliances-for-equitable-resilience.pdf.

48. US Government Accountability Office, "Disaster Assistance: FEMA Action Needed to Better Support Individuals Who Are Older or Have Disabilities," GAO-19-318, May 14, 2019, https://www.gao.gov/products/gao-19-318.

49. FEMA officials provided the following update in February 2023 related to the status of the GAO recommendations: "FEMA's Office of Disability Integration and Coordination (ODIC) addressed the two outstanding GAO recommendations referenced in this article by comparing the conditions that gave rise to them in 2019, to the changing nature of weather systems in terms of frequency and intensity today. The recommendation to standardize performance expectations across regions was considered, however, deemed unfeasible given the extreme differences in how disasters impact regions and communities in widely varying ways.

"Instead, ODIC incorporated measures of effectiveness that guide actions based on adaptability to uncertainty and equity-focused outcomes that go beyond merely implementing standard operating procedures. These measures entail measuring risk assessment, problem anticipation, efficacy of communication, and adaptation to uncertainty. This alternative approach honors the respective chains of command that govern steady state and disaster response in the regions, while unifying expectations from a macro view provided by ODIC.

"Additionally, ODIC had incorporated [an] Independent Study course (IS-368, Including People with Disabilities) into FEMA's learning management system in 2019. The course was taken by 12,779 users from federal, state, local, tribal, private, military, and

other sectors between 1/1/2019 [and] 4/26/2022. This GAO recommendation is currently under review for closure." Source: email to
author from FEMA News Desk, March 6, 2023.

50. US Department of Homeland Security, Federal Emergency Management Agency (FEMA), "State Mitigation Planning Policy Guide," FP
302-094-2, April 19, 2022, https://www.fema.gov/sites/default/files
/documents/fema_state-mitigation-planning-policy-guide_042022
.pdf.

51. FEMA, "State Mitigation Planning Policy Guide," 4.

52. See specific requirements in section 3.2 of FEMA, "State Mitigation
Planning Policy Guide," 19.

53. FEMA, "State Mitigation Planning Policy Guide," 42.

54. US Department of Homeland Security, Federal Emergency Management Agency, "Local Mitigation Planning Policy Guide," FP 206-21-
0002, April 19, 2022, 31, https://www.fema.gov/sites/default/files
/documents/fema_local-mitigation-planning-policy-guide_042022
.pdf.

55. US Department of Housing and Urban Development (HUD),
"Allocations, Common Application, Waivers, and Alternative
Requirements for Community Development Block Grant Mitigation
Grantees," Docket No. FR-6109-N-02, HUD Exchange, June 20,
2019, 10, https://www.hudexchange.info/news/hud-publishes-cdbg
-mitigation-notice/.

56. HUD, "Allocations, Common Application, Waivers."

57. US Department of Housing and Urban Development, "Request
for Information for HUD's Community Development Block Grant
Disaster Recovery (CDBG-DR) Rules, Waivers, and Alternative
Requirements," Docket No. FR-6336-N-01, *Federal Register* 87, no.
243 (December 20, 2022), https://www.govinfo.gov/content/pkg
/FR-2022-12-20/pdf/2022-27547.pdf. For the author's submitted
comments in response to this call from HUD, see "Comment Submitted by Danielle Arigoni," posted by the Department of Housing
and Urban Development, February 20, 2023, https://www.regulations
.gov/comment/HUD-2022-0083-0023.

58. US Department of Housing and Urban Development (HUD),
"Community Resilience Toolkit," 2020, accessed October 1, 2022,
https://files.hudexchange.info/resources/documents/HUD-Commu
nity-Resilient-Toolkit.pdf.

59. HUD, "Community Resilience Toolkit."

60. Centers for Disease Control and Prevention and Agency for Toxic
Substances and Disease Registry, "At a Glance: CDC/ATSDR Social

Vulnerability Index," https://www.atsdr.cdc.gov/placeandhealth/svi/at
-a-glance_svi.html.

61. US Environmental Protection Agency, EJScreen: EPA's Environmental Justice Screening and Mapping Tool (Version 2.11), accessed
January 2, 2023, https://ejscreen.epa.gov/mapper/.

62. US Environmental Protection Agency, EnviroAtlas Interactive Map,
accessed January 2, 2023, https://www.epa.gov/enviroatlas/enviro
atlas-interactive-map.

63. US Department of Agriculture, Economic Research Service, "Food
Environment Atlas: Go to the Atlas," accessed January 2, 2023,
https://www.ers.usda.gov/data-products/food-environment-atlas
/go-to-the-atlas.aspx.

64. US Department of Commerce, US Census Bureau, "OnTheMap for
Emergency Management," accessed January 2, 2023, https://onthe
map.ces.census.gov/em/.

65. United Nations Office for Disaster Risk Reduction (UNDRR), "What
Is the Sendai Framework for Disaster Risk Reduction?," accessed
October 11, 2022, https://www.undrr.org/implementing-sendai
-framework/what-sendai-framework.

66. A 2021 article in *Progress in Disaster Science* analyzes the challenges
and opportunities resulting from the US commitment to the Sendai
Framework, noting that the United States has experienced significant
data challenges in reporting its progress to the Sendai Monitor, in
part because of the decentralized role of disaster management across
local, state, and national authorities along with logistic, administrative, political, technical, and operational challenges that act as barriers
to gaining a complete picture of disaster losses—and further impede
the ability of the framework to drive US action. Aleeza Wilkins et al.,
"Challenges and Opportunities for Sendai Framework Disaster Loss
Reporting in the United States," *Progress in Disaster Science* 10 (April
2021): 100167, https://doi.org/10.1016/j.pdisas.2021.100167.

67. UNDRR, "What Is the Sendai Framework?"

68. United Nations Office for Disaster Risk Reduction (UNDRR),
"Sendai Framework for Disaster Risk Reduction, 2015–2030," March
18, 2015, https://cdn.who.int/media/docs/default-source/health
-security-preparedness/drr/sendai-framework-for-disaster-risk
-reduction-2015-2030.pdf?sfvrsn=8aa55898_23&download=true.

69. Villeneuve et al., "DIDRR Framework and Toolkit."

70. Villeneuve et al., "DIDRR Framework and Toolkit," 7.

71. Villeneuve et al., "DIDRR Framework and Toolkit," 15–17.

72. Alina Engelman et al., "Assessing the Emergency Response Role of

Community-Based Organizations (CBOs) Serving People with Dis-abilities and Older Adults in Puerto Rico Post-Hurricane María and during the COVID-19 Pandemic," *International Journal of Environmental Research and Public Health* 19, no. 4 (2022): 2156, https://doi.org/10.3390/ijerph19042156.

73. National Voluntary Organizations Active in Disaster, "About Us," accessed December 4, 2022, https://www.nvoad.org/about-us/.

Chapter 4: Strategies for Age-Friendly Resilience

1. Scott Neuman, "One Florida Community Built to Weather Hurricanes Endured Ian with Barely a Scratch," NPR, October 6, 2022, https://www.npr.org/2022/10/05/1126900340/florida-community-designed-weather-hurricane-ian-babcock-ranch-solar; Babcock Ranch, "Media Kit," accessed January 9, 2023, https://babcockranch.com/media-kit/.

2. Kim Fernandez, "An Autonomous Future Right Now," International Parking & Mobility Institute, accessed January 9, 2023, https://www.parking-mobility.org/2019/02/03/an-autonomous-future-right-now/.

3. Babcock Ranch, "Media Kit."

4. Ciara Nugent, "Climate-Proof Towns Are Popping Up across the U.S. but Not Everyone Can Afford to Live There," *Time*, October 28, 2022, https://time.com/6225970/climate-proof-towns-extreme-weather/.

5. William Shiflett and Lori A. Trawinski, "Fact Sheet: Older Consumers: Especially Vulnerable to Utility Price Increases," AARP Public Policy Institute, September 2018, https://www.aarp.org/content/dam/aarp/ppi/2018/09/older-consumers-especially-vulnerable-to-utility-price-increases.pdf.

6. Brian Barth, "Backup Generators Can Give Your House Some Juice," AARP, October 7, 2021, https://www.aarp.org/home-family/your-home/info-2021/backup-generators.html.

7. Juliana Bilowich, "HUD Announces New Round of COVID-19 Payments for Housing Providers," LeadingAge, September 17, 2021, https://leadingage.org/hud-announces-new-round-covid-19-payments-housing-providers/.

8. National Housing Trust, "The Inflation Reduction Act: Opportunities to Preserve and Improve Affordable Housing through Resilience," August 2022, https://www.nationalhousingtrust.org/sites/default/files/page_file_attachments/Inflation%20Reduction%20Act%20Affordable%20Housing%20Policy%20Brief.pdf.

9. Pennsylvania Department of Human Services, "Heating Assistance/ Low-Income Home Energy Assistance Program (LIHEAP): About the Program," accessed January 7, 2023, https://www.dhs.pa.gov/Services /Assistance/Pages/LIHEAP.aspx.

10. January Contreras, "LIHEAP and Extreme Heat: How the Low-Income Home Energy Assistance Program Is Assisting Families with Staying Safe, Healthy, and Prepared for Extreme Heat Events," US Department of Health and Human Services, Administration for Children and Families, blog post, April 22, 2022, https://www.acf.hhs .gov/blog/2022/04/liheap-and-extreme-heat.

11. US Department of Health and Human Services, Administration for Children and Families, "LIHEAP and Extreme Heat: How the Low Income Home Energy Assistance Program (LIHEAP) Is Helping People Stay Safe, Healthy, and Prepared to Combat Heat Stress," accessed November 13, 2022, https://liheap-and-extreme-heat-hhs-acf.hub .arcgis.com/.

12. AP News, "PG&E to Plead Guilty to Involuntary Manslaughter in Deadly 2018 California Wildfire," CNBC News, March 23, 2020, https://www.cnbc.com/2020/03/23/pge-pleading-guilty-to-involun tary-manslaughter-in-wildfire.html.

13. Emma Newburger, "California Finds PG&E Equipment Responsible for Massive Dixie Fire," CNBC News, January 5, 2022, https://www .cnbc.com/2022/01/05/california-finds-pge-equipment-responsible -for-massive-dixie-fire-.html#:~:text=California%20finds%20PG% 26E%20equipment%20responsible%20for%20massive%20Dixie% 20Fire,-Published%20Wed%2C%20Jan&text=Pacific%20Gas%20 %26%20Electric%20transmission%20lines,to%20a%20new%20 state%20investigation.

14. Kurtis Alexander, "PG&E Proposes Another Rate Hike in 2023— 18%—to Boost Wildfire Safety," *San Francisco Chronicle*, June 30, 2021, https://www.sfchronicle.com/bayarea/article/PG-E-proposes -another-rate-hike-in-2023-to-boost-16285643.php.

15. US Department of Commerce, US Census Bureau, "Historical Census of Housing Tables: Units in Structure," 2020, https://www.census .gov/data/tables/time-series/dec/coh-units.html#:~:text=The%20 types%20of%20homes%20people,period%2C%20in%20the%20 60%20percents.

16. Statista, "Average Size of Floor Area in New Single-Family Houses Built for Sale in the United States from 1975 to 2021," Statista Research Department, February 18, 2022, https://www.statista.com /statistics/529371/floor-area-size-new-single-family-homes-usa/.

17. For a comprehensive overview of missing middle housing and its benefits, see *Missing Middle Housing: Thinking Big and Building Small to Respond to Today's Housing Crisis* by Daniel Parolek (Washington, DC: Island Press, 2020).

18. Dr. David Eisenman and Enrique Huerta, "Climate Chats #2—A Conversation on Extreme Heat: How You Can Adapt, and Help Combat," webinar, AARP California, September 21, 2021, https://states.aarp.org/california/climatechats.

19. The "AARP HomeFit Guide" is a free and easy-to-use resource that supports the ability of renters, owners, and builders to incorporate design and functional elements that better enable people of all ages and abilities to live safely in their homes. That resource can be found at https://www.aarp.org/livable-communities/housing/info-2020/homefit-guide.html.

20. Andrew Cohen, "PVAMU Architecture Students' Winning Design Could Be a Game-Changer following Natural Disasters," *Houston Style Magazine*, June 7, 2022, http://stylemagazine.com/news/2022/jun/07/pvamu-architecture-students-winning-design-could-b/.

21. The book *Gray to Green Communities: A Call to Action on the Housing and Climate Crises* by Dana L. Bourland (Washington, DC: Island Press, 2021) presents a thorough and in-depth analysis of the Green Communities criteria and the value of using them to create more resilient communities.

22. In the interest of full disclosure, the author of this book notes that she works for National Housing Trust.

23. Enterprise Community Partners, "Green Communities Criteria and Certification: The Standard for Sustainable Futures," accessed January 27, 2023, https://www.greencommunitiesonline.org/.

24. Enterprise Community Partners, "Climate Safe Housing: Strategies for Multifamily Building Resilience," accessed January 27, 2023, https://www.climatesafehousing.org/.

25. Enterprise Community Partners, "Climate Safe Housing: Strategies for Multifamily Building Resilience; About This Book," accessed January 27, 2023, https://www.climatesafehousing.org/about-book.

26. Learn more about how National Housing Trust is working to advocate for the needs of multifamily affordable housing residents through Inflation Reduction Act implementation at https://nationalhousingtrust.org/.

27. Pam Jenkins, PhD, retired professor of sociology, University of New Orleans, interview with the author, January 18, 2023.

28. Todd Folse, Louisiana Housing Corporation, in-person presentation

at National Council of State Housing Agencies Annual Conference & Showplace, Houston, Texas, October 24, 2022.

29. Kezia Setyawan, "Amid Push for More Storm-Resilient Builds, $11M Affordable Housing Community Opens in Lafourche," WRKF, June 2, 2022, https://www.wrkf.org/2022-06-02/amid-push-for-more -storm-resilient-builds-11m-affordable-housing-community-opens -in-lafourche.

30. Louisiana Housing Corporation, Office of Public Affairs, "LHC Announces Completion of Storm Resilient Housing Community Les Maisons de Bayou Lafourche in Lockport, LA," press release, July 11, 2022, https://www.lhc.la.gov/press-releases/lhc-announces-completion -of-storm-resilient-housing-community-les-maisons-de-bayou-la fourche-in-lockport-la.

31. Setyawan, "$11M Affordable Housing Community Opens in Lafourche."

32. US Department of Homeland Security, Federal Emergency Management Agency, "Risk Mapping, Assessment and Planning (Risk MAP)," accessed November 13, 2022, https://www.fema.gov/flood -maps/tools-resources/risk-map.

33. These and are other actions taken by localities count toward the Community Rating System (CRS) score, which can make individual property owners within a community eligible for discounted flood insurance through the National Flood Insurance Program. To learn more about the CRS, see US Department of Homeland Security, Federal Emergency Management Agency, "National Flood Insurance Program Community Rating System: A Local Official's Guide to Saving Lives, Preventing Property Damage, and Reducing the Cost of Flood Insurance," FEMA B 573/2018, https://www.fema.gov/sites /default/files/documents/fema_community-rating-system_local-guide -flood-insurance-2018.pdf. See *Understanding Disaster Insurance: New Tools for a More Resilient Future* by Carolyn Kousky (Washington, DC: Island Press, 2022) for a comprehensive and accessible analysis of how more effective insurance pricing and policy can support resilience.

34. US Department of Homeland Security, Federal Emergency Management Agency, "Risk Rating 2.0 Is Equity in Action," fact sheet, April 2021, accessed April 29, 2023, https://www.fema.gov/sites/default /files/documents/fema_rr-2.0-equity-action_0.pdf.

35. National Oceanic and Atmospheric Administration, National Centers for Environmental Information, "Billion-Dollar Weather and Climate Disasters: Disaster and Risk Mapping," accessed November 13, 2022, https://www.ncei.noaa.gov/access/billions/mapping.

36. National Oceanic and Atmospheric Administration, National Integrated Drought Information System, "Data and Maps: U.S. Drought Monitor (USDM)," accessed November 13, 2022, https://www.drought.gov/data-maps-tools/us-drought-monitor.

37. LeadingAge LTSS Center @UMass Boston, "Enhancing Service Coordination in HUD-Assisted Senior Housing Communities: Lessons for Implementation," January 2022, https://ltsscenter.org/reports/Enhancing_Service_Coordination_in_HUD-Assisted_Senior_Housing.pdf.

38. *Affordability and Accessibility: Addressing the Housing Needs of America's Seniors: Hearing before the US Senate Committee on Banking, Housing, and Urban Affairs*, 117th Cong. (March 31, 2022) (statement of Shannon Guzman, MCP, senior strategic policy advisor, AARP Public Policy Institute), https://www.aarp.org/content/dam/aarp/politics/advocacy/2022/03/sen-banking-hearing-testimony-3-31-22.pdf.

39. Susan Shaheen, Stephen Wong, and Adam Cohen, "Can the Sharing Economy Be Leveraged in Disaster Relief?," University of California, Berkeley, Institute of Transportation Studies, September 12, 2019, https://its.berkeley.edu/news/can-sharing-economy-be-leveraged-disaster-relief.

40. Deborah Matherly et al., "A Guide to Regional Transportation Planning for Disasters, Emergencies, and Significant Events," Project No. NCHRP 20-59(42), National Cooperative Highway Research Program, Transportation Research Board, December 2013, https://onlinepubs.trb.org/onlinepubs/nchrp/nchrp_rpt_777supplemental.pdf.

41. Matherly et al., "Guide to Regional Transportation Planning."

42. US Department of Homeland Security, Federal Emergency Management Agency, "Disaster Relief Trials Pedal toward Community Resilience," June 2016, https://community.fema.gov/story/disaster-relief-trials-pedal-toward-community-resilience#:~:text=Through%20DRTs%2C%20Cobb%20and%20other,must%20include%20several%20essential%20elements.

43. April Ehrlich, "Ashland Cyclists Bring Water, Food to People Stuck in Evacuation Zones," Jefferson Public Radio, September 11, 2020, https://www.ijpr.org/wildfire/2020-09-11/ashland-cyclists-bring-water-food-to-people-stuck-in-evacuation-zones.

44. Stephen Wong and Susan Shaheen, "Current State of the Sharing Economy and Evacuations: Lessons from California," UC-ITS-2019-19-a, University of California, Berkeley, Institute of Transportation Studies, May 2019, https://doi.org/10.7922/G2WW7FVK.

45. Skye Seipp, "CapMetro Expands Free Rides to Cooling Centers. Advocates for Homeless Austinites Push for More," KUT 90.5, August 9, 2022, https://www.kut.org/austin/2022-08-09/capmetro -expands-free-rides-to-cooling-centers-advocates-for-homeless -austinites-push-for-more.

46. City of Philadelphia, Pennsylvania, "City Opens Four Cooling Bus Locations during Heat Health Emergency," press release, July 22, 2022, https://www.phila.gov/2022-07-22-city-opens-four-cooling -bus-locations-during-heat-health-emergency/.

47. Chicago Transit Authority, "CTA Provides Assistance during Heat Emergency," August 1, 2006, https://www.transitchicago.com/cta -provides-assistance-during-heat-emergency/.

48. US Department of Transportation, Federal Transit Administration, "Enhanced Mobility of Seniors and Individuals with Disabilities Program Guidance and Application Instructions," FTA C 9070.1G, July 7, 2014, https://www.transit.dot.gov/sites/fta.dot.gov/files/docs /C9070_1G_FINAL_circular_4-20-15%281%29.pdf.

49. National Rural Transit Assistance Program, National Center for Mobility Management, and National Aging and Disability Transpor- tation Center, "Writing a Coordinated Public Transit Human Services Transportation Plan," July 2021, https://nationalcenterformobility management.org/wp-content/uploads/2021/07/Writing_a_Coordin ated_Public_Transit_Human_Services_Transportation_Plan.pdf.

50. Washington State Department of Transportation, "Coordinated Pub- lic Transit–Human Services Transportation Plan Guidebook," M 3139, July 2021, https://wsdot.wa.gov/sites/default/files/2021-10 /PT-Guide-CoordinatedHumanServicesTransportationPlanGuide book-2021.pdf.

51. National Center for Mobility Management, "State of the State: Transportation Coordination and Mobility Management Efforts in Florida," April 2021, https://nationalcenterformobilitymanagement .org/wp-content/uploads/2021/04/FINAL-Florida-State-of-the-State -Profile.pdf.

52. An article featured in the American Society on Aging's *Generations* journal eloquently describes this need and compares the US experi- ence with that of other countries. See Kasley Killam, "Lessons from COVID-19: Improving Social Health to Build Community Resil- ience," *Generations*, Summer 2022, https://generations.asaging.org /improving-social-health-community-resilience.

53. Investments in social connectedness have positive impacts on under- lying health, particularly given that extended isolation and loneliness

among older adults is a contributor to heart disease, infections, depression, and premature cognitive decline. One study likens detrimental health effects of isolation to those associated with smoking as many as fifteen cigarettes every day. Lynda Flowers and Claire Noel-Miller, "Social Isolation: Detrimental to Older Adults' Health and Costly to Medicare," AARP Public Policy Institute, blog post, July 18, 2018, https://blog.aarp.org/thinking-policy/social-isolation-detrimental-to-older-adults-health-and-costly-to-medicare.

54. Learn more about how age-friendly communities advance work on Respect and Social Inclusion, Civic Participation and Employment, and other age-friendly domains at the interactive AARP Livable Communities Map, https://livablemap.aarp.org/#/view=details.

55. AARP Livable Communities, "Age-Friendly Greenwich, Connecticut, Responds to COVID-19," May 22, 2020, https://www.aarp.org/livable-communities/network-age-friendly-communities/info-2020/greenwich-connecticut-COVID-19-response.html.

56. US Department of Health and Human Services, Centers for Disease Control and Prevention, and Agency for Toxic Substances and Disease Registry, Geospatial Research, Analysis, and Services Program, CDC/ATSDR Social Vulnerability Index, interactive map, accessed November 29, 2022, https://www.atsdr.cdc.gov/placeandhealth/svi/index.html.

57. US Department of Health and Human Services, Centers for Disease Control and Prevention, "Identifying Vulnerable Older Adults and Legal Options for Increasing Their Protection during All-Hazards Emergencies: A Cross-Sector Guide for States and Communities," 2012, 16, https://www.cdc.gov/cpr/documents/aging.pdf.

58. Florida Department of Health, Florida Special Needs Registry, "Welcome to the Florida Special Needs Registry," accessed January 14, 2023, https://snr.flhealthresponse.com/.

59. Orange County, Florida, People with Special Needs Program, "Orange County People with Special Needs Program Frequently Asked Questions," accessed January 14, 2023, http://www.orangecountyfl.net/portals/0/library/emergency-safety/docs/specialneedsprogramfaq.pdf.

60. Federal Communications Commission, "Dial 211 for Essential Community Services," accessed December 4, 2022, https://www.fcc.gov/consumers/guides/dial-211-essential-community-services.

61. Cristin Severance, "'There Was No Information about the Heat Wave at All': 211 Helpline Failed Hundreds during Historic Oregon Heat Wave," KGW8, July 8, 2021, https://www.kgw.com/article/news

/local/the-story/211-helpline-failed-during-historic-heat-wave/283
-020af8f9-ef2f-423f-93fc-01b6df62526c#:~:text=The%20Story-,'
There%20was%20no%20information%20about%20the%20heat
%20wave%20at%20all,the%20information%20line%20starting%20
Monday.

62. Erik Neumann, "County Alert System Left Many without Notifications during the Almeda Fire," Jefferson Public Radio, September 19,
2020, https://www.ijpr.org/disasters-and-accidents/2020-09-19
/county-alert-system-left-many-without-notifications-during-the
-almeda-fire.

63. County of Mendocino, California, "MendoAlert, the Mendocino
County Emergency Alert and Notification Service," accessed January
14, 2023, https://www.mendocinocounty.org/government/executive
-office/office-of-emergency-services/
emergency-notifications-and-alerts.

64. Pew Research Center, "Internet/Broadband Fact Sheet," April 7, 2021,
https://www.pewresearch.org/internet/fact-sheet/internet-broadband/.

65. US Department of Commerce, National Telecommunications and
Information Administration (NTIA), "Digital Equity Guide for the
States: How to Prepare for Success in Your State," November 28,
2022, 5, https://broadbandusa.ntia.doc.gov/sites/default/files/2022
-12/Digital_Equity_Guide_for_States_11.28.22.pdf.

66. Pew Research Center, "Internet/Broadband Fact Sheet."

67. Universal Service Administrative Company, "Additional ACP Data:
Total Enrolled ACP Subscribers by Method of Verification," accessed
January 14, 2023, https://www.usac.org/about/affordable-connectivity
-program/acp-enrollment-and-claims-tracker/additional-acp-data/.

68. The NTIA's "Digital Equity Guide for the States," cited earlier, is a
useful guide for advising states—which serve as a critical organizing
level for subsequent local and regional action—as they develop digital
equity plans, which are required for subsequent Infrastructure Investment and Jobs Act (IIJA) capacity-building grants.

69. Institute on Aging at the University of Pennsylvania, "Digital Equity:
A Growing Focus on Seniors," April 28, 2022, https://penninstitute
onaging.wordpress.com/2022/04/28/digitalequity/.

70. Climate Health Action, "U.S. Call to Action on Climate, Health, and
Equity: A Policy Action Agenda," 2019, https://climatehealthaction
.org/media/cta_docs/US_Call_to_Action.pdf.

71. LeadingAge, "Emergency Preparedness Toolkit," accessed December
11, 2022, https://leadingage.org/emergency-preparedness-toolkit/.

72. US Department of Homeland Security, "Disaster Planning Guide for

Home Health Care Providers," accessed December 4, 2022, https://
ndocsoftware.com/wp-content/uploads/2017/09/Disaster-Planning
-Guide-for-Home-Health-Care-Providers.pdf.

73. Healthcare Ready home page, accessed January 14, 2023, https://
healthcareready.org/.

74. Tamar Wyte-Lake et al., "Education of Elderly Patients about Emergency Preparedness by Health Care Practitioners," *American Journal
of Public Health* 108 (2018): S207–S208, https://doi.org/10.2105
/AJPH.2018.304608.

75. Jennifer Marlon et al., "Yale Climate Opinion Maps 2021: Estimated
% of Adults Who Discuss Global Warming at Least Occasionally
(Nat'l Avg. 35%), 2021," accessed December 4, 2022, https://climate
communication.yale.edu/visualizations-data/ycom-us/.

76. Florida Clinicians for Climate Action, "Our Goals and Vision,"
accessed December 4, 2022, https://www.floridaclinicians.org/about/.

77. Martha Bebinger, "Has Your Doctor Talked to You about Climate
Change?," NPR, July 13, 2019, https://www.npr.org/sections/health
-shots/2019/07/13/734430818/has-your-doctor-talked-to-you-about
-climate-change.

78. Robert J. Ursano, Joshua C. Morganstein, and Robin Cooper,
"Resource Document on Mental Health and Climate Change," American Psychiatric Association, accessed February 10, 2023, https://
www.psychiatry.org/File%20Library/Psychiatrists/Directories/Library
-and-Archive/resource_documents/2017-Resource-Document
-Mental-Health-Climate-Change.pdf.

79. Mobile Health Map, "American Public Health Association Annual
Meeting: Making the Case for Mobile," November 22, 2022, https://
www.mobilehealthmap.org/
american-public-health-association-annual-meeting/.

80. S.958—Maximizing Outcomes through Better Investments in
Lifesaving Equipment for (MOBILE) Health Care Act, 117th Cong.
(2021–2022), https://www.congress.gov/bill/117th-congress/senate
-bill/958/text.

81. US Department of Homeland Security, "National Preparedness
Goal," 2nd ed., March 2015, 1, https://www.fema.gov/sites/default
/files/2020-06/national_preparedness_goal_2nd_edition.pdf.

82. US Department of Homeland Security, Federal Emergency Management Agency (FEMA), "National Response Framework," 4th ed.,
October 28, 2019, ii, https://www.fema.gov/sites/default/files/2020
-04/NRF_FINALApproved_2011028.pdf.

83. FEMA, "National Response Framework," ii.

84. National Oceanic and Atmospheric Administration, National Centers for Environmental Information, "Billion-Dollar Weather and Climate Disasters," accessed December 11, 2022, https://www.ncei.noaa.gov/access/monitoring/dyk/billions-calculations.

85. State of North Carolina, "CDBG-MIT Action Plan: ReBuild NC Substantial Action Plan Amendment 3," January 18, 2022, 57, https://www.rebuild.nc.gov/media/2220/download?attachment.

86. State of North Carolina, "CDBG-MIT Action Plan," 99.

87. State of North Carolina, "CDBG-MIT Action Plan," 100.

88. Learn more at the Partnership for Inclusive Disaster Strategies' website, https://disasterstrategies.org/.

89. US Department of Homeland Security, Federal Emergency Management Agency (FEMA) and AARP, "Guide to Expanding Mitigation: Making the Connection to Older Adults," July 2022, https://www.fema.gov/sites/default/files/documents/fema_mitigation-guide_older-adults.pdf.

90. AARP Livable Communities, "The 8 Domains of Livability: An Introduction," https://www.aarp.org/livable-communities/network-age-friendly-communities/info-2016/8-domains-of-livability-introduction.html.

91. Results were derived from a keyword search of the AARP Livable Communities Map, https://livablemap.aarp.org/#/view=details, on December 12, 2022.

92. For more information, see the Urban Sustainability Directors Network's Resilience Hubs website, http://resilience-hub.org/.

93. Urban Sustainability Directors Network, "Resilience Hubs: Core Components," accessed December 13, 2022, http://resilience-hub.org/core-components/.

94. Miami-Dade County, Florida, "Miami-Dade Parks to Host Community Resilience Pod," press release, April 1, 2021, https://www.miamidade.gov/releases/2021-03-31-parks-resilence-pod.asp.

95. City of Tempe, Arizona, "EnVision Tempe," accessed December 13, 2022, https://www.tempe.gov/government/human-services/envision-center.

96. City of Tallahassee, Florida, "Human Services—Resilience Hubs," accessed December 13, 2022, https://www.talgov.com/neighborhood services/hs-reshub.

97. Thayanne G. M. Ciriaco and Stephen D. Wong, "Review of Resilience Hubs and Associated Transportation Needs," *Transportation Research Interdisciplinary Perspectives* 16 (December 2022): 100697, https://doi.org/10.1016/j.trip.2022.100697.

98. Alzheimer's Association, "2022 Alzheimer's Disease Facts and Figures," *Alzheimer's & Dementia* 18, no. 4 (April 2022): 700–789, https://doi.org/10.1002/alz.12638.

99. Alzheimer's Association, "2022 Alzheimer's Disease Facts and Figures."

100. Alzheimer's Association, "2022 Alzheimer's Disease Facts and Figures."

Chapter 5: Community Resilience for All Ages in Action

1. US Department of Health and Human Services, Administration for Community Living (ACL), "2021 Profile of Older Americans," November 2022, 10, https://acl.gov/sites/default/files/Profile%20 of%20OA/2021%20Profile%20of%20OA/2021ProfileOlderAmeri cans_508.pdf.

2. US Department of Health and Human Services, Centers for Disease Control and Prevention, "Morbidity and Mortality Weekly Report: Deaths Associated with Hurricane Sandy—October–November 2012," May 24, 2013, https://www.cdc.gov/mmwr/preview/mmwr html/mm6220a1.htm#:~:text=Decedents%20ranged%20in%20age %20from,indirectly%20related%20to%20the%20storm.

3. The state's age-friendly effort is a complement to commitments made under the Prevention Agenda (which began in 2008) and Health Across All Policies (HAAP, initiated in 2017) efforts. Learn more about the Prevention Agenda at https://www.health.ny.gov/preven tion/prevention_agenda/2019-2024/ and about HAAP at https:// www.health.ny.gov/prevention/prevention_agenda/health_across_all _policies/.

4. State of New York, "Executive Order No. 190: Incorporating Health across All Policies into State Agency Activities," New York Governor's Office, November 14, 2018, https://www.governor.ny.gov/sites /default/files/atoms/files/EO_190.pdf.

5. Paul Beyer, New York State director of smart growth, interview with the author, January 27, 2023. See also the New York State "Down-town Revitalization Initiative Guidebook," July 2021, 26–28, https:// www.ny.gov/sites/default/files/2021-07/DRI_Five_Guidebook.pdf.

6. Beth Harrington, age-friendly volunteer with Tompkins County, New York, email to the author, February 3, 2023.

7. AARP Livable Communities Map, search by the author on January 16, 2023, https://livablemap.aarp.org/#/view=list.

8. Tab Hauser, "City's Age-Friendly Initiative Celebrated," *Long Island*

Herald, December 1, 2022, https://www.liherald.com/stories/citys-age
-friendly-initiative-celebrated,152646.

9. Lindsay Goldman et al., "Resilient Communities: Empowering Older
   Adults in Disasters and Daily Life," New York Academy of Medicine,
   July 2014, 4, https://media.nyam.org/filer_public/64/b2/64b2da62
   -f4e7-4e04-b5d1-e0e52b2a5614/resilient_communities_report_final
   .pdf.

10. Lindsay Goldman, chief executive officer, Grantmakers in Aging,
    interview with the author, December 20, 2022.

11. Read project briefs (as of December 2021) for each of the Age-
    Friendly Centers of Excellence that participated in the Learning
    Collaboratives in this final report: New York Academy of Medicine,
    "Health and Age across All Policies: Health Collaborative Teams
    Briefs; Breakdown by County," December 2021, https://media.nyam
    .org/filer_public/0c/66/0c665883-02cd-45fb-af5d-3005552e6b9e
    /haaap_county_briefs_updated_21822.pdf.

12. New York Academy of Medicine, "HAAAP in Action: Age-Friendly
    Emergency Response," PowerPoint presentation, May 14, 2020,
    46–59, https://media.nyam.org/filer_public/d1/fd/d1fd493d-b81b
    -4664-a727-60d1ee20fd47/webinar_slides_5-14-20_for_email.pdf.

13. Tompkins County, New York, County Office for the Aging, "Tomp-
    kins County Age Friendly Center for Excellence," accessed January
    25, 2023, https://www.tompkinscountyny.gov/cofa/age-friendly.

14. Caryn Bullis, deputy director, Tompkins County Office for the Aging,
    interview with the author, January 25, 2023.

15. The workshops were provided by the Southern Tier's Population
    Health Improvement Program, and the Human Services Coalition
    sponsored several of them, including the one described here.

16. Wilma Lawrence, age-friendly volunteer, interview with the author,
    January 25, 2023.

17. Read more about the ways in which a range of New York State
    agencies contributed to the statewide age-friendly commitment in
    New York Department of State, Office for the Aging, Department of
    Health, "Age-Friendly New York State," March 3, 2021, https://aging
    .ny.gov/system/files/documents/2022/12/age-friendly-report-to-aarp
    -final.pdf.

18. Greg Olsen, acting director, New York State Office for the Aging,
    interview with the author, January 24, 2023.

19. Beyer, interview, January 27, 2023.

20. Olsen, interview, January 24, 2023.

21. Olsen, interview, January 24, 2023.

22. According to its 2021 annual report, the agency served 1.3 million New Yorkers out of a total of 4.6 million residents aged sixty or older —roughly 28 percent. New York State Office for the Aging, "2021 Annual Report," https://aging.ny.gov/system/files/documents/2022 /07/2021-annual-report.pdf.

23. New York State governor Kathy Hochul, "Executive Order No. 23: Establishing the New York State Master Plan for Aging," November 4, 2022, https://www.governor.ny.gov/executive-order/no-23 -establishing-new-york-state-master-plan-aging.

24. California Department of Aging, "Master Plan for Aging: Five Bold Goals for 2030," January 2021, https://mpa.aging.ca.gov/.

25. California Department of Aging, "California's Master Plan for Aging, 2023–24 Initiatives: Delivering Results for Older Adults, People with Disabilities, and Caregivers," January 2023, 6, https://www.aging .ca.gov/download.ashx?lE0rcNUV0zbnAiDTiMJXxA%3d%3d.

26. New York State Climate Action Council, "New York Scoping Plan," December 2022, 64, https://climate.ny.gov/-/media/Project/Climate /Files/NYS-Climate-Action-Council-Final-Scoping-Plan-2022.pdf. (The term "elderly" is used in the report.)

27. Olsen, interview, January 24, 2023.

28. Beyer, interview, January 27, 2023.

29. Elana Kieffer and Mario Rubano, New York Academy of Medicine, interview with the author, January 4, 2023.

30. Goldman et al., "Resilient Communities," 46.

31. Jerry Cohen, former state director, AARP Oregon, interview with the author, January 19, 2023.

32. Age-Friendly Portland Advisory Council, "Action Plan for an Age-Friendly Portland," October 8, 2013, 29, https://agefriendlyportland .org/sites/agefriendlyportland.org/files/docs/AFP_ActionPlan_2013 .pdf.

33. Multnomah County, Oregon, "Multnomah County Age-Friendly Action Plan," April 2016, 6, https://agefriendlyportland.org/sites/age friendlyportland.org/files/docs/AFMC_ActionPlan_April2016.pdf.

34. Austin De Dios, "Oregon Reaches at Least 15 Suspected Heat-Related Deaths during Lengthy Heatwave," *The Oregonian*, August 1, 2022, https://www.oregonlive.com/news/2022/08/oregon-reaches-at-least -15-suspected-heat-related-deaths-during-lengthy-heatwave.html.

35. Erin Grahek, former community services manager, Multnomah County Department of County Human Services, interview with the author, January 19, 2023.

36. City of Portland, Oregon, Portland Bureau of Emergency

Management, "Resources for NET Volunteers," accessed January
31, 2023, https://www.portland.gov/pbem/neighborhood-emergen-
cy-teams/crt
resources.

37. Alan DeLaTorre, Age-Friendly City program manager, City of Portland, interview with the author, December 19, 2022.

38. Sarah Clay and Jeremy Spoon, "Portland/Multnomah County Joint
Volunteer Information Center (JVIC) and Community-Based Organizations during the COVID-19 Pandemic: An Analysis of Engagement and Collaboration," Portland State University (prepared for the
Portland Bureau of Emergency Management), Summer 2022, 7.

39. Jonna Papaefthimiou, "Overview of Joint Volunteer Information
Center," Portland Bureau of Emergency Management, accessed January 23, 2023, https://www.portland.gov/sites/default/files/2020-07
/jvic-presentation.pdf.

40. Jonna Papaefthimiou, chief resilience officer, City of Portland, interview with the author, January 5, 2023.

41. Grahek, interview, January 19, 2023.

42. Grahek, interview, January 19, 2023.

43. Ari Shapiro, Mia Venkat, and Ashley Brown, "Lessons from Portland's 2021 Heat Wave That Can Help Us Prep for the Hot Summer Ahead," interview with Dr. Jennifer Vines, NPR, July 1, 2022,
https://www.npr.org/2022/07/01/1109470590/lessons-from-port
lands-2021-heatwave-that-can-help-us-prep-for-the-hot-summer-ah.

44. DeLaTorre, interview, December 19, 2022.

45. City of Portland, Oregon, "About the PCEF Heat Response Program," accessed January 23, 2023, https://www.portland.gov/bps
/cleanenergy/heat-response-program#toc-eligibility-and-vulnerable
-populations.

46. DeLaTorre, interview, December 19, 2022.

47. City of Portland, Oregon, Portland City Auditor, "Emergency
Management: Pandemic Highlights City's Long-Standing Neglect of
People with Disabilities," December 8, 2021, https://www.portland
.gov/audit-services/news/2021/12/8/emergency-management-pan
demic-highlights-citys-long-standing-neglect.

48. Grahek, interview, January 19, 2023.

49. Grahek, interview, January 19, 2023.

50. Joan Brunkard, Gonza Namulanda, and Raoult Ratard, "Hurricane
Katrina Deaths, Louisiana, 2005," *Disaster Medicine and Public
Health Preparedness* 2, no. 4 (2008): 215–223, https://doi.org/10.1097
/DMP.0b013e31818aaf55.

51. Howard Rodgers, executive director, New Orleans Council on Aging, interview with the author, January 5, 2023.
52. Rodgers, interview, January 5, 2023.
53. Rodgers, interview, January 5, 2023.
54. Louisiana uses parishes as the regional unit of government, between the state and cities; the parishes serve roughly the same functions as counties do in other states.
55. Emily Woodruff, "In Best of Times, New Orleans Is Hard on People with Disabilities. In Hurricanes, It's Deadly," June 11, 2022, *Times-Picayune/New Orleans Advocate*, June 11, 2022, https://www.nola.com/news/healthcare_hospitals/article_df0265d4-e803-11ec-b4e6-af58cbe03909.html.
56. Ryan Nelsen, "Senior Apartment Regulations Approved in New Orleans following Ida Deaths; See New Rules," WWNO—New Orleans Public Radio, October 21, 2021, https://www.wwno.org/news/2021-10-21/senior-apartment-regulations-approved-in-new-orleans-following-ida-deaths-see-new-rules.
57. Suzy Khimm and Laura Strickler, "U.S. Scrutinizes Nursing Home Evacuation Rules after Hurricane Ida Deaths," NBC News, September 30, 2021, https://www.nbcnews.com/news/us-news/u-s-scrutinizes-nursing-home-evacuation-rules-after-hurricane-ida-n1280492.
58. Rodgers, interview, January 5, 2023.
59. Peter Edmondson, disaster accessibility coordinator, NOLA Ready, interview with the author, January 26, 2023.
60. Learn more at Together New Orleans, "Community Lighthouse Project," accessed January 26, 2023, https://www.togethernola.org/home.
61. Asia Ognibene, project organizer, Together New Orleans, interview with the author, February 3, 2023.
62. Edmondson, interview, January 26, 2023.
63. Edmondson, interview, January 26, 2023.
64. Pam Jenkins, PhD, retired professor of sociology, University of New Orleans, interview with the author, January 18, 2023.
65. The Road Home program was not without controversy, including a lawsuit brought against HUD (ultimately settled) that stated that the appraisal process was not equitable, resulting in lower payouts to owners in communities of color. See David Hammer, "Behind the Key Decision That Left Many Poor Homeowners without Enough Money to Rebuild after Katrina," ProPublica, December 13, 2022, https://www.propublica.org/article/why-louisiana-road-home-program-based-grants-on-home-values.
66. Jenkins, interview, January 18, 2023.

67. Marla Nelson, professor of planning and urban studies, University of New Orleans, interview with the author, January 10, 2023.

Chapter 6: Lessons Learned and How to Move Forward

1. Jonna Papaefthimiou, chief resilience officer, City of Portland, interview with the author, January 5, 2023.
2. Papaefthimiou, interview, January 5, 2023.
3. San Francisco Department of Aging and Adult Services, "An Action Plan for an Age and Disability Friendly San Francisco 2018–2021," 2019, 50, https://www.aarp.org/content/dam/aarp/livable-commun ities/livable-documents/documents-2019/action-plans/San-Francisco -CA-Action-Plan-2019.pdf.
4. Montana Disability and Health Program, "Emergency Preparedness Tools and Resources Developed by MTDH and Partners," accessed February 4, 2023, https://mtdh.ruralinstitute.umt.edu/?page_id= 6945.
5. Together New Orleans, "Community Lighthouse," accessed February 4, 2023, https://www.togethernola.org/.
6. Peter Kaldes, president and chief executive officer, American Society on Aging, interview with the author, January 18, 2023.
7. Bill McKibben, environmentalist, author, advocate, and founder of Third Act, interview with the author, January 20, 2023.
8. Claire Schoen, journalist and host of *Stepping Up* podcast, interview with the author, October 21, 2022.

INDEX

___